Legends in Sail

Main titles by the same author:

Skoleskipene
Shipping and Culture
Viking to Victorian
Gamle Dampen
Slepebåten Oscarsborg
Legendariske Skuter

Prepress & graphics: Håkon Engvig and Pirforlaget/Terje Olsen
Paper: 157 gsm Art paper gloss
Set in ITC Officina Serif 12/19
Endsheets: Marbled
Printed in Shanghai by Bigger Printing Group
First Printing 2013
Published in the USA

***

The book is a rewritten and redesigned issue of
Legendariske Skuter, Pirforlaget, Trondheim 2012
Support for the translation is provided by NORLA

THEMO Publishing
Los Angeles
themopublishing@earthlink.net

***

ISBN 978-0-578-11756-0

Library of Congress Cataloging-in-Publication Data
Engvig, Olaf T
Including preface, introduction, bibliographical references and index.
Maritime history, shipping, transport, polar exploration, sail training, windjammer, film, travel

Front Cover: LANCING in Storm. Oil on canvas, 70 x 100 cm.
Courtesy Frank G. Dean, Maryland

Olaf T. Engvig

Legends in Sail

THEMO Publishing
MMXIII

This book is dedicated to my team members
Mona, Tormod, Håkon and Einar

Content

Foreword

ailing ships made Norway known internationally. Not only the hundreds of cargo vessels that displayed the Norwegian flag in ports and on the high seas around the world, but more so the ships that at one point made headlines internationally. The history of these famous ships is not well known. This book presents their interesting stories for an international audience.

When I moved to the U.S., I worked closely with the librarians at the Maritime Museum of San Francisco to find material for my books *Viking to Victorian* and *Shipping and Culture*. I was highly surprised to find that historians in the U.S. knew very little about Norway's distinguished history as one of the major shipping nations of the world. Most of the ships I write about in this book were not known to these scholars.

I soon discovered the reason for this lack of knowledge. The memory of Norway's great days in sail has faded because of language issues. Documentation of accomplishments is all in Norwegian. Cited scholarly maritime research is written in English by researchers who do not have command of the Norwegian language, leaving Norway on the sideline.

This discrepancy is the main motivation for publishing this book in both English and Norwegian. It is never too late to share exciting stories about famous ships contributing to maritime history. There are successes and tragedies in these stories. CHRISTIAN RADICH, famous from the Windjammer movie, and the polar research vessel FRAM are success stories. The dismantling of Norway's memorial ship LINGARD and the sad history of the MAUD are examples of tragedies. This book reveals exciting knowledge that has never before been known to the public.

It is my hope that this book will educate, engage and create debate. Ships were always of great importance to nations around the world. The harbors were crucial for contact among nations before commercial air traffic. These ships were expected and welcomed and gave our forefathers something to be proud of. With the exception of the CHRISTIAN RADICH, all the ships presented in this book are gone as seaworthy vessels.

This book represents a wonderful opportunity to learn more about the many unique and astonishing accomplishments of our shared maritime heritage and pride. It should also remind us of the importance of saving ships as a memory of a time long gone and as a proud artifact of our ancestors' achievements. Once a ship is broken up, it is lost forever.

Olaf T. Engvig

Introduction

For thousands of years the wind, current, paddles and sail have helped vessels with humans and cargo onboard across any body of water. In Egypt, vessels carrying a square sail and oars were in use approximately 5,000 years back. The Kyrenia wreck was built around 400 BC. Even today the majority of the world's transport is by water. No wonder drawings and pictures with boats have been prevalent since ancient times.

Why did Norway become a maritime nation?
The simple answer is that it had to. Let me elaborate:
The further north men traveled, the more they became dependent on seagoing crafts.

Back in the Stone Age the very long, rugged and mountainous coast of Norway, with all its islands, fjords and ocean inlets, demanded that the people settling there had to have seagoing crafts to survive. Cliffs and steep terrain made transport over land a major challenge if not impossible. Therefore, the people of the land became very good at handling boats.

Boats are documented by hundreds of petroglyphs all along the coast of Norway. They commonly depict men, ships and food. Ships are prevalent, as well as food. Typical rock carvings of food are elk or moose,

Petroglyph from Skjomenfjord, Northern Norway depicts halibut fishing from a boat 5000 to 6000 years ago.

reindeer and halibut, a fish that can feed many. Some human figures are distinctly male. Archaeologists have excavated remains of ships well over 2,000 years old and are adjusting the dates of new vessel remains back continuously. From the Stone Age on, people living by the coast had good seagoing vessels.

By the Viking Age the iron riveted light and open boat using oars and sail had become the basic ship design. This is an extremely able and seaworthy all-purpose construction for transport, harvesting, raiding abroad as well as adventures and expeditions. The Vikings became the ultimate mariners, staking out a course no one else dared to pursue; going into some of the coldest, windiest and most demanding waters of the world. People from other countries of Europe in sturdier ships and from better climates would try to stay close to any coast as not to fall off "the edge of the world" into the abyss.

The Vikings' adventures were rooted in the belief that the gods and the wind would take them across the ocean. If the wind changed, they would obey and go home. It is impossible to miss such a huge target as the Norwegian coast. We have thousands of artifacts from all aspects of life during the Viking Age, but no navigational instruments. The explanation is simple. They had none. They relied on the sun to show the way in their swift and seaworthy boats. The wind would take them where they needed to go if their pagan gods would approve of the journey. They only feared the fog.

The Viking ship from Gokstad, Sandefjord, built close to 890 AD.

They had no other way of life. They knew no other options. That made them fearless navigators. Sailing to the islands to the west became quite common. On clear days it would be possible to see land to the far west both from Iceland and Greenland due to the image of high mountains, if they were in an elevated spot or sailed well off the coast.

The Norse set sail to find the seen land far away. They found *skrælinger*, indigenous people and Stone Age tribes in America. The Iron Age Vikings were ahead in development. They did find some items for trading, but no gold and silver. They also found dense forests, unlike the bare land in Greenland, that the *skrælings* seemed to have little use for. They set up shipyards like in the Old World, discarding some of the old or wrecked boats, bringing new built tonnage back to Greenland.

The Medieval Ages saw a great development in ship design. The steering oar was replaced by a stern rudder. Ships became larger and got more permanent decking. One mast and a square sail developed into several masts and new masts on top of the lower masts. The larger ships needed larger sails, and they became so large that they had to be divided into smaller sails so they could be handled. More ballast or cargo could support a taller rig and lead to better sailing performance. The square sail always does best with the wind from abaft.

The elite would send cargo ships with whetstones to England and other commodities to different countries in Europe. Norwegian fur from the dense and desirable winter coat of furry animals would be highly appreciated among the nobility of Europe. Fish and lumber were always important export articles. Amsterdam was built on Norwegian oak.

Ships of the Hanseatic League would come to their Bergen office to fill the hold with dried cod fish. It was brought there from the north by square sail *jækt* rigged vessels, a further development of the Viking ship and its rigging, and a forerunner to the brig. The Baltic grain fleet would stop over in Southern Norway waiting for accommodating wind to continue the journey. Norway was well equipped with good ship building materials. Dense forests were easy accessible close to the fjord. Merchant ships were built by the hundreds, and like always, on location. They were rigged and fitted out for commercial trading.

The two mast brig became the signature vessel for merchant shipping. This speedy and maneuverable sailing ship was used for transport across and around the North Sea, the Baltic Sea and far beyond. Merchant vessels from Norway would sail the high seas, not only shipping goods like oak logs, milled lumber, ice, fish and some industrial products, but even offering a return cargo, or a cargo to some other ports at a good rate. Captains and mates were able seamen and well educated navigators. They could take the shipment to a foreign port never heard of at an agreeable price.

In the 1800s, the Norwegian merchant fleet was fast growing

The swift and maneuverable brig became the merchant vessel of choice.

to become one of the largest in the world. Petter Malmstein has registered 100,000 names of commercial sailing vessels from this period, most of them being Norwegian at one point in time. This lingered on as owners in Great Britain and other nations converted their merchant fleets to steam, selling off large numbers of fine and not so fine sailing ships to other countries.

Norway, with small capital means, became the principal buyer of surplus sailing vessels. Most of them were great windjammers built of iron, and of steel after the 1880s. These beautiful large ships with three and four masts were manned and sailed by Norwegians. An important reason was that Norwegian banks could not afford to let ship owners make the costly conversion to steam, leaving the owners with no alternative but to purchase tall sailing ships that were on sale at a fair price. With the help of these ships and good freight rates they would accumulate capital to be able to convert to steam at a later date.

The fact is that the "romantic days of white sails" were a struggle against all odds for the last magnificent generation of sailing ships that had ruled the oceans for thousands of years. Backbreaking work with heavy yards and tall masts on long voyages became common. The crew was reduced, and they lacked good food, causing outbreaks of scurvy. The ship's hold would often consist of cargo that steamers would try to avoid, or the rate per ton would be lower than they could accept due

Norwegian STOREGUT of 2,557 tons.

On June 13th, 1917, this ship, the four mast bark STOREGUT, built 1892, was sunk by gunfire 235 miles west of England by a German U-boat shelling it. The crew survived.
On July 31, 1917, the four mast bark ALSIDES, of same size and rigging, built the same year, was sunk by another German U-boat west of Ireland. All the 23 hands onboard perished.

to higher running costs. This became the destiny for many of the beautiful tall ships with white sails and a crew of devoted sailors. That formed the ultimate romance of the sail ship era.

Many becalmed Norwegian sailing ships became easy targets of German submarines during WWI in a merciless killing where the U-boat did not even need to use torpedoes, just shelling the ship until it went down with all sail set, the crew desperately trying to escape the rage of the killing machine in their open lifeboat. Norway stayed out of the war, but its sailors became caught in it. Almost 2,000 lost their lives.

During the interwar period the shipping fleet was renewed with speedy ships propelled with the new combustion engine, while other nations still preferred the well known steam engine. By

the outbreak of WWII, Norway had a larger fleet of speedy motor tankers, liners and 18 knot produce ships. This became a crucial advantage for the Allies. Many were too fast for the slow convoys. Thus they were allowed to sail individually. They became hard to hit as the German U-boats needed time to aim their torpedoes.

Their quick turn-around became famous. One such ship managed to do 51 crossings of the Atlantic to Great Britain between 1940 and July of 1943. Prime Minister Winston S. Churchill praised the Norwegian Merchant Navy when it came to securing the crucial supply lines between America and the Allied forces struggling to survive in Europe. More famous still is President Franklin D. Roosevelt's "Look to Norway" speech in 1942.

But the Allied merchant fleet paid a high price. Sailors from every country suffered. Again, half of the Norwegian merchant tonnage was lost and 3,500 seamen also lost their lives. Rebuilding of the fleet after the war once again made Norway one of the largest shipping nations in the world only surpassed by the U.S. and Great Britain. Thanks to its international shipping activities, Norway became able to rebuild its large merchant fleet and damaged infrastructure, even if the monetary system had been decimated. "Hard currency" became the international shipping's great contribution to the countries rebulding. With the discovery of oil in the North Sea maritime engagement expanded to include the oil industry.

Of the thousands of ships belonging to the period when sailing merchants ships became legends, this book discusses nine. Each one in its own way tells about maritime history and outstanding accomplishments on sea and on land. It is interesting to keep in mind that the three expedition ships in the book became famous not as merchant ships but as vessels that could carry people further north and south than men had ever been before. The spirit of moving to the rugged coasts of Northern Europe after the Ice Age still lingers on. This connects us back to the ancient times when a ship was the ultimate vehicle for enrichment and prosperity of life. The ship still is.

THE WORLD, built in Rissa, Mid-Norway, in 2002; the first condo ship ever to be built.

Oldest know photo of the GJØA sailing.

GJØA
-The Conqueror

On June 16th 1903, around midnight and in pouring rain, the 30 year old Norwegian sloop GJØA was towed out the Christiania Fjord in Norway. Her voyage would forever make the little Hardanger sloop known as one of the world's great exploration vessels. It took 69 years before the GJØA returned home to Oslo on June 2nd, 1972.

The GJØA's departure was highly unconventional. Together with his crew of six, the Arctic explorer Roald Amundsen quietly ran away from merchants who threatened to stop the expedition to the Northwest Passage by seizing the ship as a settlement for unpaid equipment. It would take 69 years before the then 100 year old GJØA returned to Norway and the city which in the meantime had changed its name to Oslo. In 1997 Norway celebrated the 25 year anniversary of the GJØA's return. At the same time it was 125 years since the GJØA was launched and Roald Amundsen was born. That year was 1872.

The GJØA moored at Framnæs in Frognerkilen, ready and equipped for her voyage through the Northwest Passage. In the background is Hovedøya. After 69 years the ship returned to Frognerkilen and was put ashore at Bygdøynes.

The sloop (*jakt* in Norwegian) GJØA was built in Hardanger by Knut Johannesen Skaala for Captain Asbjørn Sexe and named after Sexe's wife Gjøa. The GJØA was a common coastal freighter similar to so many others built in those days. They had a single mast with a main fore and aft rig and also a square sail. She was 69 feet long, 20.5 feet wide and drafted eight feet when loaded.

Roald Amundsen in 1906.

The GJØA originally measured 61.5 tons. When Amundsen owned her she was less than 50 tons and had a normal looking rigging with three staysails, a main fore and aft sail, and a top sail often referred to as a *breifokk*. The GJØA was known as a speedy sailing ship for her size.

When she was ten years old the GJØA was wrecked and sank off Northern Norway and was written off. The shipwreck was sold twice and ended up with Ice Skipper Hans C. Johannesen. He repaired the ship and took her to the Kara Sea and King Carl's Land, and other islands in the Arctic. The GJØA had quite a track record as an Arctic trader when Roald Amundsen bought her in Tromsø on March 28th, 1901. First Mate Roald Amundsen then owned and became skipper of a vessel that was smaller than any of the other ships he had sailed on.

Roald Amundsen was a young, ambitious seaman with some Arctic and Antarctic experience who was obsessed with finding a navigable route through the Northwest Passage from the Atlantic Ocean to the Pacific Ocean north of Canada. This was the only reason he bought the GJØA. It was also the start of a brilliant career as leader of various expeditions to both the Arctic and the Antarctic. Roald Amundsen is still seen as one of the world's foremost polar explorers.

Navigating the Northwest Passage was the goal of many Arctic pioneers. This would shorten the route between the Far East and the North Atlantic by several thousand nautical miles. This search went on for 300 years. Because of the extremely difficult ice conditions the passage was abandoned as a navigable trade route between east and west after Sir John Franklin, the last in a long series of world renowned explorers, had disappeared with two ships and 129 men. In 1850, after 12 rescue operations over four years, the remains of the Franklin Expedition were found. Although reports from sleigh riding explorers on the ice indicated that there might be a navigable route, finding it was no longer seen as a priority.

When Roald Amundsen 50 years later re-launched the old idea of finding the Northwest Passage, nobody was impressed enough to invest in the project. His plans came too late to have any practical value. But if he was to succeed, it would bring a successful end to the longest, largest and most costly exploration ever to find a navigable route around one of the world's continents.

This image from the port of Christiania in 1903 bears the following inscription: "Gjøa's crew on deck at departure time. From left: Amundsen, Lund, Lieutenant Hansen, the pilot, Wiik, Helmer Hansen, Ristvedt and Lindstrøm."

Amundsen was fully aware that in order to gain support, the expedition needed to have a scientific goal. The Earth's magnetism was a major research field in the 1800s. Norway's first professor of astronomy and applied mathematics, Christopher Hansteen, did a lot of research on terrestrial magnetism. Fridtjof Nansen was a great admirer of Professor Hansteen. Hansteen encouraged Amundsen to search for the magnetic North Pole, which was believed to be in the area of the Northwest Passage.

Only when Amundsen promised to determine where the magnetic North Pole was located was he able to get international attention and some financial support. This was in 1900, and Roald Amundsen bought the GJØA the following spring. He tested the ship through oceanographic work that summer in order to gain

The GJØA has been stopped by ice.

20

more research experience, familiarize himself with the ship and get broader support for the project. The GJØA was reinforced and equipped to handle pack ice and a harsh winter climate. An early type of combustion engine was installed. This was a simple and reliable two cylinder engine, but with the imminent danger of fire in the wooden engine room. A 20,000 liter oil tank was also fitted.

Besides Captain Roald Amundsen the expedition consisted of six men. Godfred Hansen was the chief officer, navigator, geologist and photographer. Anton Lund was the mate, having a lot of experience as a polar skipper, fisherman and trapper. Helmer Hansen, an experienced navigator, became the second mate. Peder Ristvedt was the GJØA's second engineer and meteorologist. Gustav Juel Wiik was the engineer and responsible for the magnetic measurements. Adolf Henrik Lindstrøm was the cook; an Arctic veteran who also took care of the animals that made up the ship's main food supply. These seven men were the GJØA's crew on the three year long expedition through the Northwest Passage. It was one of the greatest expeditions in the history of discovery, carried out by one of the smallest expedition ships ever used for such a long and arduous voyage. The mission headquarters, the GJØA's cabin, measured six by nine feet.

After the remodeling of the GJØA and depositing of equipment and dogs in Greenland, Amundsen had little money left to buy food and equipment in Christiania. He hoped for donations or that he could get what he needed and pay when returning home. The merchants felt that this was too uncertain and asked Amundsen for payment within 24 hours. It was then that Captain Amundsen took the daring decision to confide in his men, after which the GJØA cast off in the bright summer's night and was towed out the Christiania Fjord. Early in the morning the GJØA was taking on the Skagerrak with all sails set. The ship crossed the North Sea and the Atlantic Ocean and did not approach land until five weeks later when she reached the remote Disko Island, way up by the west coast of Greenland. The expedition could no longer be stopped. Dogs, sleds, and other equipment for winter in the Arctic were taken onboard together with additional provisions and fuel. The 69 foot sloop was loaded to the brim when the ship left Disko Island.

The first stop was Beechey, where the expedition performed a series of measurements. The journey continued through the Peel Sound and the Franklin Strait. Until then, nobody had sailed west of this point and the GJØA continued into uncharted territory. Amundsen was often in the crow's nest looking for reefs and submerged rocks. Despite the caution, the GJØA ended up on a reef, but managed to get off. The expedition experienced fire in the engine room and survived a storm that was so fierce none of them had seen anything like it before. Officer Anton Lund's extensive experience with severe weather in the Arctic came in handy. He got a lot of credit for the GJØA's survival.

The GJØA frozen in and covered up at Gjøahavn.

This happened in September, and winter was just around the corner. In order to survive they had to find a good, sheltered harbor. A small bay on the south side of King William's Land was selected and named Gjøahavn (today known as Gjoa Haven). Here they built a land station with material they had brought along. During their stay in Gjøahavn the expedition managed to determine the location of the magnetic North Pole.

The indigenous people of the region, the Inuits, came to visit. They had never seen a white man, but had been told about Sir James Clark Ross and his men 70 years earlier and decided to get

The only known picture of the Arctic schooner CHARLES HANSON of San Francisco. For Amundsen, meeting the vessel became a moment of truth. This is when he realized that he was the first to navigate the Northwest Passage.

Last winter by Kings Point in the Arctic. Here the GJØA is visiting the wreck of the whaler BONANZA which had been pushed ashore by the ice. The salvage operations were unsuccessful, but some of the equipment is still mounted, as seen in this picture. The infamous spirit, fur and whaling station Hershel was close by, many Americans whalers spent the Arctic winter there.

to know the men onboard the GJØA, where Amundsen welcomed them. An entire village of huts was built next to the sloop. Amundsen managed, through barter, to obtain Inuit artifacts showing all phases of daily life in these regions of the Arctic. These artifacts are on display at the Historical Museum in Oslo.

The GJØA stayed in Gjøahavn longer than expected. The weather during the summer of 1904 was miserable. Early in the summer

the sea froze solid again before they could sail on. Amundsen made several long sledge trips to the area close to the magnetic North Pole and found that the pole was constantly moving. That was a new discovery. The documented material he collected from this expedition was extensive.

In April 1905 Hansen and Ristvedt embarked on an 800 mile trip to explore what was later named the Queen Maud Gulf and the coast along the Victoria Land to prepare for the continued voyage. They returned on Midsummer Day. Shortly thereafter the ice broke up, and the GJØA could once again head west after 22 months in Gjøahavn. The voyage continued across the waters Amundsen later named Queen Maud Gulf after Norway's new queen. The weather in the short and hectic Arctic summer changed rapidly from bright sun to fog. Beautiful sailing conditions became voyages in ice and difficult waters with reefs and rocks. Amundsen rowed around in the dinghy to find openings where the GJØA could sail through. On August 26th, 1905 the expedition sailed past the western side of Cape Colborne, the winter harbor of Sir Richard Collinson and his ship, the ENTERPRISE. Collinson arrived there after sailing from the Bering Strait

The GJØA arrives in Nome on August 31st, 1906 after three years in the Arctic.

in 1850. At this time, the GJØA crew knew that they had sailed through the unknown part of the passage north of the American continent and proved that it was possible to navigate these waters. The expedition continued westward with sail and motor through what is now called the Amundsen Gulf and continued to follow the coastline.

Nine days later they met the first vessel since they left Greenland. It was the schooner CHARLES HANSON from San Francisco. The captain was the famous Arctic skipper James McKenna. The ships exchanged short greetings and the GJØA continued the voyage until reaching Herschel, which was a winter harbor for American whalers in Canadian territory. Here the GJØA was once again stopped by ice. Amundsen and his men realized that they would not get any further that year.

In March of 1906 Gustav Wiig died. He was the youngest of the crew and was the last one who died in the search for the Northwest Passage. Many had died earlier during the centuries these explorations had taken place.

The GJØA being towed into its final port in San Francisco.

San Francisco in 1906. A city in ruins met the expedition after the earthquake and fires the same year.

On July 11th, 1906 the ice opened up and the GJØA set sail for Point Barrow and the Bering Strait and then on to Nome, Alaska, where the first celebration took place. The old and worn Hardanger sloop then sailed all the way to San Francisco where it arrived on October 19th, 1906 and the voyage ended. The GJØA had sailed 3,460 nautical miles since it left Disko in Greenland, where the scientific part of the expedition started.

The great earthquake and fires in San Francisco had happened only six months earlier, and the city was in ruins. Still, the GJØA crew received a royal welcome. The Norwegian community was obviously very excited. Little GJØA was paraded past three U.S. battleships which in turn saluted the vessel that had conquered the Northwest Passage. Amundsen and his crew paraded through the city. San Francisco gave a banquet for the heroes at the world famous St. Francis Hotel with 250 invited guests. The celebrations continued for a week, after which Roald Amundsen traveled by train all the way to Washington D.C. to meet with President Theodore Roosevelt.

During the celebration, discussions started about the future fate of the GJØA. The local Norwegian Club suggested that the U.S. Navy should take care of the sloop until the planned canal through Panama was built and the GJØA could take the voyage back to Christiania as the first and only vessel to sail around North America. Amundsen stated that he would like the GJØA to sail to Norway around Cape Horn, but the ship was 37 years old and had received harsh treatment through the Northwest

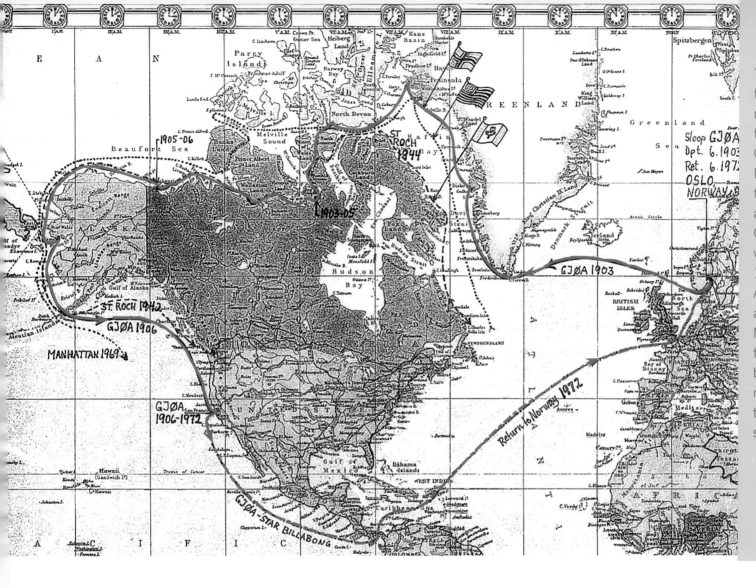

Passage. She would not be seaworthy without major repairs and new equipment. Who would pay for it?

Amundsen had new plans and was constantly looking for money to make amends with the Norwegian merchants he had run away from, and also embarked on new expeditions. The ship remained in San Francisco and became the Norwegian-Americans' pride and problem. The Norwegian community had raised money, taken ownership and given her to the City of San Francisco as a museum ship in honor of Arctic exploration and the pioneering spirit. Thus, GJØA became San Francisco's first historic ship. She

25

was hauled ashore and placed in Golden Gate Park in 1909. In the 63 years that followed, the members of the Norwegian community became her guardians. The GJØA became quite a liability for the city. There were always other budget items that received money that should have gone to the maintenance of the world famous GJØA. This old lady's valiant struggle to survive the elements on an exposed spot by the ocean only increased her fame.

During the next two decades the GJØA was left to deteriorate. Only occasionally did she get a coat of paint. Wind, sun, rain, sand, salt, termites, fungus and rot damaged the ship to the point that it was finally clear that something drastic had to be done before the ship was lost forever. Vandals trespassed and stole and destroyed what they could. All this occurred despite many reports in the city's newspapers and well-meant advice. Already in 1910

The GJØA with small sails in an Arctic storm, painted by Nils Hagerup. The title of the painting is "The Northwest Passage 1903-1906," and it covers a part of a wall in the old stock exchange building in San Francisco. It was Fritz Olsen, Fred Olsen's representative on the U.S. West Coast, who commissioned the painting and gave it to the stock exchange.

A characteristic ship painting of the GJØA under full sails.

there were proposals to erect a building around the ship. In 1932, repairs and improvements were undertaken. This revealed that the ship was in very poor condition. The restoration took five months. However, the work masked the main problem; that almost all of the GJØA had been infested by destructive organisms that had greatly damaged the hull. In 1933 a spokesman for the city noted that the GJØA had at that time been restored as close as possible to her original condition.

The GJØA had become a landmark and received a great deal of attention. Roald Amundsen himself contributed to this. After the GJØA expedition his fame rose to new heights with his conquest of the South Pole in 1911, the MAUD expedition, his flight to 88 degrees north and the journey over the North Pole by the airship NORWAY. He retired at the age of 54. Polar exploration had been the focus of his whole life. Roald Amundsen lost his life in 1928 when the flying boat LATHAM was lost in the Arctic Ocean where he had started his career as a crew member onboard a seal catcher 34 years earlier. When he died he was searching for Captain Nobile, who had gone down with the airship ITALY north of Svalbard.

A large pillar of granite was erected next to the GJØA in Golden Gate Park with a bronze relief

The successful expedition was celebrated for the first time since the ship arrived in Nome in Alaska. A significant number of ladies are among the local visitors onboard.

and the inscription "Roald Amundsen 1872-1928" without this contributing much to the ship's upkeep. Still, poetry, paintings, postcards and collages had GJØA as the main theme. Small, unpretentious models of the GJØA were made of materials from the ship and sold to raise funds for further restoration. The local newspapers continued to write about the ship's demise, including an editorial called "The Shame of the Gjoa" in 1939. "The city's shame is longstanding. If sufficiently strong demand is made on the City Hall, something will be done. Thus far the only formal

Beach life in 1909. The ladies are wading in full clothing, while the man on the right with a suitcase and an umbrella is assisting. This shows a typical day at the beach; very different from today.

2091 – CAPT. ROALD AMUNDSEN'S ARCTIC EXPLORING SLOOP "GJOA", GOLDEN GATE PARK, SAN FRANCISCO, CALIFORNIA. (FIRST VESSEL TO MAKE THE NORTHWEST PASSAGE).

The GJØA leaves the water for the last time. This happened over 100 years ago, on the West Coast of the U.S.

"The ship in the park" was San Francisco's tourist attraction and the city's first historic ship, rescued at a time when it was very uncommon to preserve old ships and boats. The world famous hand-colored postcard was made shortly after the GJØA was pulled ashore, and was mailed all over the world.

The GJØA's final journey on her own keel was short. From her mooring place in port the ship was towed out to Pacific Beach by Golden Gate Park and pulled ashore at high tide as part of the 4th of July celebration in 1909.

protests have been made by citizens of Scandinavian birth residing here. Why should we leave it to them? Where are our native sons and first families?" the editorial noted.

People of Norwegian descent must have felt very upset with this situation. It was their forefathers who had given the ship to the city. In 1939 they decided to create a formal institution named the Gjoa Foundation to help the city take care of the ship. The mayor had just cut $25,000 to restore the GJØA from the budget. At the gala dinner with 300 guests during the Norwegian Crown Prince and Crown Princess's visit to San Francisco on May 17th, 1939 the city pledged funds for immediately restoring the GJØA.

The work started in the spring of 1940 and it turned out that the ship was in worse condition than expected and that the funds would not suffice. It was therefore decided to erect a temporary shelter over the ship; rigging it all the way down and securing the GJØA until it could be properly restored. The Gjoa Foundation was an important participant in planning this restoration. The members refused to give up the ship and realized that the rescue operation would take several years. They set a long term goal: To stabilize the vessel in a proper building where it could be exhibited along with other artifacts from the Arctic and thus be secured for future generations. The plan was to create a museum of Arctic research with the GJØA as the main attraction.

The GJØA was thus saved from destruction and was temporarily kept inside a protective shelter for the first and last time. It was a good thing that the decision to save the vessel was made at that time. World War II was in full development. The people in San Francisco got other things to think about. Five long years without any extra help would have destroyed the last remnants of the GJØA. The restoration was an ambitious project. The plans included provisions for restoring her back to her former glory using material of original dimensions. This would give the ship a solid and nice look, but would leave little of the original vessel from 1872.

Not much happened during the war. In the fall of 1945, the city was reminded of its promises. The response was that the restoration would have to wait for two more years. The Gjoa Foundation

Shortly after the landing, the newspapers started discussing enclosing the ship in a building. This picture, from about 1910, reveals parts and details that are no longer found onboard the GJØA. It also shows that parts of the ship have started to rot.

members therefore started their own fundraising and provided much of the money needed to finish the project. A full restoration of the ship took place in the following years. "We hope that in 1972 on the 100 year anniversary, both of Roald Amundsen's birth and the original launching of the GJØA, those in charge of the ship's welfare will acknowledge that what was done here in her 76th year really gave the GJØA continued lease on life," said Chairman Erik Krag of the Gjoa Foundation at a ceremony in May, 1949 when the restoration of GJØA was finally finished. The ship looked beautiful and was admired by old and young. Her nickname was no longer only "The Ship in the Park," but also "The Pride of San Francisco." The Hardanger sloop had become the city's maritime pride.

Unfortunately, regular maintenance was not performed. Only six years later it was clear that the decay had started anew. The Parks Department had not painted and protected the wood. "The ship should never be permitted to get into disrepair now that she has been so basically restored," stated the Gjoa Foundation in 1955 in its first meeting since 1949.

The deck with equipment before it was taken off. It followed the GJØA back to Norway.

However, a new generation of counterculture followed; some of them were vandals who took possession of the ship. They smashed the doors, cut the rigging and used open flames onboard. The fence was repaired to no avail. Somebody tried to set fire to the ship. The fire was luckily extinguished before major damage was done. Late one night a week later the same thing happened. An off duty police officer who drove by smelled smoke and alerted the fire brigade who extinguished the fire. They found that a pyromaniac had lit paper soaked in ignition fluid and thrown it through the hole made by the first fire. The GJØA was rescued minutes before it would have become a formidable bonfire. Only three months later did a severe winter storm break the mast. Amundsen's old

This famous postcard has been reprinted and used many times, here as an illustration for a book cover.

GJØA became the pride of Norway. This postcard was made and sold during the Panama Pacific World Exposition in 1915.

Captain Roald Amundsen himself helped make the ship even more famous through a series of grand expeditions in the years that followed. Amundsen returned to San Francisco and was, of course, depicted next to the GJØA, his first command.

32

The retired polar explorer Roald Amundsen in 1927. This image, taken in San Francisco, is thought to be one of the very last portrait photographs of the man who conquered both the South and the North Pole. He died in a plane crash the following year.

Terry No Longe Means Toweli

Fashion models aboard the historic ship Gjoa in Golden

By Ninon

TERRY CLOTH was whisked off the towel racks and into sportswear styles several years ago; and each season the designers outdo themselves in creating eye-catching playtime togs of the erstwhile Turkish toweling.

Terry cloth in all the colors of a summer rainbow—in brilliant dots as big as two-bit pieces, in stripes wide as rulers or narrow as peppermint sticks, and terry printed in amusing motifs and Hawaiian flowers—all contribute to the gaiety of vacation wardrobes. Fashions on

this page were se cloth collections stores and photo the Gjoa, located Pa k meets the G

The Gjoa is most historic sh landmark of San was the ship in w sen made the the Northwest of the ship fro to Argonaut B one of the pr San Francisco

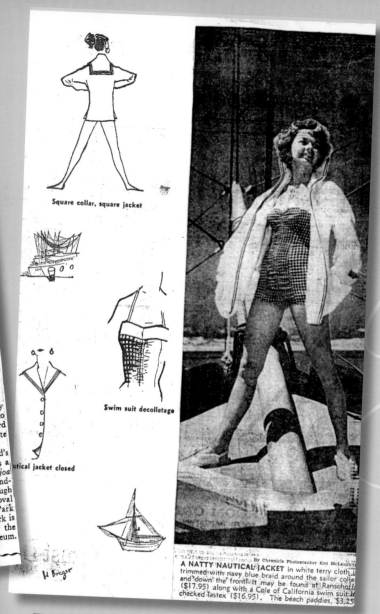

Square collar, square jacket

Swim suit decolletage

nautical jacket closed

A NATTY NAUTICAL JACKET in white terry cloth, trimmed with navy blue braid around the sailor collar and down the front. It may be found at Ransohoff ($17.95) along with a Cole of California swim suit in checked Lastex ($16.95). The beach paddies, $3.25.

H Br-ger

The GJØA even became a location for fashion models. A four page photo shoot presenting new swim suit designs was printed in the Sunday issue of the San Francisco Chronicle on May 24th, 1953.

After more than 60 years as American property, the GJØA was released and transported back to Norway.

Some persons responsible for the GJØA's return. From left: Rolf Schou of the Gjoa Foundation, Consul General Finn Koren and Captain Einar Øxnevad of the STAR BILLABONG. The two ship owners behind the "Home Going Project," Christian Blom and Per Waaler, were not present when the picture was taken.

The GJØA was sent home to Oslo in 1972, 69 years after the ship left. She traveled as deck cargo onboard the STAR BILLABONG. This picture was taken just before the GJØA passed under the world famous Golden Gate Bridge.

The Bill of Lading.

crow's nest was crushed against the rig and the railing.

This happened shortly before journalists and other visitors from Norway came to see the GJØA on their way to the Winter Olympics in Squaw Valley in 1960. Polar explorers Amundsen and Nansen were excellent skiers and early ambassadors of winter sports. They contributed a lot to increasing interest in skiing as a sport. The City of San Francisco refused to repair the mast on such short notice. The Gjoa Foundation had to find workers and pay for the job.

In the 1960s, the Maritime Museum in San Francisco conducted many minor repairs on the rig and the hull. The museum director Karl Kortum worked together with the Gjoa Foundation to get the city to move the ship to the collection of boats in the Aquatic Park. The plan was again and again delayed due to real estate issues. During his visit to the city in 1968 King Olav of Norway was informed about these plans and thought they were interesting. It would be great if the GJØA could be seen by more people, His Majesty noted.

In 1970 Oslo's Mayor Brynjulf Bull sent a formal request to San Francisco's Mayor Alioto regarding moving the GJØA home to Oslo. The ship had been a landmark in San Francisco and a meeting point for Norwegians for over two generations. A survey conducted in 1971 showed that all 12 Norwegian organizations in the San Francisco Bay Area supported moving GJØA back to Norway. Hippies, vandals, poor maintenance and difficulties conserving the ship under challenging environmental conditions were important reasons cited.

The wish to send the GJØA home did not originate in Norway. It was the ship's closest friends, people of Norwegian descent in San Francisco, who in despair over the city's lack of commitment, pushed for relocation. They saw this as their only option, even if they would lose their beautiful old ship and their ancestors' pride. Norwegian ship owners promised to pay for the move and also fund a full restoration of the GJØA outside the FRAM museum on Bygdøynes in Oslo. The Fish Club in San Francisco and the Gjoa Foundation provided planning, insurance and shipping. Christian Blom, Rolf Schou and Consul General Finn Koren became officers of the committee in San Francisco that worked closely with ship owner Tom Wilhelmsen in Norway and Director Molaug of the Norwegian Maritime Museum in Oslo.

The main problem was to get the City of San Francisco to give up ownership of the GJØA. Once again newspapers started writing

When the GJØA came to Oslo, yet another major restoration started, undertaken by Kristian Djupevåg from Hardanger. After two years the ship was once again rigged and ready for display outdoors on Bygdøynes as a reminder of the voyage through the Northwest Passage and polar exploration and research.

about Amundsen's old polar ship. Many locals did not want to give up ownership of the GJØA. She was San Francisco's first and, for a long time, their only historic ship, and had been a well known and popular fixture of the city. But many also remembered the city's neglect and found that the proposed relocation was reasonable. The letter from Mayor Brynjulf Bull to Mayor Joseph Alioto was positively received. In the spring of 1972, the GJØA was released in part due to the cooperation between good friends Mayor Alioto and Christian Blom and could return home. It was quite a job to get the GJØA out of the sand pit at the bottom of the Golden Gate Park. The transport of the ship was even more challenging, as overhead electrical wires needed to be cut and repaired as the transport passed.

The GJØA was transported home by the STAR BILLABONG from the Billabong Shipping Company in Bergen. The GJØA finally took the voyage through the Panama Canal, but not on her own keel. On June 2nd, 1972 the cargo ship arrived in Oslo with the GJØA on the aft hatch. The OSLOKRANA took the GJØA the final stretch to Bygdøynes where the ship was set down on cushions. Sixty-nine years after the GJØA left Christiana, now Oslo, she was handed over to the Norwegian Maritime Museum at Bygdøynes with much pomp and circumstance. Boat builders from Hardanger were commissioned to restore the GJØA for the third time. This restoration was as complete

36

Gjøahavn at Bygdøy has a great collection of traditional boats, some even older than the good old GJØA.

as the one in the 1940s, leaving even less of the original ship. But the ship kept a good number of solid redwood knees as a memory of her time in San Francisco, while an original pine knee from the GJØA's construction in Hardanger, is still on display at the Maritime Museum in San Francisco. This knee was used as a template for the new knees. After two summers of hard work, the polar exploration sloop was once again restored and rigged to her former beauty. Later the aft cabin was restored. Upkeep on the GJØA is being done on an ongoing basis.

Boy Scouts from San Francisco's Troop 14 attending an international jamboree in Norway. They were allowed onboard the GJØA and gathered for a picture on the forecastle to honor San Francisco's first historic ship.

The Norwegian Maritime Museum still continues some of the traditions from Golden Gate Park. The GJØA is sitting outside, exposed to the elements. But she is at least maintained on an ongoing basis and is also covered up during the winter. She sits behind a high fence and is usually off limits to the public. At least people no longer break through the fence. The bow is, as always, pointing towards the sea, although no longer towards the north. The polar seas are far away. The GJØA is a symbol of the research and exploration that characterized the battle over the Northwest Passage. A statue of Roald Amundsen sits outside the fence and a bronze plaque shares information about the ship's voyages and her time in San Francisco in both English and Norwegian. Many Americans nod in recognition when they come to visit the ship at the new Gjøahavn at Bygdøynes.

At Ocean Beach in Golden Gate Park we can still find the fence and the statue of Roald Amundsen. Some maps of San Francisco even today show "The ship GJØA" in Golden Gate Park. Lured by such maps visitors come to the site to see the GJØA, and some of them contact the San Francisco National Maritime Museum to find out what has become of "The Ship in the Park." Paintings and artifacts from the ship and the expedition surface from time to time. Some time ago the author was shown a small fishing net Amundsen had used for fishing during his expedition. It ended up in San Francisco when the famous explorer used it to barter with a merchant in the city after the ship arrived there in 1906.

Some of the locals were sad to see the GJØA leave San Francisco.

They would have liked to keep her, but the city lost its first historic ship. This vessel was saved at a time when it was far less common to preserve historic ships than it is today. The GJØA was an early inspiration for many, and encouraged people interested in preserving old vessels. She was saved long before the FRAM was rescued and placed in a museum. The GJØA was brought home and placed next to FRAM, thanks to expatriate Norwegians in California, mainly in San Francisco.

The small, but accomplished Arctic sloop GJØA has yet to get her own boathouse. She is very old. Only a few ships on the coast of Norway are older. In her current condition, she is a symbol more than a real historic ship. From a distance she may look real: The

GJØA's forecastle facing Oslo Harbor.

lines are beautiful, the mast and the rig powerful. The GJØA was a very good example of the Norwegian boat building tradition. A closer inspection of the ship, however, shows that what currently is left of the GJØA is very different from the weather beaten old hull, anchors and rig that we can see in the photos from 1910. The images were taken immediately after the GJØA was retired, and show a ship with iron bands around the bow. The bands were added by Amundsen and are similar to those the FRAM still have. The pictures also show her damaged bow; a result of damages sustained in the Arctic. The gray and weathered extra oak hull she got for added protection as she sailed through the Northwest Passage is missing today.

The GJØA has something to tell us today, and should inspire future generations. We have no time to lose when it comes to preserving buildings and ships that are related to significant events or document traditions from a time long gone. Securing, repairing and maintaining these historic artifacts are required and must be based on good planning. We are the ones responsible for future generations having something to learn from.

"Only a culturally deprived society will leave little behind and provide the new generations with less ballast and a smaller platform to build their lives on. It is a good generation that saves for its children things to see and learn from, to make them feel important and proud of themselves and their ancestors' achievements." (From the book *Shipping and Culture*, 1997.)

Countless models and paintings have been made of the GJØA. This large scale painting is at the Norwegian Club in San Francisco.

The Dutch Windmill, Amundsen's *bautastein* and GJØA's fence are still left at the west end of Golden Gate Park.

The GJØA at Bygdøynes is almost a full copy of Amundsen's polar ship. Deteriorating forces the vessel has been exposed to since the voyage through the Northwest Passage have damaged the vessel to a point where there is very little left of the original ship. Some frames and beams of redwood are still inside. They are reminders of restoration work done in San Francisco.

A bronze plaque with a map and information by the *bautastein* of Roald Amundsen in Golden Gate Park in San Francisco. It is fairly new. Here is the text:

Roald Amundsen, the Norwegian polar explorer, was the first to locate the magnetic North Pole and to navigate the Northwest Passage, the Arctic water route from the Atlantic to the Pacific. He left Norway with a crew of six on June 16 of 1903 in a 69-fot long converted herring boat named Gjoa. Amundsen spent three years on the perilous journey. The Gjoa continued on, sailing through the Bering Straits and anchored off Point Bonita, outside the Golden Gate, on October 19, 1906. The San Francisco Norwegian community purchased the Gjoa from Amundsen and donated the ship to the people of San Francisco in 1909. In 1911, Amundsen became the first explorer to reach the South Pole. The Gjoa remained at this site at the west end of Golden Gate Park until 1972, when it was returned to Norway. The restored ship is now on display at the Maritime Museum in Oslo.

The Amundsen monument is a stone Bauta, or a pilar of Norwegian granite which was donated by Bay Area Norwegians March 1st 1930.

A close-up of Amundsen's relief. The monument, of Norwegian red granite, was erected in front of the ship shortly after Amundsen's death.

Oslo's first sailing training ship, the brig STATSRAAD ERICHSEN, became an international legend. She took young men on sail training missions for three generations.

Statsraad Erichsen
-Longest In Sail

The naval brig STATSRAAD ERICHSEN was in 1901 taken over by the Norwegian organization Christiania Skoleskib to become the capital of Norway's first active sail training vessel for cadets seeking a career in the merchant marine. This wooden brig is in a class all by herself among Norwegian sailing ships. She set records that will stand forever.

Of all the Norwegian sailing ships the STATSRAAD ERICHSEN is the most unique. No other sailing vessels, from the days of white sails, verge upon breaking the records that this brig set during many decades in military and civil service. The STATSRAAD ERICHSEN was the last "white swan" of the good old type, built of wood and with only sails for propulsion. When she finally was given up as a result of war and strife she had become the world's oldest vessel of her kind. The solid oak ship had survived the era of the sailing ship by many decades and the golden age of its ship type, the brig, by well over 100 years. She was the last Norwegian brig. No Norwegian sail training ship comes close to matching the years of service given by this old lady.

During the first part of the 1900s all sailing ships with machinery were registered as "auxiliary sail ships." They were not considered pure sailing ships, but motor ships with sails. For example, the bark STATSRAAD LEHMKUHL, another well known Norwegian sail training ship, was a vessel of this type since she was built with an auxiliary engine. The older sail training ships in Norway were tall ships with sails only. The first Norwegian built sail training ship with an engine was actually the CHRISTIAN RADICH. She was built only 13 years before the middle of the Twentieth Century and remains the last great sailing vessel built in Norway. Times and standards change. Today no one would dream of calling Norway's three sailing ships "auxiliary sail ships;" they are definitely known as sailing vessels. In the old days the perspective was different. Machines were rare and considered such a great improvement that a ship with sails and motor was no longer seen as only a sailing ship, one example is the hybrid Pacific steam scooner.

Except for the bark LINGARD which never sailed after being saved in Norway as a memorial, the training brig STATSRAAD ERICHSEN was the last pure sailing ship with home port in Oslo.

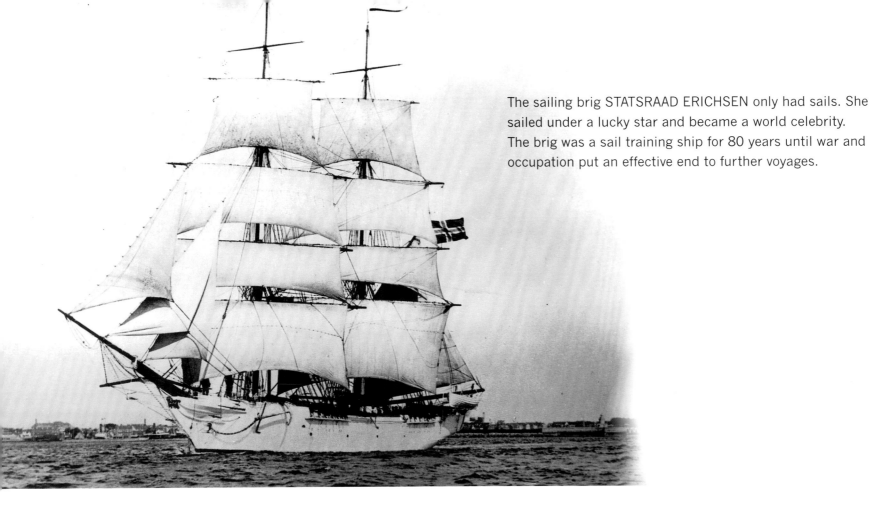

The sailing brig STATSRAAD ERICHSEN only had sails. She sailed under a lucky star and became a world celebrity. The brig was a sail training ship for 80 years until war and occupation put an effective end to further voyages.

She only had her sails for propulsion and, naturally, when the wind died down she could not proceed in the desired direction. There is a significant difference between this and modern sailing ships that simply start their engines when the wind dies or changes direction, or when the currents might cause trouble. In the old days, the current and changing winds were always dangerous for sailing ships, which could end up on shore due to their dependence on the elements. Many a seaman perished because of this simple fact. Sailing ships often had short service lives, but the STATSRAAD ERICHSEN survived to become very old.

It could be said that this small naval brig was born under a lucky star and lived among giants. The Norwegian Navy Yard's next ship was the huge KONG SVERRE, a sail and steam powered frigate with 50 cannons. Referred to as "The Nordic Horror," her

The Navy's cadet brig in place between the buoys outside of Akershus Castle in Oslo. She became the city's sailing training ship in 1901.

hull was no. 43. The sail training ship for cadets, the STATSRAAD ERICHSEN, was no. 42. The year was 1858 and the training vessel was built with great care. Only first class oak was used. Many measures were taken so the vessel would be as solid and safe as possible. The brig had a displacement of 215 tons when fully equipped. She measured 84 feet at the water line, was 23 feet wide and 11 feet deep, and was equipped with four 18-pound cannons and one 12-pound metal howitzer. On the test run she reached a speed of 11 knots! The ship served as the main vessel for naval cadets, with the naval city of Horten as her home port. She had a crew of between 68 and 92 men.

The STATSRAAD ERICHSEN was the youngest of the three naval brigs of the Royal Norwegian Navy. The oldest, the LOLLAND, originally belonged to the Danish-Norwegian fleet and took part in the Napoleonic Wars. When Norway was separated from Denmark in 1814 the entire Royal Norwegian Navy's officer corps consisted of 39 men. The largest ships were the brigs, of which the LOLLAND was the leader. The six other ships were soon decommissioned, and the brigs KIEL, SEAGULL, LANGELAND, ALLERT, ALSEN and LOUGEN were sold.

The brig FREDRIKSVERN was built in 1814, based on the LOLLAND's drawings, but was not commissioned until 1817. She measured 100 feet with 448 tons displacement and had a crew of between 107 and 140 men. Her armament consisted of 16 cannons. The FREDRIKSVERN served the Norwegian Navy until 1848 and was scrapped in 1854. She logged 10.5 knots while on patrol off Gibraltar. The three naval brigs were used for training purposes. While the first two regularly participated in expeditions to distant seas such as the Mediterranean, the Bay of Biscay, the Baltic Sea and the White Sea in Russia, the smaller STATSRAAD ERICHSEN was used for training in domestic waters, with occasional voyages to Stavanger in the west and Strømstad in Sweden to the east.

The oldest known image of the Royal Norwegian Navy's cadet ship STATSRAAD ERICHSEN under sail. The ship carries single topgallants and royals.

The period after the 1815 Vienna Peace Congress was a comparatively peaceful period in European history, even though Norway's warships, together with the Swedish Navy, were used to harass the Barbary States and were on call during the Danish-German War of 1864. The STATSRAAD ERICHSEN, built also to serve as a Man-o-War, nonetheless became more and more of a pure cadet ship. She was built to be able to go to war, performing blockade service or defending against smaller ships off the coast. By virtue of her small size she could easily hide among the islets and reefs, or act as a boarding vessel against enemy or rebellious merchant ships. A high gunwale with room for sandbags gave her sailors and marines good protection. Extra equipment and parts, magazines for weapons and ammunition, and a sick bay were included in the ship's features. The brig could be equipped for and function in a service role not unlike the Norwegian Coast Guard cutters that patrol the coast and board and inspect foreign vessels today. But the advent of steam and iron quickly rendered such warships obsolete. This happened while the STATSRAAD ERICHSEN was still a young ship.

The board of the organization Christiania Skoleskib was fully aware that their old, stationary sail training ship CHRISTIANIA no longer served its purpose. The merchant captains who hired the graduates wanted boys who were used to the sea. It became more and more important to find a sail training ship that could actually sail. But the organization lacked the needed funding. The board's sole asset was the old CHRISTIANIA. It was essentially a lodging ship, more than 40 years old. Scrapping her would not yield much. A simple solution to the problem did not exist. Some suggested that they take over the naval brig STATSRAAD ERICHSEN which was being decommissioned. The board had previously kept in touch with the Navy and in 1896 they sent a letter to formally request a swap since the Navy needed a lodging vessel. The response was positive. Some of the board members inspected the brig and were convinced that the STATSRAAD ERICHSEN would fulfill their needs. But the process took time. Several years went by before formal negotiations started. The board minutes noted that it was important to "stride into action" as soon as possible.

The yearly general meeting held in the spring of 1900 voted unanimously that the new goal for the organization was to secure a seaworthy sail training ship. That same summer Trondheim acquired the *skolebriggen* TORDENSKJOLD. The Norwegian capital was starting to lag behind the provinces. The board sent an application to the Ministry of Defense to buy the STATSRAAD ERICHSEN for 5,000 Norwegian kroner. The insurance company Nora donated the money. They bought the ship and gave it to the Christiania Skoleskib organization. The Navy included a lot of extra equipment with the purchase. On July 1st, 1901, the Norwegian naval ensign was lowered and the merchant flag hoisted onboard

The brig TORDENSKJOLD became Norway's first training ship actually sailing. All previous training vessels were stationary.

During a cruise, laundry is up for drying in calm weather at Frederikshavn, Denmark. Mother's clothes pegs will not do. The white uniforms must be tied up with twine so as not to be blown overboard.

the STATSRAAD ERICHSEN in the city of Horten. The brig had been decommissioned from the Royal Norwegian Navy.

On *Olsok*, or St. Olav's Day (July 29th) 1901, the stationary CHRISTIANIA's last cohort of 45 boys transferred to the brig. A photo taken by the famous photographer Anders B. Wilse, dated August 6th, 1901, is likely from STATSRAAD ERICHSEN's arrival in Christiania. The brig arrived at new moorings in Pipervika close to the old ship. The capital had finally received its seaworthy sail training vessel. In retrospect, this was a good choice. Like in the past, it was the private promoters and philanthropic efforts that created the progress and helped young people become seamen.

Old wooden ships deteriorate and can become dangerous to sail as they age. Even in our time old wooden ships have gone down with loss of life as a result. Wooden ships were seen as old long before they turned 30, if they even managed to survive that long. The STATSRAAAD ERICHSEN had been in service for the Navy for over 40 years and was a very old brig, but she was superbly maintained. In 1901 nobody would have thought that the brig was only halfway through her career as a sail training ship. A good example for comparison is the ship the brig replaced. The CHRISTIANIA was built in 1853, just five years prior to STATSRAAD ERICHSEN, but she stopped sailing in 1877, 24 years old. At that

A bow image with beautiful ornaments. Two of the cadets are busy rigging the jib boom.

Rigging aft under the supervision of the captain.

time she was considered unfit for further work on the high seas. She would probably have been broken up or converted to a barge or some other stationary service if not sold to Norway.

It was obviously important to the board that the brig was well kept, safe and solid. The responsibility for the ship and the lives of many young people was theirs. Stories about tragic accidents and loss of sail training ships from other countries caused the members to worry. The captain and the officers, together with the board, put great emphasis on keeping the ship in excellent condition and had 50 cadets eager to perform the work. The number of applications for admission was unusually large. Those who were admitted were counted among the lucky ones. The ultimate reward for good effort was to get to handle a fine old ship with genuine square sails on a summer cruise.

When the STATSRAAD ERICHSEN arrived in the capital, it was a naval vessel, painted black and with the broad hedge that was so typical for ships in the mid-1800s. She still had her original, powerful rig, with large mainsails, topsails, topgallant sails, and royals. With a deep keel and lots of ballast she could withstand bad weather and make good speed.

The new commercial flag was not the only symbol of the change from naval to civilian service. The brig's hull was painted white. The masts and poles were oiled, and she got brightly colored scrollwork on the bow and stern. The deep and heavy topsails were re-rigged to more "modern" rigging with upper and lower topsails, to make them easier to handle, but also to give her a more modern

New cadets are arriving onboard the brig, which is about to break the winter hiatus. Yards, running rigging and sails are to be put in place.

Old and new meet. Photographer Wilse's beautiful image from the Port of Christiania at sundown; probably taken on a fall day after students have left the ship. The down-rigged STATSRAAD ERICHSEN is waiting for the winter, while a steam freighter is waiting for a berth.

49

Twelve boys rigging.

rig that would facilitate the training. Steel wire rigging with turnbuckles replaced the old hemp rig with deadeyes after a few years. Some other minor adjustments were also made, but basically the STATSRAAD ERICHSEN sailed for 36 years with only regular, general maintenance. No major repairs were needed.

The brig is a type of ship superbly suited for the training of future seamen. Brigs were rarely larger than 300 tons. The rig was therefore lightweight and easy to handle compared to the heavy rig on the big bark rigged cargo ships that dominated the end of the age of sailing ships. Yet the brig's smaller rig required the same kind of training and knowledge as on the large ships. No other sailing ship needed larger crews in terms of tonnage, and no square rigged ship had better maneuverability than the brig. It could sail up rivers and into narrow and difficult harbors without assistance if the wind

and current conditions were good. The clipper ships were world famous, but in home waters the brig was perfect for coastal sailing. If at war, just like the Viking ships, they could choose to attack or run, and few other ships could catch them, let alone outmaneuver them in shallow water amongst islets and reefs. The naval brig LOUGEN's endeavors off the Norwegian coast during the Napoleonic Wars were legendary. The brig SEAGULL chased and captured larger English ships.

In international trade the brigs disappeared early as the need for more transport volume increased. This kind of ship was not very

Learning to row a lifeboat was important. The first thing the guests would notice when visiting the ship was the boys' skills with the oars.

The brig STATSRAAD ERICHSEN back in the city after completed summer missions.

financially competitive compared to larger vessels with bark rigs. Only on shorter routes did the brigs retain their position for a while longer. But after the mid-1800's, when the steamship also entered the competition, their era was over.

The brig was, however, very well suited for cohorts of 35 to 55 cadets. As long as this remained the target class size for the institutions in the cities of Christiania and Trondheim, the brig served very well. The two brigs STATSRAAD ERICHSEN and TORDENSKJOLD would honor their hometowns through fine sailing and brilliant maneuvers in the years up until WWI. The best evidence for the appropriateness of this ship type was that the number of applications increased sharply. A total of 167 boys submitted their application for admission the first full season onboard the STATSRAAD ERICHSEN in 1902. Only 46 were accepted. The class size increased gradually, and the sail training ship would have up to 57 students.

Captain Torkildsen's report from the first season in 1902 show how the officers would familiarize themselves with the ship. It is evident that the ship had some shortcomings. The report refers to how difficult it could be to get into Christiania's port with a sailing ship. Let us take a look at Captain Torkildsen's voyage report from 1902:

The class of 1928. The ship's crew and cadets are gathered around Captain Fredriksen for a final picture before the boys are scattered around the world. Most of them are only 16 years old.

The captain's report includes humorous and time specific details. The first voyage took about two months. Between the lines one can read that this was the ship's trial run. Gradually the range was extended after the captain had been back in town and conferred with the management. Before radio and telephone service, this was the way to do it to ensure the cadets were operating in a safe environment. The bowsprit was affected by rot; a new one was made and changed in five days. The boys' hands were sore due to working the ropes. Many suffered from seasickness. The ship was totally dependent on the weather. The report reveals how difficult it was to sail up to Christiania without an auxiliary engine, and explains why cargo ships in the old days went to Son, a port farther out in the fjord, instead of trying to sail all the way up to the city. Three to five days to sail all the way to the capital should be ample time for a brig. Yet it took 10 days of tacking back and forth without making much headway. When the winds finally turned, it was a piece of cake to reach Christiania. The STATSRAAD ERICHSEN arrived in Christiania a week behind schedule. This was part of the game when traveling by sails alone.

A sail training ship that could actually sail helped gain support. The STATSRAAD ERICHSEN expanded her horizons and ventured out of the fjord. The following year she sailed to Frederikshavn in Denmark, doing eight knots on her best watch, with a lot of seasick city boys who later would become sailors. From 1906, Leith in Scotland was the turning point of the cruise. The first crossing was quite dramatic. The brig had to turn around in bad weather

The cadets demonstrate what they have learned at an anniversary show. An interested Majesty, King Haakon, a Navy admiral himself, pays careful attention. He is seen to the right of the mast.

with a damaged rudder. After 12 days of drifting in the North Sea, the weather took the brig into Larkollen where the rudder was repaired. The ship set sail again, and with a fresh breeze from the northeast, crossed the North Sea once again. Outside the Firth of Forth the ship met fog, but managed to sail right into the harbor and cast anchor. When the fog lifted they saw that the TORDENSKJOLD was anchored close by. She had arrived after a 23 day voyage from Trondheim, Norway. It was not a coincidence that

His Majesty King Haakon VII arrives onboard
STATSRAAD ERICHSEN on September 9th, 1931 in
conjunction with Oslo Skoleskib's 50th anniversary.

The King and the captain.

The King enjoying conversing
with celebrities.

His Majesty's first task was to inspect the students.

The King and invited gues

After the demonstrations and the tour of the ship, King Haakon was served traditional ship's food. Note the hooks for attachment of the hammocks and the height of the deck.

A STATSRAAD ERICHSEN cadet in the ship's dark blue parade uniform with an Oslo Skoleskib cap, used for festive occasions and on shore leave. The white canvas uniform was used during summer sailing parades.

two Norwegian training brigs met in Leith, a popular destination in those days. In addition, the British royal yacht VICTORIA AND ALBERT with escorting naval vessels as well as the Dutch warship FRIESLAND had arrived in the harbor. The cadets in their white uniforms from the two Norwegian ships got a job ferrying dignitaries to and from the ships in the harbor. They were praised and often received a token tip in appreciation of a job well done. The first mate on the STATSRAAD ERICHSEN deposited the money into the ship's coffers, although it was intended for the boys. When the cadets found out that the TORDENSKJOLD's cadets got to keep their tips, uproar occurred among the boys. There was widespread dissatisfaction. The result was that 11 cadets signed off and three more ran away. The annual parade for the press and invited guests after the ship's return had to be canceled. A newspaper editorial concluded that although the ship's funds were meager, they should be able to do without confiscating the tips. The cadets should have been allowed to keep their money.

The morale was usually good, but a few incidents show that there, as always, were some issues. Two boys ran away in Larkollen after a storm in the North Sea, and the captain noted that they were probably scared of the many challenges in the life of a sailor. Another time a boy was sent ashore with the note: "Not fit to be a seaman." The most dramatic way to react was to run away. From time to time students disappeared, and we do not always know the cause. There could, of course, be reasons that had nothing to do with the ship.

After 1905, the students signed on with an understanding that there would be a relationship of mutual obligations. Upon graduation they were given a certificate to document their training, with the following grades: Excellent, Very Good, or Good. They were given physical and mental training; focusing on cleanliness, order, alertness, and quick responses to the challenges of the sea.

The training was linked to the upkeep of the STATSRAAD ERICHSEN, keeping her in seaworthy condition. The season started with the rigging of the ship as well as regular maintenance to prepare her for the summer cruise. The cadets were given basic knowledge of the ship, the rig and the work routines onboard. Lifeboat drills and practice in rowing and basic seamanship were included. The training also included a "modern" subject: All students had to learn to swim. At that time, few people knew how to swim. Many drowning accidents at sea could have been prevented if more seamen knew how to swim. The method was quite rough. As soon as the sea was "warm" enough (60 degrees Farenheit), the boys were taught the basic moves while still onboard the ship. The boys then had to swim without any additional practice, knowing that they were in deep water. Those who did not voluntarily jump in were thrown overboard. The instructor was waiting in the dinghy and grabbed the poor guys who could not stay afloat on their own. Both the instructors and the students alleged that everyone could swim after the cruise.

There was only one area of specialization. All the boys were mustered on deck, although some boys were tasked with assisting the cook. New plans and procedures for training had been established after 1912. These provided good insight into what the STATSRAAD ERICHSEN focused on in the effort to turn boys into men. For many decades the curriculum was the same. With some modifications it actually stayed the same until the 1950s and even longer in some respects. The good curriculum was one of the explanations for why the STATSRAAD ERICHSEN sailed as long as she did.

When the students were admitted, they were given a list of the things they needed to bring when they first embarked: Clothes

The STATSRAAD ERICHSEN boys participated in the May 17th celebration, parading past the Royal Palace in Oslo. They were easily recognized in their blue uniforms and always did well because they could march in step. King Haakon and Queen Maud can be seen on the terrace.

"The last in sail." This stylish photo was taken by photographer Wilse on August 6th, 1901, when the handsome Navy brig came to Christiania to become the capital's sail training ship. The ship ended up becoming a world-renowned legend.

Three Norwegian sail training ships gathered for a celebration in 1930. Closest and to the left is the brig STATSRAAD ERICHSEN. In the middle is the bark STATSRAAD LEHMKUHL of Bergen. To the right is the bark TORDENSKJOLD, which replaced the brig with the same name after World War I.

and shoes, rain gear and boots, flatware, washbasin, toilet soap, comb, mirror and toothbrush, towel, clothes, hairbrush, shoe brush, shoe polish, sewing kit, wool blankets, sneakers, and a folding knife. All their personal items had to be marked with the student's initials and packaged in a sailor's bag. The students were required to arrive clean and with short hair.

The list of personal property above represents the seafarer's life in a nutshell. This was what the seaman needed as he moved from one boat to the next. Stationery, the New Testament, a picture or two and a few other items were added as the cadet became a "real" seaman. Going to sea was something completely different

from moving to the city or taking a job on a farm. It could be several years between each time a sailor came home. They could normally only carry with them what they could bring onboard or to a boarding house in Boston or other ports in wait for their next ship. The education onboard the sail training ships was a preparation for this kind of life. Most of the students became career seamen. Onboard the STATSRAAD ERICHSEN all students were issued a dark blue uniform for going ashore, and a white uniform of canvas to be used onboard the ship. The boys had to wash and keep their uniforms in order.

The STATSRAAD ERICHSEN was an old Navy vessel built strong and deep. Thus, she was pretty heavy for her size and had a big rig, and could reach high speeds in good weather. On the return from a visit to Trondheim in 1930 she took part in an unofficial race, competing with the full rigged ship SØRLANDET. She was built of steel two years earlier, and should have been able to sail faster than the old wooden brig STATSRAAD ERICHSEN, but this was not to be. As the two ships passed the island of Hitra outside the Trondheims Fjord, they sailed side by side. After that they did not see each other until they rounded the cape of Lindesnes, the southernmost point of Norway. At that time, the SØRLANDET was closer to land and a little bit ahead. The competition continued as they sailed up the coast and ended with the STATSRAAD ERICHSEN anchoring at Horten one hour before the SØRLANDET arrived. The distance was about 650 nautical miles.

On September 9th, 1931 the Skoleskib organization celebrated its 50th anniversary. This nonprofit, idealistic organization that had spent four years securing the *Skoleskibet* CHRISTIANIA and converting the old clipper ship had gained a lot of respect and admiration over the years. Even if the capital had the smallest and oldest sailing ship of all the Norwegian cities (and the only still remaining built of wood), this brig had high status. The sail training organization that started in Christiania was the oldest in Norway and in many ways set the stage for similar organizations in other parts of the country. Proximity to the Ship Owner's Association, the Parliament and the governmental offices made it easier to get noticed. The newspapers in the city often wrote about STATSRAAD ERICHSEN and CHRISTIANIA before her.

The era of the white sails had passed. There were few pure sailing vessels left. The STATSRAAD ERICHSEN was a breath of fresh air from a bygone era. Visits by members of the Royal Family onboard sail training ships were not that uncommon. But it was rare that the King himself visited such small vessels. This exception occurred in 1931. The institution's 50th anniversary celebration started with His Majesty King Haakon VII of Norway's visit onboard the STATSRAAD ERICHSEN. Together with representatives from the Department of Trade, the Navy and the entire board of the Oslo Skoleskib organization, His Majesty the King experienced a show where the students demonstrated their knowledge and skills, on deck and aloft. Student portfolios were exhibited and the ship sported shining brass and new paint all over. After the students' performance the visitors all gathered at the dinner table. King

Haakon had himself received maritime training as a young man and showed great enthusiasm during his visit. The next two days the students gave repeat performances for other visitors such as official representatives, donors and friends of the old brig.

The brig STATSRAAD ERICHSEN was the last white swan. She only had sails for propulsion, and moved quickly or slowly depending on the wind and the currents. There was no modern equipment onboard which could disturb the sense of close, genuine interaction between people and nature. The officers and students had to rely on their own knowledge and seamanship, as well as the anchor, to stay safe. The STATSRAAD ERICHSEN sailed under a lucky star and experienced 80 years as a sail training ship for the Navy and the cities of Christiania and Porsgrunn without being blown ashore, and without significant breakdowns or other accidents involving the ship or the crew. It is important to note that the majority of wooden sailing ships did not get very old. Shipworms, rot, fungi and accidents left their mark even if the ship had been among the lucky ones and avoided major accidents. Old ships under sail were highly unusual. Those which did not have major leaks were often left without their rig in rivers and straits and used for different purposes.

The STATSRAAD ERICHSEN continued to undertake long voyages after World War I. She overcame one challenge after another, both at sea and on land. The Skoleskib organization checked out newer, better and larger vessels to find a ship that could replace the brig. All were rejected, except for the 35 year younger and

One of the last photos taken of the STATSRAAD ERICHSEN shows her in Porsgrunn River and still at work as a sail training ship. Shortly after this, the aristocratic ship was seized by German invaders to be used as an accommodation ship for the occupants through five long years of war.

full rigged TRANSATLANTIC. She was purchased and made a trip with students from the STATSRAAD ERICHSEN as crew. But because of the war the new acquisition was soon resold. The brig was retained. But the days of the white sails were definitely over. In the period after World War I there was a huge surplus of old sailing ships no one wanted. Many of them were in poor condition. The scrappers were busy recycling the steel and iron; some of which was for use in the burgeoning weapons industry.

At the end of the 1920s the brig was 70 years old. She was used about 140 days a year, of which 80 days were spent at sea in the North Sea, Skagerrak and Kattegat. This went on until 1935, when the board decided to start planning for the transfer of their operation to a new ship. Drawings were made and the

shipyard at Framnæs signed the contract for a new ship; a full rigged ship with room for 100 cadets. She was named CHRISTIAN RADICH and was delivered in 1937. The 21st of June that year 57 students from the brig mustered onboard their new training vessel. The old naval brig was moved to the city of Porsgrunn, where a local sail training organization took ownership. They bought the STATSRAAD ERICHSEN in 1937 and equipped the ship for voyages in 1938 with young boys from the district. The school soon faced problems due to Nazi Germany's aggression at sea. The CITY OF FLINT and the ALTMARK incidents were indications of things to come.

For the old STATSRAAD ERICHSEN, World War II in Norway became fatal. Like for all the other sail training ships this was a devastating period. The brig was taken over by the Germans and used as accommodation ship in the Porsgrunn River until 1945. In the fall of that year she was sold to the municipality of Sandefjord for 20,000 Norwegian kroner. The STATSRAAD ERICHSEN's days as a sail training ship had come to an end. Sandefjord sold it on, and most of the ship's rig was removed. In 1947, the Arntzen Yard in Stathelle converted her to a motor ship for L. Nygaard Nilsen of Bodø. The ship was used in coastal shipping under her new name KJEØY. She was at that time 156 gross tons, 92.7 feet long, 25.2 feet wide and 11.2 feet deep.

The KJEØY did not have much success as a freighter. Since the ship was originally built for sail and dimensioned for other uses, she was too soft for heavy loads and her hull started to leak. In addition, she was deeper than normal vessels on the coast. Many small places did not have enough water at low tide, and she often had a hard time reaching the pier. But she was so solid that she continued to move all kinds of cargo between Fredrikstad in the south and Kirkenes in the north of the country for another 15 years. With her distinctive poop the ship was often recognized as the former sail training ship. In 1962 KJEØY sank off the island Sula by Sognefjord. The ship was salvaged and scrapped. The wreck was sold to a shipyard in

The STATSRAAD ERICHSEN was a lucky ship. She sailed for more than 80 years.

western Norway and removed from the ship's registry.

The STATSRAAD ERICHSEN became 104 years old. For well over 80 of those years the ship was a cadet training ship. Long before she ended her career, the STATSRAAD ERICHSEN had a reputation for being the oldest sail training ship in the world and a living legend. Many understood that the STATSRAAD ERICHSEN was an historic vessel, but at the time, the focus was on larger ships and

The STATSRAAD ERICHSEN on the Porsgrunn River, one of the last pictures of the brig as a training ship. Many flags indicate an important event. It could be the liberation in 1945 or May 17th, 1939.

the brig was too small. Both the LINGARD and the KONG SVERRE were younger, but they were large ships, and would be something for little Norway to show to the rest of the world. The LINGARD was saved and was Norway's national heritage ship for a while. "The Committee for Kong Sverre's preservation" struggled with their major project, and in 1932 decided to try to preserve the training vessel STATSRAAD ERICHSEN as a last alternative and temporary solution to preserve an old Navy vessel. Not even this minimum solution was feasible.

Of all the Norwegian sail training ships, the STATSRAAD ERICHSEN is the most accomplished. Norway has hardly ever had a more outstanding ship than her. During her entire career, she only relied on her sails and her anchor to stay safe. She was built for training and coastal defense at a time when the larger sailing ships were starting to be replaced by steam. The ship survived the brig era by 100 years. The days of the sailing brig made of wood came to an end before the brig turned 50. Only iron and steel ships were left behind. Wooden ships were phased out. The best of them became barges. The other training brig in Norway, the TORDENSKJOLD, sailed her final season in 1914. Researchers have determined that only the STATSRAAD ERICHSEN was in continuous service without a break or major repairs over such a long period of time. The ship was built at a time and in a manner that can only be reproduced with a replica in our time. If a similar ship would be built she would automatically get a motor, while the old brig was in her 90th year before this happened to her. The full rigged ship

CHRISTIAN RADICH, which replaced the brig, was a sail training ship for the Norwegian merchant marine for 61 years. Although this is a respectable achievement, she was in service much shorter than the STATSRAAD ERICHSEN.

The STATSRAAD ERICHSEN deserves to be remembered and given a place in history in line with that of the CHRISTIAN RADICH. She had a unique and distinguished service.

Pipervika, photographed around the year 1900. The sail training ship CHRISTIANIA is moored in the fjord outside Akershus Castle. The harbor was once characterized by close contact between the city and the fjord. The park in the foreground was named Tordenskjolds Plass.

Training Vessel *Christiania*

1877 – 1903

The sail training ship CHRISTIANIA's original certificates from 1853 as the American built clipper ship the STAR OF EMPIRE.

When the first Norwegian sail training ship was broken up in 1903, a maritime treasure of international stature was lost forever. Nobody knew at the time. The history of the once world famous, but later forgotten, STAR OF EMPIRE has been a mystery for over 100 years.

For more than 25 years, the venerable old training vessel the CHRISTIANIA was moored at the Christiania Harbor, now the Oslo Harbor. Speculations about the history of this old ship have been many. But nobody could find out where this proud ship came from or where and when it was actually built. It was known that it was purchased as the bark LADY GRAY in 1877. It would be much more than a hundred years, however, before anyone found out where the ship originally came from and what it had done before it came to Christiania. This is where she ended her career as Norway's first sail training ship; preparing city boys who wanted to go to sea.

The initial investigation into the history of the CHRISTIANIA started with the research pertaining to a book about sail training ships in Norway (*Skoleskipene*, Gyldendal, 1981). Several newspaper reports from the 1880s and 1890s show that many were interested in the ship's history. Many conflicting accounts added to the confusion and made the research more difficult. Ship registries lacked the necessary data on the LADY GRAY regarding where and when she was built and who the original owners were. One clue pointed to Port Elizabeth in South Africa as her oldest registered home port. There was only one hitch; a ship like the LADY GRAY

Jack Spurling's painting of McKay's Boston clipper the FLYING CLOUD is one of the world's most famous paintings of a sailing ship with all sails set. The picture could just as easily have been McKay's the STAR OF EMPIRE. The rig was similar and the proportions were the same. One can well imagine that the sail training ship CHRISTIANIA, with the artistic freedom a painting gives, looked like this in her prime.

Akershus Castle in the 1880s as seen from Ekeberg. The training ship is easily spotted in front of the castle.

could not possibly have been built in this part of Africa at that time, it looked more like an American built ship.

Thereafter, several archive searches and requests around the world did not lead to additional clues. But one day a letter arrived from the museum in Port Elizabeth in South Africa. It stated that a local newspaper article from the spring of 1857 contained applicable information. It noted that among the ships in the harbor was the full rigged ship LADY GRAY, formerly known as the STAR OF EMPIRE. This was a new name to work with, but it only made matters more confusing. The information did not make

sense. Which ship was actually the LADY GRAY, previously known as the STAR OF EMPIRE and Oslo's first sail training ship?

When reviewing numerous books on sailing ships from this period the author found a lot of information about the STAR OF EMPIRE. The ship was a classic full rigged ship and in fact a "big sister" to the legendary FLYING CLOUD built two years before. Many authors mention the STAR OF EMPIRE as one of the finest and most expensive clipper ships built by the famous shipbuilder Donald McKay in Boston. The owner was Enoch Train. He also built the clipper ship FLYING CLOUD, maybe the world's most legendary

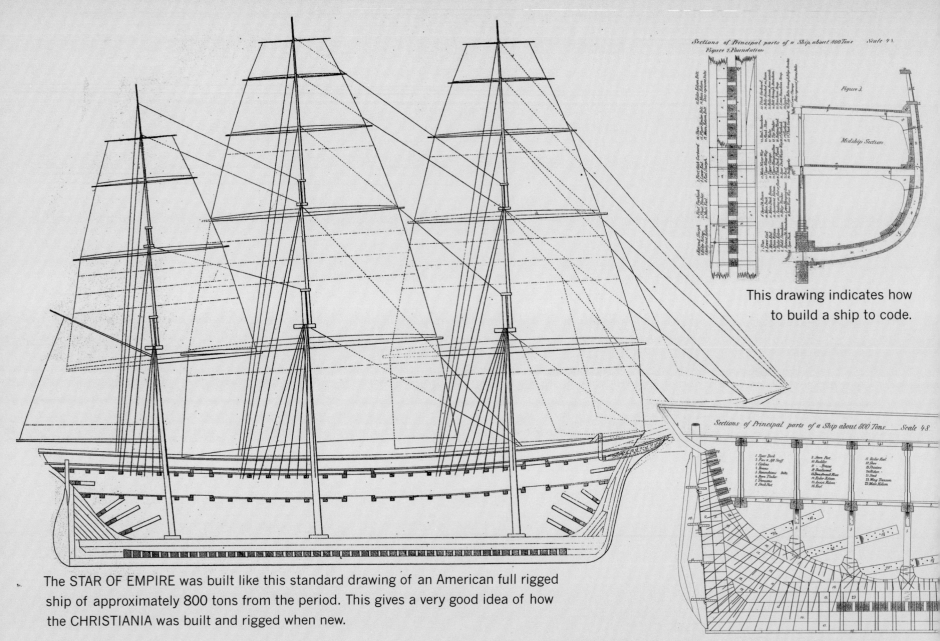

Sections of Principal parts of a Ship about 800 Tons   Scale 48.
Figure 2 Foundation

Figure 3.

Midship Section

This drawing indicates how
to build a ship to code.

Sections of Principal parts of a Ship about 800 Tons____ Scale 48.

The STAR OF EMPIRE was built like this standard drawing of an American full rigged
ship of approximately 800 tons from the period. This gives a very good idea of how
the CHRISTIANIA was built and rigged when new.

The back section reveals many interesting details, including
several layers of wood, bolted together with long metal bolts. They
became the main asset when the CHRISTIANA was broken up.

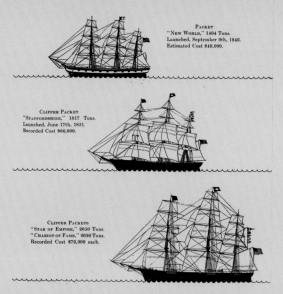

An example of the development of ship design in the classic era of clippers. Never before were so many large sailing ships built of wood. Never did they have larger crew or more sails. Never did they sail faster!

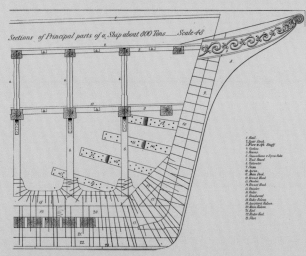

The bow section of an American clipper from the classic period early in the 1850s. It shows how solidly a world trader had to be built in order to be approved.

sailing ship. She set the world speed record on the voyage from New York to San Francisco via Cape Horn, and is depicted in several famous paintings.

Enoch Train had a so called "packet-line" of emigrant ships sailing between Boston and Liverpool. The STAR OF EMPIRE was one of these ships; 2050 tons with three decks, built in 1853. She was considered among the most prominent and fastest sailing ships built in America and was an extreme clipper, with hull and rig designed to achieve maximum speed under sail. The famous shipbuilder Donald McKay had also built the classics WASHINGTON IRVING, FLYING CLOUD and SOVEREIGN OF THE SEAS in the years just before and launched the GREAT REPUBLIC, 3,356 tons, in October 1853, the same year as the STAR OF EMPIRE.

The launch of the STAR OF EMPIRE on April 14th 1853 was given wide publicity in the newspaper The Boston Atlas. The ship was described as the most beautiful Boston clipper built until then. This sailing ship would compete with a growing fleet of steamers in terms of speed, price and quality. The ornaments around the stern included the prophecy "Westward the Star of Empire takes its way" - "The guiding star shows the way to the west." The figurehead was a trumpet-playing goddess with flowing wings, painted in white and gold. In the folds of the dress were a series of miniatures of famous Americans. The ornaments were carved floral decorations.

The clipper ship STAR OF EMPIRE was a magnificent ship

69

The training ship CHRISTIANIA laid up for the winter in Pipervika around 1890.

met with great expectations. She did not disappoint. The first crossing to Liverpool took 19 days, but she also had slower voyages. One return voyage with 830 passengers took 45 days. On January 13th, 1854 the STAR OF EMPIRE left Boston, arriving in Liverpool on January 28th. The 3,058 nautical mile voyage took 14 days and 15 hours from port to port. This record is still recognized as one of the classic sailing records, and is the fastest ever between these two main ports. The STAR OF EMPIRE sailed as well as the FLYING CLOUD. After this fantastic accomplishment all traces in the sources disappear. Only one informant mentions that

the STAR OF EMPIRE was wrecked off North Carolina in 1857. All other sources note quite simply that the STAR OF EMPIRE arrived in Algoa Bay in South Africa on June 28th, 1856; leaking and with major sea damage. The sources note that the ship was condemned and auctioned away to be scrapped.

The information about the STAR OF EMPIRE's final wrecking in South Africa has obviously created confusion in the U.S. and has led American researchers astray. None of the many books that mention the ship offer any explanation. Did a local 1857 news article from the museum in Port Elizabeth indicate that the ship was repaired after the accident in 1856 and sank again off North Carolina the following year? And where does the LADY GRAY, formerly known as the STAR OF EMPIRE, fit in?

The LADY GRAY just does not fit into the story of Donald McKay's big and full rigged Boston clipper the STAR OF EMPIRE. The LADY GRAY was considerably smaller. It seems unreasonable that the clipper ship should have been downsized so much after the accident.

Researchers were only interested in Donald McKay's clipper, and did not register that the ship that was in Port Elizabeth in the spring of 1857 and later ended up in Norway as the CHRISTIANIA could have been another STAR OF EMPIRE. They found sources that indicated that the full rigged ship STAR OF EMPIRE, built in 1853, had been condemned in Africa in 1856 and thought it was McKay's proud ship that the sources mentioned. This is one of the reasons why the CHRISTIANIA's early history remained a mystery for such a long time. The Lloyd's Register lacked a building year and location for the LADY GRAY, which meant that she remained an unexplored topic until recently.

The key to the enigma of the LADY GRAY, previously the STAR OF EMPIRE and later the CHRISTIANIA, is that two ships, both built in the U.S. in the same year and both with the name STAR OF EMPIRE, were confused with each other. They were rigged the same way and looked fairly similar from a distance. Only the size was significantly different. They even worked within the same type of trade when they both were damaged and wrecked less than a year apart.

Below follows the solution to this centuries-old riddle. The story

Christian Krogh's drawing of the legendary Captain Torkildsen of the CHRISTIANIA. He became the ship's captain in 1882 and followed when the students transferred to the brig STATSRAAD ERICHSEN in 1901. Captain Torkildsen disembarked from the ship in 1907.

of the CHRISTIANIA pertains to both international and Norwegian maritime history, detailing the adventures of an American ship that became a legend on the seas far away from the U.S.

The history of the sail training ship CHRISTIANIA starts simultaneously with the history of the legendary McKay clipper STAR OF EMPIRE. Likewise, Norway's first sail training ship was built in 1853, but not in Boston as the ship that also bears her name, but rather in Maine. Both ships were fully rigged and worked in the cargo traffic between the Far East and Australia and the Atlantic coast of America in the years from 1853 to 1856.

It was the STAR OF EMPIRE from Maine, later the LADY GRAY and the CHRISTIANIA, that ended up in Port Elizabeth with major sea damages. It survived and became a real legend. The ship would go on to impress international shipping even more than many of the great and world famous clipper ships. Clippers from this period have always been romanticized as the fastest sailing ships the world has ever seen.

Norway's the STAR OF EMPIRE was one of the many full rigged ships built at the Down East yards in Maine. In the Nineteenth Century this area was one of the world's major manufacturers of durable, beautiful and fast cargo vessels operating on all oceans. Maine had all the special timber and equipment that a sailing ship built of wood needed. Ships from Maine eventually earned the prestigious Down Easter designation.

The STAR OF EMPIRE was built of oak, pine, larch and pitch-pine, with copper bolts and a single hull. It was built by the St.

Croix River in 1853 by Albert Babcock of Robbinston, Maine. The ship measured 628 tons, had two decks and a length to width ratio normal for clipper ships of that size. She was rigged and equipped in Robbinston and got Passamaquoddy, a cove on the Canadian side of the river St Croix, as her first home port. As with many other ships from Maine, she was immediately sold to New York. The STAR OF EMPIRE received worldwide certification. The full rigger was one of the many American fast and famous sailing ships that transported goods all over the world. She could bring general cargo out and tea, rice, exotic wood, porcelain and spices on the rebound. The STAR OF EMPIRE sailed around the world until June 1856. On the journey from Rangoon to Falmouth, loaded with rice, she met her fate.

With all sails set the STAR OF EMPIRE was suddenly hit by a freak wave east of the Cape of Good Hope. This was a monster wave of the kind that occasionally occurs in these waters and has maimed many ships. These giant waves are caused by undersea storms or earthquakes on the seabed. Today they are called tsunamis. The wave struck the ship stem, splintered the bow, cleared the deck and took out the rudder head. The wave left the STAR OF EMPIRE crippled and with severe leaks.

With great difficulty the crew managed to repair the ship and close the leaks well enough to sail the ship into the Algo Bay on the evening of June 26th 1856. But the drama was not over. It was winter in the Southern Hemisphere, and during the night there was a full storm. The STAR OF EMPIRE had two anchors out

This magnified view reveals the high activity level onboard the training ship. At least four white-clad boys can be seen at work on deck. The lifeboat has been launched. The watchman is standing by the gangway, a small ferryboat with the oarsman and one other person can also be seen.

and the pumps going. The ship was only three years old and the equipment onboard was new and solid. The next day one of the anchors broke and the ship began to pull the remainder of the anchoring gear towards land. In a last desperate attempt to save themselves, the ship and the cargo, the captain and the crew chose to cut down the big rig to reduce the wind pressure. The masts, the yards and the sail went overboard. Through superb seamanship and luck the ship stopped dragging. She was saved from further damage from being driven ashore. It was a very close call, but the STAR OF EMPIRE was saved from a total loss. The rig and sails drifted ashore.

The ship was brought to Port Elizabeth after the weather had improved. She was badly damaged and had major leaks, but she was after all a fairly new and strong vessel. After the cargo was unloaded the ship was inspected, condemned and sold at auction. This was the standard procedure at that time when ships suffered major damages and were left in ports far away. Furthermore, salvage and restoration would cost more than the insurance covered. Thus began the transformation of the ship.

T. W. Gubb in Port Elizabeth bought the wreck, and must have believed that it would be possible to repair it and make the ship profitable again. The STAR OF EMPIRE was repaired and the rig was restored. Sometime later, the local newspaper in Port Elizabeth wrote something that solved the riddle: "Among the ships in the harbor is the LADY GRAY, former STAR OF EMPIRE." The ship likely was named after the wife of the popular governor of the Cape Province, Sir George Gray.

The full rigger LADY GRAY received a brand new certificate stating that she was 597 tons, with a 17 foot draft. She remained in Port Elizabeth until April 1857, when she departed for London under British flag and with a new name. When the LADY GRAY left Africa, she sailed out of the story without any original data intact. This occurred at the same time that Donald McKay's STAR OF EMPIRE was wrecked off Currituck in North Carolina, according to sources in the U.S..

Port Elizabeth was the LADY GRAY's home port until 1862 when she was transferred to London. It took until 1874 before she was recorded in Lloyd's; this time only with name, new tonnage and the new ship owner C. Tate of North Shields. In 1875, the now 557 ton LADY GRAY was transformed to a bark, which was a common occurrence at that time. Even then, the LADY GRAY had managed to survive longer than most wooden ships.

An oil painting, dated 1963, from an old drawing of the sail training ship CHRISTIANIA.

Two years later, at the age of 24, she was sold from Great Britain to Norway. The buyer was a committee charged with finding a vessel that could be used as a sail training ship. She was renamed CHRISTIANIA and put in moorings in Christiania Harbor. She was a stationary vessel for training boys from the city who had not been out to sea before, and was also the first Norwegian sail training ship for the merchant marine. Despite some support from benefactors, it was difficult to fully fund the project. Several rounds of fundraising and four years of hard work were needed to get the program started. It took until June 7th, 1881 before the first boys could embark on the sail training ship CHRISTIANIA. The project was a success, and the city leaders got to see what kinds of skills these city boys were mastering after their training. The leaders were even able to get all the program graduates signed on to work on merchant ships in international trade. Continued funding was secured, and the following year the board was able to accept 25 students.

The sail training ship's escapades received wide coverage in many newspapers. The spirit of the times and the charitable focus were expressed with flair: "Most of the boys are orphans raised by relatives. Almost all of them come from poor homes, where much is lacking in regard to their upbringing and education." (translated from Norwegian)

The good citizens' strong support for the sail training ship prevented the young boys from being idle and getting in trouble. The newspapers agreed that training onboard the CHRISTIANIA already had prevented many boys from becoming criminals.

The board minutes noted that, in addition to orphans and poor boys, there were also sons of a priest, a lawyer, a master mariner, a pilot, a typographer and a master carpenter onboard. The sail training ship's board accepted students from all walks of life. The sail training ship CHRISTIANIA, first stationed in Bjørvika, not far from where the Norwegian Opera now is located, was later moved and moored in Pipervika just below the Akershus Castle, where the ship lay until it was scrapped after the turn of the Twentieth Century. The CHRISTIANIA became a legend; well known in the capital for which she was named (Oslo was named Christiania until 1925). The CHRISTIANIA's success was also an important precursor to Norway's most famous sail training ship, the full rigged windjammer CHRISTIAN RADICH.

The aging British LADY GRAY had to undergo extensive modifications in order to become the sail training ship CHRISTIANIA. The 'tween deck was converted into quarters for approximately 40 boys between the ages of 15 and 18. The bunks were fixed, with the short end against the hull side. Between the bunks there were square windows providing good light for teaching, which took place at the big table in the middle of the room. This table was also the students' dining table. Windows in the "gun ports", wide stairways from the main deck and skylights for light and air were incompatible with a seaworthy ship and the CHRISTIANIA became a stationary sail training ship that never again went out to sea.

In the next 25 years, the CHRISTIANIA was firmly moored

The view from Akershus Castle of the previously American-owned clipper ship shows a proud old lady dressed for an occasion.

between buoys in the harbor, except for two special occasions when the ship ventured out. The CHRISTIANIA was rented for the transport of military personnel from the city during a mobilization in the vicinity of the Oscarsborg Fortress. The ship was also used as a quarantine station during a contagious epidemic, and as such she was towed to a deserted anchorage on the fjord.

During the entire period as a sail training ship in the Port of Christinia, it was emphasized that the ship should be perceived not as a discarded wreck, but as a real sailing ship and training institution. She was laid up in the winter months, but during the summers the ship came to life. She was taken out of winter storage, rigged and painted. The CHRISTIANIA was rigged with flags for special occasions, where she added a festive touch. Sails were set and given up. Boys were at the helm, learning the compass and the appropriate command calls. They were constantly at work on deck and in the rig and learned about knots, splicing and how to row a skiff. They learned to wash clothes, be tidy and clean the forecastle, and took turns serving food.

Most official visitors to the capital arrived coming up the Oslo Fjord. They were always greeted by the CHRISTIANIA, and respectfully signaled back as they approached the harbor. Members of the Swedish-Norwegian Royal family visited the ship during one of their stays in the city and inspected the students' skills and work. Crown Prince Oscar

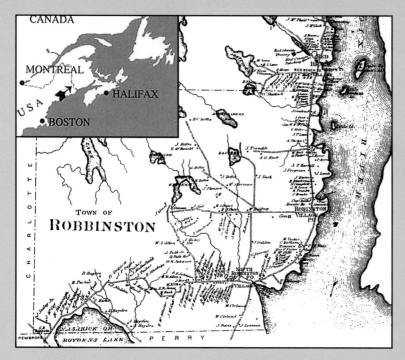

This old map from 1881 shows Robbinston, Maine, where the CHRISTIANIA was built in 1853 as the STAR OF EMPIRE. The St. Croix river, to the right, borders the U.S. and Canada.

No trace of any old ship building activity was found during a recent visit to Robbinston. Even the local post office looked deserted. The lone car belongs to the photographer.

shared a meal with the boys and the captain, and was served a portion of regular ship's food. His Royal Highness noted that the food was both good and nourishing, according to the newspapers.

Going for a Sunday promenade on the ramparts of Akershus castle was a popular summer activity. Couples in love enjoyed the bright summer evenings. This location allowed for a great view of the harbor and all the activity there. In the foreground lay the CHRISTIANIA. In the city's newspapers from the 1880s and 1890s there were frequent reports about the sail training ship, including speculation about the vessel's previous life and work. Without knowing the ship's history some guessed that she was a former East India trader, maybe a clipper. The conclusion was that she must have been a good and fast ship from distant oceans. The painted gun ports which had been turned into windows gave the

77

One of the last pictures of the CHRISTIANIA. The new sail training ship STATSRAAD ERICHSEN has arrived, but is not rigged yet. In the background is the sail training brig TORDENSKJOLD of Trondheim.

impression that she could have been a real warship. Such decor might have given protection against pirates. From a distance the CHRISTIANIA could maybe have been perceived as a naval vessel with a lot of guns, and pirates would stay at a respectful distance. It is, however, unlikely that the ship as the STAR OF EMPIRE or the LADY GRAY was painted in the same way as the CHRISTIANIA.

All pictures of the CHRISTIANIA reveal some interesting details about the ship's past life. She has the lines of a clipper; the lower masts are clearly original. These are very over-dimensioned compared to the rest of the rig and typical for a ship with a big rig and a large crew from 1853. During the ship's first period on the world's oceans as STAR OF EMPIRE, the rig was much larger and more powerful; she had a lot of sails and could reach high speeds. The many full rigged ships from this particular period were known as clipper ships. The RED JACKET and the RED GAUNTLET, both from 1853, were two of the best known ships from Maine. These two were probably quite like our STAR OF EMPIRE. The usual Down Easter was built later, had more room, a simpler rig, a small crew and was a more appropriate cargo ship for carrying larger loads.

Fate is unpredictable. It is odd that this proud ship, which even was mistakenly believed to be a Boston clipper, ended up in a Norwegian fjord. Over a period of 20 years, 731 young city boys were given a good start in life with an education from the sail training ship CHRISTIANIA. They mustered out and proved just as qualified as children who had grown up along the coast. These young boys often went to sea right after graduation. Statements from the captains who employed these boys from the city confirmed that their time onboard the CHRISTIANIA had taught them well, both in regard to behavior and seamanship.

When the chosen boys boarded the CHRISTIANIA it was often their first experience away from home. Captain Torkildsen and his wife did an excellent job making the youngsters' first stay away from home as pleasant as possible. The students could only go ashore on Sundays. Half of the boys went to church with the captain in the morning, while the other half got shore leave in the afternoon. The next Sunday the schedule was reversed. Rowing to shore was the most popular job. Just like all other watches, this duty was assigned on a rotating basis.

The boys endured hard work and practice all day long, from the wakeup call at 6:00am until 5:30pm, when supper was served. Good routines were seen as very important. The report card gave future employers information about a boy's capability, diligence, order and behavior. It was strict discipline day after day; from rigging in the spring to washing and polishing after the ship was painted and equipped for the summer. Laundry skills and personal hygiene were taught with the same fervor. Boys who did not adapt were sent ashore. Waitlisted boys took their place.

The sail training ship usually had from two to five times more applicants than slots. For the 1883 season the board of directors received applications from 127 students. Only 30 were accepted. The capacity increased to 45 cadets in 1901.

Watches were set, day and night. The guard, perched on the deck above the captain's cabin, was responsible for everybody's safety while his shipmates slept. No wonder these young boys grew up fast under such circumstances. The student who stood watch was required to pay attention to everything that was going on onboard and in the harbor. Time was kept by signaling in synchronization with the clock in a church tower in the city. Any irregularities had to be reported immediately. Falling asleep on duty was a mortal sin.

Alert students onboard the CHRISTIANIA again and again helped others nearby. They made a difference in the harbor and in the fjord. Many got a helping hand when they needed towing or help lifting heavy goods. Two young boys were given credit for their quick response when they launched a rowboat and rescued two drowning bricklayers who had capsized not far away. The accident was observed by the lookout at the CHRISTIANIA and immediately reported to the student responsible for the rowboat. This and similar episodes were proudly recorded in the board minutes. The ship earned a reputation as a guard, helper and a lifesaver. The sail training ship was credited with saving 18 lives during the years it was stationed in the harbor.

The CHRISTIANIA was open to visitors. The ship's board and Captain Torkildsen were always focused on showcasing the ship's importance, although it was also noted that fully adequate training could only be given through a ship that sails. It was a key goal to get a sailing vessel in the future when the CHRISTIANIA would be retired. The CHRISTIANIA gave good publicity to the city, and inspired other cities to try similar projects in order to help young boys become seamen.

Of course, none of the students knew that their first ship was a former American. Several of them would, however, later end up onboard American ships where Norwegian sailors were sought after for several reasons. Their good training made them especially competitive. After passing the navigator exams and becoming citizens they could work as officers and captains. Many Americans are descendants of students from the CHRISTIANIA and other Norwegian sail training ships. This old American became a steppingstone for young people who wanted to see the world. She serve as a first stop for boys on the road to a career in America.

80

"Westward the Star of Empire takes its way" stated the prophetic epigram on the ornaments around the stern of the great Boston clipper STAR OF EMPIRE. It has symbolic value in that it was her small namesake in Norway that led sailors and navigators to America. Every summer for 21 years boys were trained onboard the sail training ship CHRISTIANIA. The old American remained on duty until 1902. In 1901 it was decided to decommission the ship after the sail training ship board had bought the Norwegian Navy's cadet ship STATSRAAD ERICHSEN, which was fit for sailing. At the dawn of the Twentieth Century, this old Navy brig became the city's new sail training ship.

There were discussions about what should happen to the old CHRISTIANIA. She had long since become part of the cityscape and harbor of the city for which she was named. She was a proud, old sailing vessel people had come to care about. They felt that she belonged to them and did not want her to be sold for scrapping. Several ideas surfaced in the newspapers. This was long before most people had a clear understanding of the concept of conservation, but the many requests for the preservation of the sail training ship testify to a nascent understanding of the matter.

The ship's owners were willing to let the ship remain a part of the cityscape, and she stayed put for a while. The board eventually decided to offer the ship to the city to be used for a bath house. The existing bath houses on the beach below the Akershus Castle were no longer sufficient. But the effort to preserve CHRISTIANIA was not easy. No permanent solution was found, and she was eventually sold at a public auction in 1903. A sail maker in the town of Moss won the bid. The sail training ship CHRISTIANIA was then towed to Moss and scrapped.

The ship that barely avoided being destroyed when she was just three years old, made it to the ripe old age of 50. This is a very respectable age for a wooden sailing ship from a time when sailing ships of her type rarely lasted for long. With the current knowledge about the history of the CHRISTIANIA it is sad that this old lady was not preserved longer. This would have given Norway a unique world treasure which would have allowed researchers to investigate aspects of an era from which very little exact knowledge has been preserved.

The definition of a clipper has been the subject of many discussions. Because fast ships commanded a large premium for their services, many ships built in Maine between 1848 and 1855 were narrower than before, with a slimmer inlet for maximum speed. These ships got a huge rig with lots of sails, and set many sailing records. The California Gold Rush and the discovery of gold in Australia were key reasons these ships were so popular. This short period of time during the middle of the Nineteenth Century provided a solid basis for the myths surrounding clippers and contributed to the later sail romanticism.

The CHRISTIANIA, previously known as the STAR OF EMPIRE, helped create this golden age of sail. In 1853 when the STAR OF EMPIRE was built, far more sailing ships than in any year before or later were launched. The concept clipper may relate to the hull shape, the rigging or the period of time. The CHRISTIANIA is clearly within these general definitions. In the half century the ship existed there were major technological advances. The ship lived through an era of development and had an international career few sailing ship would experience. The CHRISTIANIA was first the proud and fast American STAR OF EMPIRE for four years. Then she became a cargo ship under the British flag as LADY GRAY for the next 20 years. Finally, she came under Norwegian command for 26 years. The CHRISTIANIA thus carried the flags of the world's three leading maritime nations, one after the other.

The old Coolie clipper MERSEY was converted to a British cargo carrying training ship for the company that owned the TITANIC. Later it became Norway's only attempt at training seamen onboard cargo carriers. World War I effectively ended this effort.

The Transatlantic ex Mersey
- Cargo Carrying Sail Training Ship

The first CHRISTIAN RADICH from 1916 was, as the ship with the same name we know today, named after the merchant who in 1884 gave money for a sail training ship. The ship was made in Scotland. It came to be an intermezzo in the history of Norwegian sail training ships. It may not deserve a central space in the gallery of famous sailing ships. Nevertheless, the story of this great cargo ship is an informative and fascinating story about people, shipping companies, the TITANIC, money, stock speculation, cadet training and safety at sea.

A war was going on in the world when the great and internationally renowned full rigged CHRISTIAN RADICH sailed into the harbor in Christiania, soon to be renamed Oslo, with a few thousand tons of cement in the hold. She was handled by students from the training brig STATSRAAD ERICHSEN and docked with almost no help. That was an accomplishment which deserved great respect, even if the ship had had an experienced sailing crew. But most of the crew consisted of inexperienced young cadets who had not been to sea before. The cargo came from Denmark and the name TRANSATLANTIC was still painted on the stern of the ship, even if the board of the sail training organization Christiania Skoleskib had decided that the ship should be named CHRISTIAN RADICH. She became the first and the last cargo carrying sail training ship of Norway.

From before the establishment of the organization Christiania Skoleskib in 1877 many experienced officers and seamen claimed that an adequate training of cadets for the merchant marine could only be accomplished onboard a cargo carrying sailing ship. The sail training program in Norway started with an older stationary ship, *Skoleskibet* CHRISTIANIA. Twenty years later, the training included actual sailing after the city purchased the old cadet brig STATSRAAD ERICHSEN from the Norwegian Navy. This gradual development from a stationary ship to a seaworthy sailing vessel was the same in other cities. The main reason was the organization's lack of funding. A fully equipped sailing ship was expensive and beyond the reach of schools who started as charities. But there was always someone who wanted to help.

When the training of seamen started, Norway was a poor agricultural nation, unlike the wealthy welfare state we know today. The merchant fleet was an important factor in the prosperity of the country throughout the last century until oil was found. The training of new generations of sailors for this important task required effort. From the start, little of the value the merchant fleet created was used to help the training of young boys preparing for jobs in the merchant marine. Maritime cadet training schools often sailed against the wind at home but with fair wind abroad, where they won races and were good ambassadors for Norway.

The full rigged ship MERSEY in a light breeze with all sails set, including the skysail on the main mast top. This picture was probably taken while she belonged to James Nourse and transported emigrants from India.
Notice the man on top of the royal yard!

Nourse Line's the MERSEY near a harbor. Two royals are missing. The picture might have been taken in connection with the change of ownership in 1908.

The cargo ship TRANSATLANTIC was larger than any Norwegian sail training ship. She was a famous Clyde clipper that had sailed on voyages to India and Australia and was the only Cape Horner among Norway's sail training vessels. The full rigged ship was named MERSEY when built and TRANSATLANTIC when she was purchased and brought to Oslo. This happened at a time when good sailing ships were affordable and the money was available from some speculators who had seen a huge profit due to lack of tonnage, rising freight rates and insurance costs during WWI. The unrestricted submarine warfare led to the slaughter of sedentary sailing ships and their unarmed crews. This saddest chapter in Norwegian shipping history is rather unknown. Numerous sailors from neutral Norway lost their lives. Their fate was sealed because they chose the sea as a profession and were at work when the war started. To work on sailing ships became a very dangerous profession. This is the reason that the CHRISTIAN RADICH's career as a Norwegian sail training ship was short. The end of the story is tragic, but not in the way most of us may think.

MERSEY, as Norway's first CHRISTIAN RADICH was named from the start, was built of steel by the famous shipyard Charles Connell

& Co. Ltd., Glasgow in 1894 as hull no. 213 for James Nourse in London. She measured 270.7 by 39 by 22.5 feet. She was described as a Clyde built clipper ship, and all the pictures of her reveal a sleek, beautiful and well built full rigged ship with a high foremast, a lofty rig and even skysail on her mainmast. In addition, she carried studding-sails. She had a total of six lifeboats. Two were placed on the roof of the forward deck house, two at the half-deck in the middle of the ship, and two on a platform above the deck in front of the aft mast. Such peculiarities helped to identify a sailing ship from a distance. When the MERSEY was built, these were the hallmarks long established as characteristics of the Nourse Line Coolie ships. Like the MERSEY, another distinguishing feature was that all new ships were named after rivers. This fine ship belonged to the last group of swift and well equipped passenger ships built. Captain Nourse amazed the world by outcompeting everyone, including steam ships into the Twentieth Century. His ships were the last trading ships on the oceans that carried studding-sails in order to achieve greater speed in light weather. Among the sailors the Nourse ships had a reputation as having good luck and there was never a problem hiring a full crew of skilled seamen for a voyage in one of Captain Nourse's ships even after the turn of the century.

In 1861 the young Captain James Nourse was registered as owner and captain of the GANGES, a ship carrying Coolies

The White Star Line sail training ship did six cruises around the world. Today's around-the-world race is a copy of the MERSEY's voyages to Australia. This image shows 20 men at work aloft. Rust on the hull and awning stretched over the poop deck indicate that she has just arrived in port after a long voyage out from England.

from India. Between 1867 and 1909, Captain Nourse had 35 combined passenger and cargo ships in what was known as the Coolie trade. They became legendary as they transported workers from crowded Calcutta, Bombay, and Madras to the West Indies, Trinidad, Demerara in Guyana, and Mauritius where their chances for an improved life as a plantation worker were far better than living in large urban slums. The ships' 'tween decks were designed to carry up to 700 passengers, with young men before the mast, families separated by gender on each side amidships and young girls aft. The families could meet only on deck. The voyage from India could take months with stops in Cape Town and St. Helena for water and the provisioning of fresh vegetables to prevent the crew from getting scurvy.

Some of the captains were tough sailors and some of the Coolie ships held formidable distance records. One made a voyage from England to Sydney in only 65 days. But the doctor could be just as tough. Sometimes he ordered the captain to ease the pressure on the sails when the work in the hospital performing an operation became too difficult. Births were common during the voyage. James Nourse wanted to focus on safety when the cargo consisted of hundreds of Coolies. Speed sailing was for cargo ships, not for emigrant ships with seasick landlubbers onboard. It is alleged that James Nourse never lost an emigrant as a result of shipwreck, even if one of the ships went aground with 700 passengers.

The MERSEY, later the Norwegian cargo-carrying training ship CHRISTIAN RADICH, in the doldrums. Note all the port holes from the Coolie trade on the 'tween deck.

Some of Nourse's captains managed to supply Coolies to the West Indies healthier and more well-fed than when they came onboard in India. They could even be in better shape than Coolies who were transported by steamship. The transportation of Coolies was no one-way endeavor. Eventually there arose a great need for transportation of the "new rich" back to India. This trade grew and as time passed it included other nations. Chinese Coolies were known to be especially hardy and easy to deal with. They were the preferred plantation workers. The name that originated in India came to be known as a name for Chinese transported to the plantations.

The Coolie clipper MERSEY belonged to the second group of six sister ships Nourse had built in the 1890s and the ship soon became known as a good vessel. During the latter part of the 1890s through the early 1900s, C.A. Hampton & E. Bromhead are listed as owners of the MERSEY, but after 1905 James Nourse Ltd. is again listed as her owner. One of the company's well known captains, G. Rock, took over the newly built MERSEY and was her captain for 14 years until she was sold in 1908. Old James Nourse had such success with his ships that the story of the Coolie trade to and from India will forever be linked to his name. He died in 1897. In 1908 and 1909, the company decided to replace the sailing ships. The last batch all went to Norwegian owners. The MERSEY was sold the year before to become a British sail training ship.

Her buyer was the Oceanic Steam Navigation Company, Ltd. in Liverpool. The company was part of a broad based committee charged with finding a sail training ship which could undertake long open ocean journeys. The committee was given the green light from authorities. The MERSEY thereby became a pioneer in the officially approved maritime training in Great Britain using cargo carrying sailing ships. The company is better known as the White Star Line, the leading passenger line between Europe and America. Four years after the MERSEY was purchased, they launched their latest megaship and the world's most luxurious steamer. It would sail from Great Britain to New York. This was a major event in Trans-Atlantic passenger service and

White Star Line's company flag.

many VIPs boarded. The four stacker TITANIC sank on her maiden voyage; White Star Line's new flagship and the pride of the company collided with an iceberg in the North Atlantic. Chairman Joseph Bruce Ismay, son of the founder Thomas Henry Ismay, was onboard. He survived. It is very likely that former cadets from the sail training ship MERSEY sailed on the TITANIC. The TITANIC disaster ruined Ismay. The White Star Line deteriorated and the

company merged with Cunard Line in 1935.

The Ismay Line started at the same time and in a similar way as the Nourse Line. In 1867 T. H. Ismay secured the White Star Line's old sailing ships from the gold prospector trade to Australia and used them to start a shipping empire in the emigrant and passenger trade. Like the Nourse emigrant trade from India, the Atlantic passenger voyages cannot be described without mentioning Ismay. The two shipping companies had a similar start and the same early success, but the rest of their stories are different, except that both founders died in the last part of the 1890s and both were owners of the full rigged ship MERSEY. Nourse was a successful owner, but first and foremost a prudent sea captain, while Ismay was a citizen of the world who built a dynasty and befriended royals. His son, J. Bruce Ismay, continued this tradition. A focus on prestige, with ever bigger, better, more comfortable and safer ships, was the White Star Line's trademark. The company was a leader in this respect. It was an irony that this culminated with the loss of "the world's safest ship" TITANIC in 1912. It is still known as the most infamous ship disaster, even if the big, beautiful and luxurious Canadian passenger steamer EMPERESS OF

The coolie clipper MERSEY in the doldrums. The port lifeboat is used by the ship's photographer to get a picture of the ship with sails set.

IRELAND collided and sank in Canadian waters only two years later. This disaster killed more passengers than those who died onboard the TITANIC.

Also, in regard to maritime education, the White Star Line wanted to be a leader. In 1908, international shipping had largely completed the transition from sail to steam. The need for good training of new officers was not as important as on the old sailing ships where many cadets were needed to provide extra muscle power on deck and aloft, handling all the sails. But young sailors were still required to have some experience with sailing. The result was that the White Star Line concentrated on a cargo carrying training vessel to meet this requirement. The MERSEY

was White Star Line's training vessel for comprehensive training of future maritime officers. She was well equipped and suitable for the purpose.

The ship was refurbished and the deck behind the mast became quarters for up to 80 cadets, but she usually took slightly fewer students enrolled in a year long sailing education program. The boys were between 15 and 20 years old. Some came straight from school without any maritime experience, while others could have experienced up to two years on a stationary sail training ship before they signed on to the MERSEY. The deck house by the main mast was converted to a combined classroom and chapel, and was also used as the living room. Officers and teachers lived aft. The regular crew lived as they always had, before the mast. Steam equipment for heavy work was not widely used after the ship became a sail training ship. The MERSEY had enough manpower to heave anchor the old way, by turning the windlass using pure muscle power. A small oil engine generator was added and the ship got electric light throughout, a necessity for students who had to study in the evenings, when they where off watch. A doctor and a teaching staff of three were carefully chosen. In August of 1908 the MERSEY left from Liverpool for her first tour to Australia as a cargo carrying sail training ship with 60 students onboard. Cadets were exposed to a rigid academic curriculum in addition to sailing the ship. The voyage to Sydney with a full cargo load took less than three months and the vessel proved that she could sail, even if security took priority over speed.

The MERSEY had made many successful roundtrips as a Coolie ship and continued as a British cadet ship to make six trouble free voyages to Australia in as many years. She performed world wide sailings, through the Atlantic Ocean, around the Horn of Africa, and across the Indian Ocean to Sydney. "The Roaring Forties" was the major test for many future British maritime officers. The return voyage was across the Pacific Ocean and around Cape Horn, often with very strong winds and with small sails. Then they followed the Atlantic trade winds and the doldrums to London for examination of the students. Captain F. W. Corner had taken over the command of the full rigged ship after Captain Rock. The current "Around the World" races follow in the wake of the MERSEY. The voyage includes two crossings of the equator and temperatures from freezing conditions to tropical heat. After graduation, the Ministry of Transportation was full of praise for the curriculum and the quality of the graduates. All parts of the organization received great praise for good results. There was respect for the maritime training onboard the MERSEY and White Star's prestige increased. The board of the sail training organization in Norway followed closely what happened in Great Britain.

Newspapers and magazines contributed to the public interest in the sail training ship MERSEY around the world. Many postcards of the ship under sail and in port still exist. Sydney celebrated the ship's arrival and the boys experienced picnics, regattas and sports tournaments. The future British maritime officers were also popular among the city's young girls. The MERSEY cadets had a band called "The Merry Mersey Musicians" which held concerts for the benefit of the seamen's mission in Australia. The captain's wife traveled with the boys on their excursions; this was quite common in those days. Mrs. Corner was of course appreciated by the young boys who likely missed their mothers, and many of them spoke warmly of her. She was a self-taught radio operator and one of her extra jobs onboard was to assist the radio officer. In those days women could not become wireless operators.

The MERSEY became the first sailing vessel to have a wireless radio installed. This was a direct result of the TITANIC disaster. Before the full rigged ship set sails for her voyage in 1913, she had a radio station and a radio operator, thanks to J. Bruce Ismay and the White Star Line's board. The MERSEY could therefore keep in touch with the rest of the world at all times. Many sailing ships disappeared at sea without a trace. Losing a sail training ship with many young people onboard was

Two of the crew members at work painting the aft mast on the MERSEY.

particularly tragic. When Marconi invented wireless telegraphy, ships finally had the opportunity to maintain contact and report any problems. The TITANIC tragedy showed how important this was. Had telegraphy at sea and the radio contact between ships been better established, and had the procedures the year before been clearer, the majority of TITANIC's passengers would probably have been saved. This was one of the bitter lessons learned from the TITANIC disaster.

The MERSEY set another record that likely is unique. A cadet suffered from acute appendicitis. The doctor saw no alternative but to operate. This happened in a storm while the MERSEY rounded Cape Horn. The doctor was assisted by Captain Corner and a mate, while another cadet assisted holding the tray with the instruments. The boy fainted when his shipmate's belly was cut open. While this happened, the ship moved heavily in the rough sea, but even so, the Captain managed to salvage the instruments before they all ended up in the gutter. The surgery was successful and the patient could later boast that he was the only Cape Horn sailor who had had his appendix removed off the Horn.

Return trips were often easier than going out. By then the ship had a more experienced crew that knew the ship inside and out. The load on the return was often wool or grain in bags. Going out, she could be loaded with every type of cargo from heavy railway material to Scottish whiskey. All the boys received certificates after completing the mission and were free to muster out on whichever ship they wanted. But many stayed with the

The CHRISTIAN RADICH, still with her former name, discharged at Vestbanen in Christiania in 1916. The old Cape Horner has a full rig but lacks the upper yards. She is a classic British cargo carrying sailing ship from the last days of sail.

White Star since the company had a large fleet of ships and good opportunities for advancement. The White Star Line gave up the training of young cadets in 1915 as a result of the outbreak of World War I. The MERSEY was ready to sail in the autumn of 1914 and cadets were admitted, but the outbreak of the war meant that almost all were enlisted for war duty with the Royal Navy. The MERCEY was suddenly without students and staff. After some time the board decided to sell the ship and Captain Corner left her late in the autumn of 1914. Prior to that, MERSEY managed six round trips. It was alleged that the MERSEY program was the finest maritime training the British Isles could offer.

The board for the STATSRAAD ERICHSEN, her captain and cadets, maritime buffs and newspapers paid close attention to what was going on regarding maritime training in other countries. The British model with the MERSEY and similar training with general cargo sail training ships in Germany and Denmark gave inspiration to try the same, even though many in Norway felt that the German training was too militaristic. The MERSEY program in many ways became a model for what they tried to achieve, even though young boys in Norway attended shorter training, especially in regards to leadership. The reason was that Norwegian cadets at first were trained in stationary ships and after 1900 on vessels that only sailed during the summer. They had to have some time at sea before they could be accepted to navigation school before becoming officers. The British cadets could take the second mate exam at the end of their round trip with the MERSEY if they had served two years in a stationary sail training ship before the roundtrip to Australia.

Students at the MERSEY had been accepted based on previous education and experience. During their voyage they received training in practical seamanship and learned about ship rigging, sails and other equipment, knots, splicing of rope and wires, proper

Oslo's first CHRISTIAN RADICH was a former English cargo carrying cadet ship. The White Star's flag is flown from the main mast and she also has radio antennas. This image must therefore be from the last British round trip to Australia from 1913 to 1914.

loading, the use of the sextant, keeping the log and signaling with Aldis lamps and flags. In addition, there was a lot of practical training in sailing, working aloft, sail repair, and regular watch duty. Theoretical instruction included mathematics, navigation, astronomy, compass deviation, meteorology and in reading the charts. They even received foreign language training. In port, they practiced rowing and swimming, unloading and loading, ventilation of cargo stowage and securing of loose cargo, fire drills, mooring and anchoring. The Christiania Skoleskib organization wanted to give their students a similar basic training.

Norwegian sail training ships before World War I were limited to sailing summer cruises in the North Sea. The trip often went to the British Isles, where some of the best and most mature students received a diploma and were signed onto merchant vessels, while the rest of the cadets sailed the ship back to Norway. The other Nourse Coolie clippers were sold and ended up in Norway as cargo ships in international traffic. They were regarded as very good vessels. Brokers, owners, officers and crew knew that the old Nourse ships were especially well built and well equipped with many lifeboats and several sets of good sails. They also had good track records. Although they aged, those which had received good care still sailed for many years. These old ships could be had at a favorable price. When the MERSEY was offered for sale, Norwegian ship owners once again showed interest. Christopher Hannevig from Borre, close to Horten, won the bid. The contract was signed on February 19th, 1915 and the full-rigged vessel MERSEY was

transferred over to the Transatlantic Motor Ship Company in Christiania that summer. She was renamed TRANSATLANTIC and used in foreign trade.

In 1911, the sail training ship organization in Christiania decided to focus on getting a cargo carrying sail training ship to supplement the training brig STATSRAAD ERICHSEN. The foregoing developments, the fact that Sweden and Denmark had such ships, and particularly the success of the MERSEY in England motivated them. In the winter of 1916, the organization started to gain momentum. The estate of deceased merchant Christian Radich donated 90,000 Norwegian kroner (NOK) for a new sail training ship. The only condition of the gift was that the ship would carry his name. This inspired other donors, and shortly after, a total of 200,000 NOK had been secured. Ship owners and others interested in shipping saw the importance of training more and better sailors. The city of Christiania also gave a major contribution.

At the same time the Hannevig brothers offered the full rigged TRANSATLANTIC to the school ship organization for of 410,000 NOK, of which Hannevig would then contribute 25 percent. The board had already secured the rest. They thought this was a good price for a cargo ship that had already been a sail training ship and was known as a very stable, secure and fast vessel. The ship had been redesigned for training purposes and needed few modifications, although the quarters on the 'tween deck had been removed a few years earlier to make room for additional cargo space. The board accepted the offer.

In April of 1916 Christiania Skoleskib bought the full rigged ship and renamed her CHRISTIAN RADICH. She was in Aarhus in Denmark loading cement for Buenos Aires and was soon joined by her new crew. Cadets still onboard the STATSRAAD ERICHSEN prepared themselves for deep water sailing, looking ahead to the long voyage to the Southern Hemisphere. The board of Christiania Skoleskib applied for permission, to the German Embassy in Norway via the Norwegian Ministry of Foreign Affairs, for a free passage through the danger zone where German submarines operated. Permission was not granted, and the board took no chances of having the ship torpedoed with all the cadets onboard. Instead the ship was diverted to Christiania where there was also a shortage of cement.

Captain Mathisen was signed on and 20 boys and the third mate from the STATSRAAD ERICHSEN went down to Copenhagen to take the ship and cargo to Christiania. The pilot and the tugboat left and the captain set all sails for Norway. With her hull painted in light colors and with the required neutrality flag painted on both sides of the hull, the full rigged ship headed north through the Kattegat. All onboard were full of admiration for this great addition to the country's fleet of sail training ships. The old Cape Horner was a truly magnificent and stately sail training ship with a long and proud history. This was something quite different and much better for the young cadets than a small wooden

«Transatlantic» — igjen

Vi kommer tilbake til fullriggeren «Transatlantic» som vi bragte bilde av lørdag. Teksten var ikke så helt vellykket. Bl.a. skrev vi at skuta var kombinert, for både seil og damp, men der gikk vi fem på. Ved nærmere øyesyn viser det seg nemlig å ligge en steambåt b a k skuta, og der hører skorsteinen til! Det var den observante og historiekyndige Asbjørn Nygaard som gjorde oss oppmerksom på saken. Han hadde også med seg et bind av Norske Seilskuter, og der sto «Transatlantic» utførlig beskrevet. Slik:
Fullrigger «Transat-

lantic» var bygget av Donnell & Co. i Glasgow i 1894 som skoleskib for «White Star Line». Dens navn under engelsk flagg var «Mersey». Den var på 1847 tonn. I begynnelsen av 1915 blev den innkjøpt til Norge av det velkjente skibsrederfirma Chr. Hannevig, Horten, og fikk da navnet «Transatlantic». Den førtes av kaptein C. Johannesen, Fredrikstad. Det var en meget vakker og velholdt skute, hvitmalt fra «topp til tå» og førte «skysail» på stortoppen.
Under krigens omskiftelser blev den solgt, først til Kristiania for å bli skoleskib ennu en gang. Imidler-

tid fant man det nok for dyrt å ominnrede den, hvorfor den i 1917 blev solgt til Christianssands Shipping Co., Kristiansand, som i 1918 omdøpte den til «Dvergsø». I 1920 overtokes den av Lars Jørgensen, Kristiansand, som i 1922 flyttet til Svelvik. I 1923 gikk den til England for å bli opphugget.

Førere var: fra 1915 nevnte C. Johannesen, fra 1917 Nielsen, fra 1918 Chr. Olsen og fra 1920 E. A. Olsen.

Gutten i forgrunnen går på skøyter, og en isbryter er uten tvil på ferde foran skuta.

Newspaper clipping from the Fredrikstad Demokraten February 15th, 1917. It shows the CHRISTIAN RADICH, while she was owned by Christiania Skoleskib. She is frozen in. The many men onboard and the tug at her side indicate that she is in the process of breaking out.

The tugboat OSCARSBORG is breaking ice for the ship to leave Fredrikstad. A person on skates in the foreground to the right shows that the ice is pretty solid. Judging from her draft, it is likely that she has lumber in her hold.

brig. They trimmed the sails and showed great pride in proving that they could meet the challenges. The course was changed at the entrance to the Oslo Fjord and with a fair wind the full rigged ship sailed all the way into the capital as the country's first cargo carrying sail training ship. The goal was achieved after nearly 40 years of planning and hard work. Finally, Norway had a full-fledged maritime training program.

The CHRISTIAN RADICH, still with her former name TRANSATLANTIC showing, arrived in the capital by sail alone and docked without using anchors and only assisted by a single tugboat. Those present had respect and admiration for the way the officers, crew and young cadets handled the loaded ship upon arrival. The cement cargo was discharged and everyone from the

members of the board to the cadets received ample praise for the new acquisition. She was moored in the harbor of Christiania and admired by all, while the board worked hard to find new, meaningful charters for the ship. Freight revenues for the cement cargo from Aarhus had given a nice income of 29,000 NOK. The board members were excited; suddenly the organization had some earnings to spend. To get paid for carrying cargo was of course a meaningful way for a poor organization to complement the charitable contributions. The ship was purchased in the middle of the economic boom during World War I. Prices for ships, freight and shipping escalated day by day.

German submarines were a major threat to defenseless sailing ships. Neutral Norway was indirectly drawn into the war and lost much of its merchant fleet and many sailors. It made little sense to send out a cargo carrying sail training ship with many youngsters onboard into the dangerous waters of war. But there was an abundance of available jobs. The board could easily have signed contracts for well-paid voyages with non-military cargo between two neutral countries. Bids were submitted, but it was not possible to get guarantees for the ship's safety through diplomatic channels. The board was not willing to sail the ship under these circumstances, even if so many other ship owners did. The future was very uncertain. The CHRISTIAN RADICH could not function in her planned role as a sail training ship. The ship was not able to take cadets on long voyages to exciting ports in other parts of the world without the considerable risk of being torpedoed.

In addition, the board members were, like many others at the time, focused on making money. The CHRISTIAN RADICH's value increased drastically. Barely a year after she was purchased for 410,000 NOK, the board received offers of 700,000 NOK for the ship. The following month, and exactly one year after purchase, the bid had increased to 800,000 NOK. Doubling the value of a ship over only one year was incredible. The temptation was too great for the board and in April of 1917 the ship was sold. The CHRISTIAN RADICH was transferred back to the Hannevig brothers and the Transatlantic Company. This is one of the reasons why the full rigger kept the name TRANSATLANTIC. In addition, the ship's registries did not always follow up on the many transactions that occurred at this time. Additional information was avoided in time of war for security reasons. The Hannevig brothers' goal was to secure more tonnage, no matter the cost.

In May the same year, Leif Bryde of Sandefjord paid 885,000 NOK for her. The same month Christiania Skoleskib made sure that she was removed from the Christiania registry and was listed with Sandefjord as her new home port. In August, the full rigged ship was again sold with profit; this time to the Christiansand Shipping Company. She was renamed the DVERGSØ and registered in Kristiansand. Over the summer of 1917 the sail training ship had been sold three times. Under her new name DVERGSØ, she was sent out into the world; first, to the east coast of the U.S. where she arrived in October of 1917 and stayed for a while. At the end of 1918 and the beginning of 1919 she was in Rio and in the spring in Norfolk, Virginia. The ship made several runs between South and North America, including a trip from Rio to Baltimore, until the fall of 1919. In December of 1919 she left for a trip from Buenos Aires to Aalborg in Denmark, finally returning to Europe. It is reasonable to believe that she carried grain. Old DVERGSØ still relied on her sails, and as always did very well. At this time she was 25 years old and we can safely say that she was a lucky ship. The same could not be said of her new owners.

The Christiansand Shipping Company was focused on quick profit and did not have the reserves that traditional shipping companies had. The company was started in the fall of 1916 and bought all the sailing ships it could get, and at first did

DVERGSØ was the MERSEY's last name. This is a late picture of the ship with some kind of ballast, perhaps water.

well financially. But during 1917 the trend in regard to freight rates was reversed, and shipping shares began to fall after rising dramatically during the first part of the war. Fewer ships were sunk by German submarines. Military protection of merchant tonnage had become more efficient and the U.S. entered the war. The Christiansand Shipping Company had been very successful when the company took over the TRANSATLANTIC, but their income then rapidly declined. The shipping company's board had even purchased tonnage unseen. All the sudden they had ships they could no longer find freight for. These were mothballed. Times were not good for some of the companies that had survived the war. In addition, the old sailing ships got competition from newly built U.S. tonnage that also flooded the market. The shareholders of the Christiansand Shipping Company were not happy. Instead of huge profits, the company operated with a bottomless debt. The entire board was let go. This did not solve its problems. Although refinancing was attempted in 1920, there were still no jobs for the company's tonnage. The company became the big loser among the companies located in the southern part of Norway, and lost close to 12 million NOK.

Ship owner Lars Jørgensen took over the full rigged DVERGSØ in an attempted refinancing operation. This did not improve the situation for the old sail training ship. Jørgensen's new company Otra tried to salvage what was left, but it is doubtful whether the DVERGSØ was chartered at all during this period. Her owners, just like everybody else, probably expected that the financial situation would improve. Most of the old sailing ships did not experience better times and it is reasonable to assume that the DVERGSØ remained stationary. Otra changed its name to Svelvik Skipsrederi in 1922, still with Jørgensen at the helm. That fall the ship was transferred to the company. It seems that Jørgensen was not able to get rid of the beautiful and world famous sailing ship that had had such a distinguished career. He probably hoped for the longest time to sell her back to the sail training ship organization so she could continue her operation as a sail training ship. Unfortunately, he was not able to create new interest in the DVERGSØ. She was therefore sold back to the country where she was built. The former sail training ship, earlier known as the Coolie clipper MERSEY, was broken up in England in 1923.

After the financially successful venture with the CHRISTIAN RADICH the Christiania Skoleskib organization became more cautious. All the money earned ended up in the bank. Times were unstable, but a new ship to relieve the brig STATSRAAD ERICHSEN had to be found. The wooden ship was at this time over 60 years old. The board was offered many big sailing ships at very good prices. In 1921 the bark ALFHILD could be had for only 275,000 NOK, fully equipped for training purposes. The Norwegian Ship Owners' Association supported the purchase. The ALFHILD was originally known as the British steel bark MEINWEN of 1,551 tons, built in Liverpool in 1892. The board chose to refuse the offer, even if they had funds to purchase the ship.

Somewhat later the board considered an offer to take over

Christiania Skoleskib's first CHRISTIAN RADICH ex TRANSATLANTIC painted as the artist thought she looked when she came to Christiania in 1916. She was Norway's only experiment using a cargo carrying sail training ship.

the four masted bark GERTRUDE for only 175,000 NOK. The Norwegian Ship Owners' Association now pledged 150,000 NOK in support, resulting in the board only having to use 25,000 NOK of their own funds to pay for the ship. A shipping company in the city of Sarpsborg had brought her to Norway one year earlier. The GERTRUDE was none other than the Norddeutsche Lloyd's cargo carrying sail training ship the HERZOGIN SOPHIE CHARLOTTE; a four masted bark of 2,591 tons, built for Rickmers in 1894. After the turn of the century she was furnished into a sail training ship. She was part of

MERSEY fully laden with a good speed in the breeze as a British sail training cargo ship.

the war reparations and sister ship to the beautiful HERZOGIN CICILIE, the flagship of the Gustaf Erikson fleet of sailing ships.

In the years before World War I both the German school ships went on long voyages with 60 to 70 students each. These two ships were among the best sail training ships designed and were beautifully decorated. As with the TRANSATLANTIC, the GERTRUDE's stay in Norway was an investment, and just like the TRANSATLANTIC she did not change her name in the records. The GERTRUDE was sold to A. Mattson in Åland and retained her original name, HERZOGIN SOPHIE CHARLOTTE. Christiania did not get her duchess. The city of Bergen, however, secured a duke. The Deutsche Schulschiffverein's new bark GROSSHERZOG FRIEDRICH

AUGUST of just over 1,700 tons was given to the city through the support of the Norwegian Ship Owners' Association. She was an auxiliary sailing ship fitted with an engine. The ship was renamed STATSRAAD LEHMKUHL and became Bergen's new sail training ship. This city had earlier used the wooden brig ALFEN, which was then sold. The organization Christiania Skoleskib decided to wait.

It seems inconceivable that the board of Christiania Skoleskib did not buy back the MERSEY at scrap price, or accept the offer to buy ALFHILD, or even accept the extremely generous GERTRUDE offer. For next to nothing they could have had a stately and beautiful ship which needed a lot of tender loving care but could have been restored in a reasonable fashion via student training work. The board was worried about securing enough freight income for such a large cargo ship when there was far too much tonnage of old sailing ships on the market. New power driven ships had fewer challenges obtaining insurance. The HERZOGIN SOPHIE CHARLOTTE did not become a new CHRISTIAN RADICH, but went to Finland and was broken up in Germany in the late 1920s. The huge profit from the sale of the CHRISTIAN RADICH remained untouched in the bank. This reluctance proved to be a very bad choice. The bank crash in 1924 led to Christiania

Skoleskib losing most of the funds saved up for a new sail training ship. The board's task suddenly became a struggle to try to get as much as possible of their funds out of failed banks.

This story did not end well for the organization due to the financial crisis. It was a great misfortune that the money for a new sail training ship for the city just disappeared. But the Christiania Skoleskib organization had succeeded in many respects. They sure were better navigators than the Norwegian financial establishment. The banking system of Norway went belly up in 1924. Many savings just vanished.

The tragic loss of sail training ships and many young lives have shaken the world several times over the years since the training of cadets started. Norway has been lucky in this regard. With the acquisition of the TRANSATLANTIC, Norway for the first and only time experimented with using a cargo carrying sailing ship for training purposes. This cautious attitude was likely due to major tragedies with this type of arrangement. The large five masted bark MARIA RICKMERS disappeared without a trace in 1892 with many German young men onboard. She was only one year old. Since then, several large cargo ships with cadets have been lost. The Danish 3,900 ton five mast cargo ship KØBENHAVN was nine years old when she disappeared in 1928 without a trace on a voyage from Argentina to Australia. There were 45 young boys onboard. After MERSEY had retired as a cargo caring sail training vessel, the old L'AVENIR was lost with 33 cadets and later the PAMIR also went down with its 52 cadets onboard.

Norway has always been spared the loss of sail training ships as well as serious or fatal accidents with cadets onboard. This indicates that the country has a very strong tradition when it comes to safety at sea. The story of the nation's first and only cargo carrying sail training ship, the rather unknown first CHRISTIAN RADICH, gives an exciting overview not only of the ship's history, but many international socio-economic events from the early part of the Twentieth Century.

The CHRISTIAN RADICH is the windjammer from the movie with the same name. It is still remembered all over the world as the ship from the movie. Of all sailing ships, it is clearly the most famous.

Christian Radich
-The Windjammer

Nothing has contributed more to the marketing of Norwegian maritime traditions than the CHRISTIAN RADICH. The full rigged ship is one of the world's most famous sailing vessels. She belongs to the aristocrats of the oceans; always given attention and leading to discussion when visiting foreign ports. The movie Windjammer was a powerful contributing factor.

Norway's last sail training ship was also the last full rigged ship built in Norway. In June of 1937 the new sailing ship was handed over to her owners from the Framnæs Shipyard in Sandefjord. The yard had the year before been sucessful to beat 10 other Norwegian shipyards in the competition to build a genuine full rigged ship. The sailing ship era was over. A lifetime had passed since Framnæs built its last cargo carrying sailing ship.

The construction was supervised by the commander of the Norwegian Navy Yard in Horten, Christian Blom. The organization Oslo Skoleskip wanted a full rigged steel ship of similar size as the DENMARK, but Blom was given flexibility in regard to the design of the ship. The drawings he submitted indicated that this could be a fast and beautiful

Draft of figureheads including a sailor's hat askew. A lady in full figure emerged victorious. The scroll work on the bow was made somewhat simpler than shown.

The figurehead shows the way, and symbolizes the perfect interaction between elements. Muscle power, wind and good seamanship lead the ship to victory.

ship. Framnæs approached the task of building the yard's hull no. 115 with fervor and enthusiasm. In the midst of the harsh 1930s, with economic hardship and low activity in most industries, this task was a shot of energy for the yard.

In August of 1936 the keel was laid down, and in February the following year the baptism and launch took place. The ship was named CHRISTIAN RADICH after a merchant and school ship benefactor who already in 1884, just after the stationary CHRISTIANIA had come into operation, bequeathed funds for a new sailing school vessel. The one condition he had was that the ship would bear his name. Little did he know that his name, because of this, would be kept alive for generations to come.

Rigging and placement of equipment occurred during the spring, and a number of prominent guests were invited along on the ship's trial run. It was a major event that the great maritime nation of Norway had a brand new full rigged sail training ship. The newspaper reports were numerous and the verdict unanimous: "A more beautiful ship can hardly have plowed the sea."

The CHRISTIAN RADICH was 676 gross tons, 192.1 feet long, 32 feet wide and 16 feet deep, with a 128 foot tall main mast. These numbers have varied somewhat

The CHRISTIAN RADICH was the last sailing ambassador Norway had to show how we shaped future merchant marine sailors.

with repairs, new measurements and interior conversions. The ship is the same even though she now is reported to be 662 gross tons with main dimensions of 205 by 31 by 15 feet. The ship has a sail area of 14,638 square feet spread over 15 square sails, 11 staysails, and a mizzen. She also has a main engine for propulsion.

This ship can nowadays achieve an absolute top speed of 14 knots only with the help of her sails. This requires five miles of rope, raw muscle power from cadets and seamen, and capable officers' knowledge of sailing. During her last reign as a sail training ship for the merchant marine, the CHRISTIAN RADICH had ten officers, six crew members and 78, both male and female, cadets. The latter figure is down from the original 99 cadets, all boys, who graduated the first year the ship was in full operation. The year was 1938 and the ship made a presentation voyage to the Baltic Sea with visits to Stockholm, Helsinki, and Karlskrona. The previous year the cadets received training on the brig STATSRAAD ERICHSEN and then were transfered to the CHRISTIAN RADICH after she was delivered from the shipyard. The summer cruise

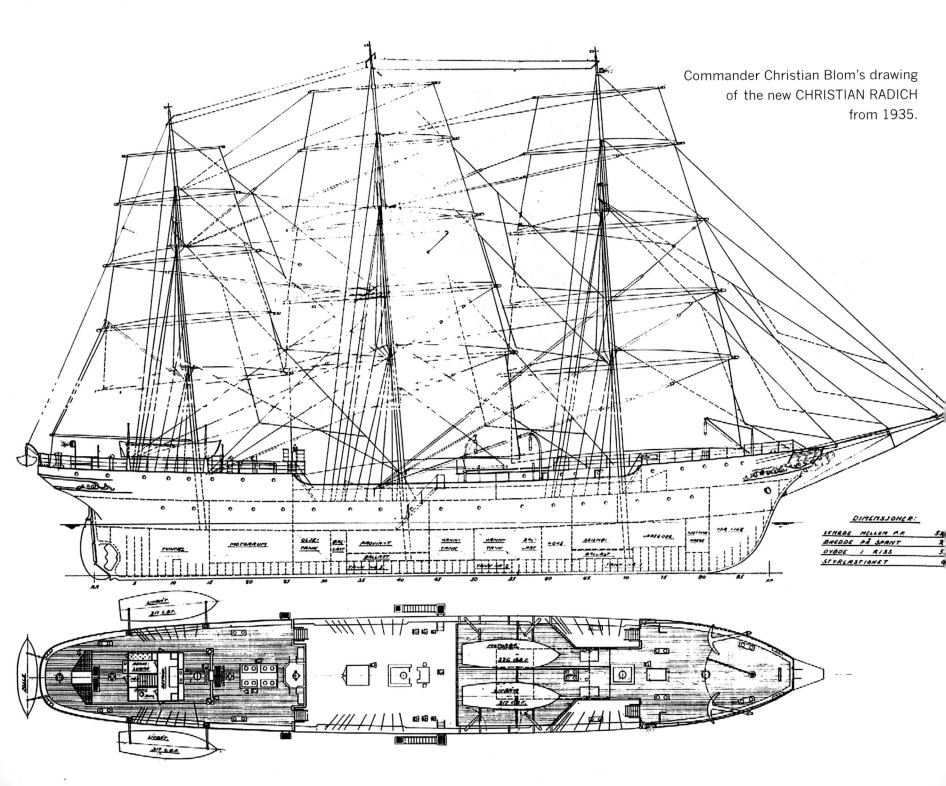

Commander Christian Blom's drawing
of the new CHRISTIAN RADICH
from 1935.

went to Fredrikshald, Kirkwall and Leith in Scotland.

In 1939, there were world exhibitions in New York and San Francisco. The CHRISTIAN RADICH was sent to New York to enhance Norway's participation at the exhibition. It was a very exciting experience for all involved. That sailors and sailing ships were celebrities was something completely new. The American media saw the new full rigged ship as very good and interesting material for a feature story and gave more coverage than anybody could hope for. Romantic dreams of the days of white sails with memories of foreign lands and exotic ports followed the ship and the crew on their American tour.

The captain decided to take the northern route on the crossing to America. On May 14th, the CHRISTIAN RADICH passed North Ronaldsey on the northern tip of the Orkney Islands. Exactly one month later, she took the pilot onboard near the AMBROSE LIGHTSHIP, outside the entrance to the New York Harbor, after a good passage of almost ten knots average speed on the best watches. The ship's ability to sail well was confirmed. On the return trip in August the log book shows that the best watch speed was over ten knots average.

The arrival was a fantastic experience for those who participated. Media representatives were onboard to cover everything. With all sails set she entered the harbor of New York under the deafening greetings coming from the steam whistles of the multitude of large and small vessels there. Many huge Atlantic passenger steamers lay in port and sounded their whistles. The CHRISTIAN RADICH received greetings from everywhere and the admiration of a lot of people. She was even photographed from the air. That was a rare event in those days.

The CHRISTIAN RADICH was given a berth at an honorary pier where as many people as possible could see her. Norwegian emigrants were very excited and did whatever they could to support this great ambassador from Norway. Young Norwegian cadets were the heroes of the day. The 16 to 17 year olds had been able to sail a new, full rigged ship across the Atlantic, utilizing "the Viking spirit," according the newspapers. His Royal Highness Crown Prince Olav and Crown Princess Märtha were at this time about to finish their great American journey. They came onboard and added luster to the CHRISTIAN RADICH's visit. The trip to America exceeded all expectations and led to the ship's owners in Oslo making grand plans. The ship itself returned to Oslo and dropped her anchors into Frognerkilen on September 3rd, 1939, on the very day that World War II started. She was rigged down for the winter.

There was no new voyage the next summer. Less than three years old, the CHRISTIAN RADICH was given other tasks than to train rookie sailors. After the invasion of Norway on April 9th, 1940, the Germans seized the vessel, just like they did with the other Norwegian tonnage they needed. She was subjected to particularly rough treatment during the war and was finally towed out of the country. Few people knew that she was taken to Germany to be used as a sail training ship for Hitler's Kriegsmarine. She was

In Boston's old dry dock, the CHRISTIAN RADICH's sleek lines come into full view.

docked in Flensburg in January 1945 during an Allied air attack. Floating docks had a high priority as bomb targets, thus hindering repairs and stopping sea transports. The dock where the CHRISTIAN RADICH lay took several hits and was severely damaged. The ship rolled off the blocks when the floating dock heeled over and sank. The ship's hull and decks were badly damaged. The CHRISTIAN RADICH sank along with the dock. When the war ended, only her top gallant yards and the mastheads were visible above the water.

This is how she was found after diligent search efforts, and in August 1945, Oslo Skoleskib took the initiative to get her back. She was towed to the Nyland Yard in Oslo and docked in December. The Norwegian Navy was liable and paid the hull value minus the scrap price. Norway's focus after five years of German occupation was the reconstruction of the country, and this of course applied to the CHRISTIAN RADICH as well. The ship looked miserable. Her furnishings were gone or destroyed. The hull and rig were badly damaged, and ropes, lifeboats and machinery were destroyed. A lot of equipment was missing. The wreck was towed to Framnæs where there were many boats in need of repair. All yards lacked basic materials. The waiting list was long, and repairs could take years. The wreck's future was uncertain also as a result of sharp price increases for iron, labor, and parts. All options were carefully considered. Should she be broken up, built down to a barge, converted to a freighter, or restored back to a sail training ship? Irony of fate meant that restoration would give the best value for the money. Dismantling and conversion would cost more.

The wreck was not suited for other alternatives because of her unique construction.

Final estimates from the yard led to Oslo Skoleskib deciding to repair the ship. They would be billed in installments as work was finished. The organization pushed to get high priority due to the inflation. Framnæs Shipyard worked on up to 45 ships within a week, while at the same time trying to raise sunken boats and repair damage to the docks, cranes and other yard equipment that had been destroyed by Allied bombing towards the end of the war. As if this was not enough, there was an acute lack of equipment and materials from steel to rivets, nuts, bolts as well as paint. Almost all the supplies had to be imported and licensed, or requisitions had to be obtained from the government due to the shortage of foreign currency. The yard was working under tremendous pressure, since all ship owners wanted their ships finished as fast as possible. The ships trading abroad usually were paid in U.S. dollars or British pounds; currencies needed for any type of import at that time.

It took until 1947 before the CHRISTIAN RADICH was finished and ready for service anew after eight long years. The spirit from before the war was still alive. Oslo Skoleskib started where they left off and got a lot of support from the Norwegian film industry, which needed to produce good, inexpensive movies about the postwar national spirit. The Norwegian filmmaker Thorolf Sandø and a film crew came onboard when the ship was ready for her summer cruise. Young boys became movie stars and the first voyage after the war went to Lisbon, Funchal, Ponta Delgada and Aberdeen. It was filmed and documented. The following year, the movie *Vi seiler* was presented to Norwegian audiences. It was shown for two years in theaters all over Norway and got a lot of attention. Many moviegoers at that time enjoyed experiencing exciting things together with young cadets in foreign ports, and also got to see how a genuine full rigged sailing ship was operated. For many old salts who had started out on windjammers around the turn of the Twentieth Century, when white sails were still common on the Seven Seas. The movie became a romantic

The captain with two of his young boys at the helm.

Three cameras rolling during the shooting of the *Windjammer* movie.

remembrance of the days when they were young. They enjoyed being taken back to the good old days.

There was a growing interest in sail training ships. The rebuilt merchant fleet needed a whole new generation of sailors. The film showed that sail training ships could offer a unique experience. The focus was on the boys and they were met with admiration and recognition. This gave self confidence and created pleasant memories for later in life. The movie was intended as entertainment, but was just as much a recruitment film for the merchant marine. The result was as expected; many Norwegian youngsters chose to start their working life with some time at sea.

For the CHRISTIAN RADICH, the first part of the 1950's was a busy time. The long summer cruises were replaced by crash courses all year around. A screaming demand for more seamen for the

merchant fleet led to an intensive training of young boys over two months before they joined the merchant fleet. Many young boys came from outside of Oslo, and the organization was renamed Østlandets Skoleskip (Østlandet is the name of the southeastern part of Norway). The name was changed to better reflect the region of the country many boys were recruited from. The ship was moved to a secluded spot by Hjortnes in Frognerkilen and started to show signs of wear and tear from lack of funds. The short courses were challenging both for the boys and the ship. Some argued that this represented exploitation of young boys' wanderlust and was detrimental to the ship's general condition. The ship was appropriate for summer courses and completely unsuitable as a winter residence for students who took crash courses that could just as well have been held in a schoolhouse on land. Cadets and crew lived through a freezing cold winter with frost condensation on the inside hull and portholes. They suffered from cold and flu during the winters, while the cold ravaged the open 'tween deck.

At all times, people at sea have had a competitive attitude. Fishermen in the old open square sail boats on the way in from the fishing ground measured forces. Some boats were clearly faster than others. The *Høvedsmann* (the chief), crew and boat shared the honor, and the boat builder was praised. For people on the coast having a good boat conferred status, just like it was important for the farmer to have the fastest horse. Adventure books and Viking sagas include stories that show the same. Racing even led to King Olav Trygvasson's demise; a majority of his flotilla that raced ahead did not see the enemy ambush in wait.

Clipper ships and grain ships competed with each other. When sailing ships met, rowing competitions and regattas were a natural expression of patriotism and the joy of achievement. Often they were spontaneous and occurred informally when it was convenient, but they could also happen in a more organized fashion. Rowing competitions are defined as the oldest organized sport in the Americas.

In 1955 the British Sail Training Ship Association took an initiative to gather the world's remaining school ships for a race from Torbay to Lisbon the following year. An appointed committee named the Sail Training Association was in charge. The idea caught on and an impressive armada from 11 nations met in Dartmouth for the first international Tall Ship Race. From Norway the CHRISTIAN RADICH and the SØRLANDET participated. In many ways this race forms the link between the voyages of the last great grain ships from Australia to Britain in the interwar period, and the international sail training ship voyages established later.

The CHRISTIAN RADICH did well in the first modern sail training ship race and secured a victory to the surprise of many foreign ships known for their superior speed. For Norwegians who had long suspected the ship to be a speedy windjammer, this was the first confirmation. The beautiful ship from Oslo has since gained a solid reputation among the world's finest sailing vessels. The year 1956 was important for sail training ships for other reasons. It appears that many ideas in the making suddenly

One of the last pictures of the four mask bark PAMIR, taken from the CHRISTIAN RADICH.

burst into full bloom. Eric Newby's book *The Last Grain Race* was released simultaneously with the Sail Training Association's first race. Famous sailing fans and writers were behind the new initiative. Eric Newby was onboard the giant ship MOSHULU with the nickname "THE WINDJAMMER", when she won the last grain race in 1939. His book became a bestseller and was translated into several languages. Sail ship romanticism inspired Hollywood to make a movie about it, with the MOSHULU as the lead ship.

But the four mast bark MOSHULU, capable of carrying 6,000 tons of whole grains and perhaps Norway's last sail cargo ship, was taken out of commission and was used as a grainary in Stockholm and Finland. Therefore, film agents went to Philadelphia to take a

Scenes from the movie *Windjammer* and the book about the film.

look at the STATSRAAD LEHMKUL. But she was about to depart to take her cadets back to Norway. Why not the CHRISTIAN RADICH? The production company got in touch with Alf R. Bjercke in Oslo, who negotiated an agreement. The CHRISTIAN RADICH was chartered for a period of six months from December 1956 for a film voyage. Onboard there were 41 young boys, some of whom were handpicked for the task, some professional actors, and a 19 man film crew as well as the ship's regular crew. The Norwegian shipping industry helped fund the film production.

Just before the departure His Royal Highness Crown Prince Olav came onboard to wish the film expedition a prosperous voyage, and to hand over a 1,000 year old Viking sword as a gift from Norway to the American people, and to remind them that it could have followed a Viking on his trip to the Norse Vinland, today's North America. Upon arrival to the U.S. the sword was handed over to President Dwight D. Eisenhower who in turn passed it on to the U.S. Naval Academy's Museum in Annapolis, where it would be exhibited as a reminder of the Viking voyages to the North American continent 500 years before Columbus.

The *Windjammer* film was the most impressive tribute ever staged for a sailing ship. People of all ages all over the world flocked to the movie theaters to see the film which was produced using a new and highly advanced video and audio system called "Cinemiracle". Three synchronous 35mm Mitchell cameras weighing 500 pounds each filmed scenes at different angles simultaneously. They covered the entire eye's field of view and gave a good

Beautiful ladies participating in a garden party for officers and cadets at Port of Spain, Trinidad. One of the Norwegian cadets later married one of the girls in the picture.

impasse in film development. The system was too complicated and expensive, but it did offer an entertainment experience nobody had experienced before, and gave memories for life for all those who went to see the *Windjammer* movie.

The film cruise went from snow, freezing temperatures and Christmas decorations in Oslo to Madeira where a sleigh ride on the cobbles down the steep, narrow streets gave the audience a first taste of what was in store for them. The movie continued with

depth perspective. A huge underwater case was used when filming under water. This monster of a system for recording and playback required a giant curved canvas over large parts of the theater and seven Hi-Fi channels around the room for sound. Playback was through mirrors and complicated electronics to synchronize all the sound with the pictures. Ten miles of film passed through three special viewers during a showing. The setup was as advanced as it was unique, expensive, and complicated. Only large cinemas were able to invest in the system. It was launched as the future of cinema, and the Colosseum movie theater in Oslo was rebuilt for this purpose. However, "Cinemiracle" turned out to be an

Old and new meet at sea. A unit from the U.S. Navy Task Force during a shooting for the movie.

113

Arthur Fiedler and the Boston Pops Orchestra playing Grieg's Piano Concerto in A Minor, dockside with Cadet Libæk as the soloist on the concert grand piano.

more and more exciting visuals, such as the cadets' encounters with exotic beauties, calypso and limbo dancing in the West Indies. The moviegoers also experienced the oil port of Curacao, where the ship had to sail through the city to get to the harbor. In New York the cadets had the experience of their lives. Their meeting with the world's metropolis was a celebration in sound, light and colors; impressively reproduced by the new movie system.

The *Windjammer* movie was truly a film of contrasts, where a rather thin storyline was compensated for with breathtaking visuals, including picturesque scenery, art and culture. This movie

114

had everything. Blond cadets, led by the young Norwegian actor Harald Tusberg, were surrounded by attractive American girls in beautiful dresses. The cadet and pianist Sven Erik Libæk was a soloist with the Boston Pops Orchestra, directed by the legendary conductor Arthur Fiedler. Grieg's Piano Concerto was played on the pier with the CHRISTIAN RADICH as a backdrop, accompanied with beautiful pictures of snowcapped mountains in Norway. This was indeed a movie with many contrasts; scene with the ship under escort by a U.S. Navy Task Force, with frigates, airplanes above and an aircraft carrier towering in the background. In rough weather with all sails set and with the sea rushing in over the bow, the CHRISTIAN RADICH comes plowing towards the audience, the bow coming out of the movie canves and into the audience. People instinctively slid back in their seats to prevent the imaginary waves from hitting them in the face. Whether eight or 80, for the audience this was a scene to remember and arguably the movie's most lasting impression in 1958 and the years that followed.

Like all sailors the CHRISTIASN RADICH cadets found playful girls in every port.

The *Windjammer* movie was shown at the world famous Grauman's Chinese Theatre in Hollywood for a long time. A bronze plaque with the ship and the commemoration of the event is still to be found in the cement outside the famous movie theater, together with the commemorations of many other movie stars from that era.

Even today, the CHRISTIAN RADICH is often only recognized as "The Windjammer" or "The ship from the movie". Most of those who went to see the movie back then still remember the film. During the more than 100 year long history of the cadet training on sailing ships, nothing has to the same extent helped bring the world's attention to the sail training ships in general, and to the CHRISTIAN RADICH specifically. Finally, in July of 1957, the ship arrived back in Oslo to a Royal reception. She had been a movie star in Hollywood; this was great promotion of the ship and of Norway.

In 1958 the race went from Brest to Las Palmas and once again, the CHIRSTIAN RADICH secured an excellent place in the race. On the return trip, she visited Hamburg to condole the tragic loss of the city's four mast bark and cadet training cargo ship PAMIR. The two tall ships had met in the Atlantic during the filming of the movie when the PAMIR was on her way to Montevideo to pick up cargo for Germany. Such a meeting between two proud sailing ships far out at sea was a rare event even in the old days when sailing ships were common

Only Sonja Henie and the CHRISTIAN RADICH from Norway have been honored by getting their names imprinted in front of the famous Grauman's Chinese Theatre in Hollywood, where the film *Windjammer* was first shown on April 8th 1958.

No single event has provided sail training ships more advertising worldwide. The film *Windjammer* had its world premiere at Grauman's Chinese Theatre in Hollywood in the spring of 1958. This picture was taken five months later, in September 1958.

cargo carriers around the world. In 1957 it was a sensation. It was filmed from the CHRISTIAN RADICH while the two ships sailed together for a while and exchanged greetings.

The PAMIR never returned to Europe. On the way home she was surprised by hurricane Carrie. Sails blew out, her cargo shifted, and she sank slowly southwest of the Azores. Only six of the 86 onboard survived the tragedy. They where found several days later. This accident put a definitive end to the training of young seamen onboard hybrid cargo carrying sailing ships.

In 1960 the large gathering of sailing ships for "Operation Sail" took place in Oslo. Not since the golden days of sail had a larger

116

fleet of sailing ships visited the capital of Norway. The harbor basin was full of proud ships with masts, yards and ropes, resembling a forest. Oslo's CHRISTIAN RADICH was the host and had performed very well during the previous races. She was charged with the task of bringing all the trophies for the awarding seremony to Ostend in Belgium.

Sixteen vessels participated. The CHRISTIAN RADICH was off to a good start and quickly left all the others behind. The captain chose a northerly route and met almost windless weather. So did everyone else in a race that lasted several days without any of the ships moving much. There were discussions about calling off the race when the wind returned, and all the ships made it to Ostend. Only the CHRISTIAN RADICH, located the farthest out to the north, got headwind and had to tack her way while the others could head straight for the finish line with a nice breeze

Louis de R

WIN

a
modern
adventure
in
CINEMIRACLE

mont's

JAMMER

The front cover of the booklet made for the movie. It contains extensive information on the ship, sailing and "Cinemiracle", a new and unique film and audio recording system.

NDOM HOUSE BOOK

from behind. That she and the awards had difficulty making it in time for the ceremony has become one of the funny stories from international regattas. The moral of the story is, of course, that in sailing all have a chance to win; it all depends on the wind and the weather.

The first races in her home waters around the North Sea were so successful that during the meetings in Oslo the race leaders discussed the possibility of going on long voyages. The CHRISTIAN RADICH was a sprinter. Many felt that a longer voyage would give the larger ships a chance to beat her. To gather the world's remaining sailing ships at the New York World's Fair in 1964 became the next big task. Britain's Sail Training Association agreed to participate. Thus the stage was set for the first Trans-Atlantic sail training ship race. It would encompass the 3,600 nautical mile stretch from Lisbon to Bermuda; longer than the distance Columbus sailed on his voyage to America.

After persistent efforts among enthusiasts in Norway, they managed to equip all three Norwegian sail training ships for the voyage to New York. In this show of maritime power, the CHRISTIAN RADICH did things right and showed that larger ships may not necessarily profit from having a longer water line, thus being able to reach greater top speeds even when the races were longer. She sailed across the finishing line after 24 days as the winner of the first Trans-Atlantic race.

The exhibit in New York was the largest collection of sail

training ships the world had ever seen. It especially attracted great attention that little Norway, with only three million inhabitants, mustered all three of her proud sail training ships for the merchant marine. No other country had as many sail training ships. This became the "Year of Norway" on the U.S. East Coast. The SØRLANDET sailed south along the coast and visited Philadelphia, Baltimore, and Norfolk before her journey home. The STATSRAAD LEHMKUHL went north to New London, Providence, Boston, and Portsmouth before she returned to Norway along the northern American route. After her visit to New York, the film diva CHRISTIAN RADICH cruised up the St. Lawrence Seaway to the Great Lakes and Chicago. The trip from Montreal through the locks was tiring with a lot of extra work. The rig was too tall, and they had to lower the top masts so that the ship would be able to pass under the many bridges. Chicago rewarded the brave Vikings well. Everyone had seen the film and wanted to go onboard "The Windjammer". That the sailing ship came right into the heart of the American continent was a sensation in itself. People stood for hours in line to see her. The visit was registered as the summer's big event in Milwaukee, Detroit, Cleveland, Alpena and Toronto; other cities the CHRISTIAN RADICH visited on her voyage to the Great Lakes. The Norwegian Foreign Service and the Norwegian Trade Council cooperated in order to coordinate the visits.

For the first and last time, Norway sent three merchant marine sail training ships with a total of 227 cadets together across the Atlantic. From the enormous press coverage found in the CHRISTIAN RADICH's archives, it appears that a better representation for advertisement of Norway would be hard to find. Other countries recognized this and started large scale building programs to get their own sailing ships and gain international recognition at the next crossroads. Orders for new vessels were placed, and many of the tall ships we see today are a result of this contracting surge.

At the same time things did not go well for the Norwegian ships that had been part of the merchant marine sail education programs for a very long time. To a greater extent than others, they inspired the world to care about this kind of education and to participate

During a race one becomes accustomed to living on an inclined plane. Crossing the deck can become an uphill battle.

in international regattas. The Norwegian sail training ships' battle for survival did not receive much interest from politicians in Norway. It became increasingly difficult for the ships to compete for students with the state run maritime schools ashore. Arguments that education on the sailing ships was not relevant for work on modern ships made matters worse and clearly showed that education by sailing around the world no longer had support among the Norwegian people. Government grants decreased and could not keep up with the actual expenses. Also, new recruitment to the commercial fleet stagnated. All these factors contributed to the end of the traditional training onboard sailing ships. The local North Sea Regatta from Falmouth to Skagen in 1966 in connection with the Royal Danish Yacht Club's 100th birthday was the last time sail training ship institutions in Oslo, Bergen and Kristiansand sent their three ships to meet and enjoy peaceful rivalry. The SØRLANDET won, while the CHRISTIAN RADICH came in second and the STATSRAAD LEHMKUL third; securing a triple victory for Norway ahead of the host country's ship, the DENMARK, which placed fourth.

That same fall the Bergen sail training ship organization closed down their operations, and the largest and oldest of Norway's sail training ships,

The CHRISTIAN RADICH sailing into the Golden Gate by San Francisco for arrival after the longest cruise the ship ever made.

Pilot Fred Andersen is taking her into port in San Francisco, while Captain Fjell Hansen is standing by.

A cruise outside the Golden Gate Bridge with the mighty Marin Headland as a backdrop makes the CHRISTIAN RADICH look small.

The tall ships are back! A forest of masts is the first visual impression when the last pack of the world's great sailing ships meet. CHRISTIAN RADICH is the fourth ship in the middle of the group.

The captain informs all how they are going to win the race from Boston to Kristiansand.

The U.S. Coast Guard bark EAGLE is coming right at the CHRISTIAN RADICH with all sails set. This could have ended in tragedy.

On top of the world. Standing on top of the main mast's royal yard, looking down. The deck below is amazingly narrow and small. The problem is to find balance while operating an old Nikon camera with both hands.

The ship is heeling over. The bottom paint is visible. With all sails set she takes off with the wind as a non-polluting energy source.

The wind increases to storm intensity and more and more sails are taken in. The ship still maintains its speed of 13 to 14 knots.

Even with only the lower sails set, the speed remains the same.

The air is filled with sea and visibility is low. The picture gives a good feel for what it really is like when it is a storm at sea.

the STATSRAAD LEHMKUL, was without duties. The SØRLANDET was smaller and younger, but she needed more funds than what was available. Although her owners struggled long and hard, it ended with the sale of the ship in 1972. Suddenly, the CHRISTIAN RADICH was the only Norwegian sail training ship left. An uncertain future awaited the CHRISTIAN RADICH as well, but the Østlandets Skoleskip board of directors and her management refused to give up. Well supported by the Friends of the CHRISTIAN RADICH support group, which was founded in 1974 with His Royal Highness Crown Prince Harald as president. Actor Lasse Kolstad and TV Producer Harald Tusberg from the *Windjammer* cruise signed on as warm supporters. The board managed to save their ship. The CHRISTIAN RADICH got the needed help so she could still be used for training of merchant mariners. The government of Norway decided to look into the matter and invited other interests to a meeting in 1975 where the conclusion was that the ship would continue to sail and that the expenses would be picked up by the government. This came after the realization that the ship had an educational potential as well as public relations and entertainment value, and would be important for cultural export, marketing

The wind increases steadily. More sails are given up while the ship keeps the same speed.

and tourism. The CHRISTIAN RADICH was also a symbol of Norway's rich cultural tradition and history as a maritime nation.

After 1975 the CHRISTIAN RADICH was to become a sailing Norwegian ambassador in connection with anniversaries and major events and used for export promotion in addition to her old focus on educating personnel for the merchant marine. The first mission under this new model was the Norwegian emigrant anniversary in America. On the day 150 years after the first organized emigration started from Norway, the CHRISTIAN RADICH left from Stavanger with wishes for a safe voyage from King Olaf of Norway and proud Norwegian supporters.

Sailors have always forged a special link between the homeland and the New World for those who emigrated. Often, sailors and letters home were the only contact the new Americans had with the country they left. It always warmed their hearts to see a Norwegian flag on the ships in the harbor and hear the crew speak the language they used as children. For cadets onboard the CHRISTIAN RADICH, this resulted in a number of social invitations from former countrymen wherever they went.

The following year was the celebration of America's bicentennial. The expedition to America in 1976 was a collaboration between the Norwegian Information Service in New York, the Norwegian Trade Council, Operation Sail, the Sail Training Association and the anniversary committee. That year the voyage would go between Plymouth and Newport via Tenerife and Bermuda. The race was challenging with little wind and several stretches cut short. The

At watch change, the cadets on duty are tired while the new watch, to the left, is fresh and ready.

CHRISTIAN RADICH was still able to place second. In the previous race four years before, there were excellent weather conditions when she sailed from Helsinki to Falsterbro and won.

The Fourth of July in 1976 was the 200 year anniversary of the U.S. Declaration of Independence. Many tall ships sailed into the harbor of New York. All were duly presented and with them the country they came from. "The Windjammer" received the greatest applause. Not only was she recognized from the movie, but she was also sailed by 16 year old boys. This was different from many of the newer ships that had arrived. They were all sail training ships for their country's navy and were sailed by considerably older students, most of them were adults.

Once again the CHRISTIAN RADICH went on a cruise to the Great Lakes and stayed there for five weeks. The ship visited numerous cities and turned around at Duluth on Lake Superior, the innermost and largest of the Great Lakes, 600 feet above sea level. She had never been higher up, or farther from home. This freshwater voyage was a long parade of unforgettable experiences for the ship. In Chicago, thousands of people met up at the dock in the middle of the night to see the ship well off and wave goodbye. The police had a full hand controlling the crowd. The boys onboard could not believe their eyes. "This they'll refuse to believe home in Norway," was a common comment.

It was fall before the CHRISTIAN RADICH started her homeward voyage and the ship encountered bad weather. On the night of the 23rd of September things could have ended very badly. In the Atlantic Ocean, 400 nautical miles west of Lands' End, the CHRISTIAN RADICH was overtaken by a hurricane with over 60 knots relative wind. It took hold of the studding sails on the fore and main mast and forced them out of their lashings one by one. It was impossible to enter the rig due to all the wire, blocks, and ropes whipping around aloft and hammering the masts and yards. Sparks flew when steel hit steel. The masts swayed like sticks when the hurricane's gusts took hold. The rig could not endure such punishment for long. It took time for the sails to blow out the way they were supposed to do, saving the ship. This

124

The sea is getting ugly with huge waves rolling in from behind. The ship tips over the top and plows down into the valley between two waves, while a new wave is rising behind. Sea washes onto the deck as the aft part gets ready to accommodate a new wave.

The wave passes. It is a mountain of water to the left in the picture. Only the smallest sails are set. The speed is still measured at around 13 knots. All the larger ships are behind.

experience showed that the far too solid Dacron sails nearly led to CHRISTIAN RADICH's demise. During the time of the sailing ships the hemp fabric in the sails served as a safety valve. They quickly blew to shreds and relieved the pressure on the rigging during excessively high winds. While the hurricane raged a distress message went out. The international press reported that the CHRISTIAN RADICH was in trouble. Several ships approached to help while the captain and crew struggled to save the ship. The skipper himself took the helm for a while. All hands were gathered aft, nobody could be forward or on the main deck. The ship drifted north in the rough sea with a lot of surface water on deck. The hull was checked on a regular basis and the vessel was sound, but water penetrated from above and made it wet and unpleasant under the deck, especially in the cadet quarters on the 'tween deck.

Conditions stabilized later in the day and a French frigate, coming to the rescue, was lying nearby. Other vessels eventually arrived. The next day the CHRISTIAN RADICH could raise some undamaged staysails and use the engine. The ship got back on course and headed for the Isles of Scilly and the English Channel while the assisting ships could go back to their courses. The ship and crew had made it through the storm, but it was a narrow escape. The fore topgallant mast was broken and the rig had sustained vibration and strain damages. The hurricane was a highly dramatic end to an otherwise wonderful cruise.

The number of applicants for the courses the next two years

125

Coming home. Sailing into Oslo Harbor without the mizzen gaff to carry the flag. It was taken away in the Atlantic storm, but otherwise the ship was fine after a voyage that was only 850 nautical miles short of the Earth's circumference.

was very high. In the fall of 1977 there were three times more applicants than the ship's capacity. Some girls even demanded a slot. The regatta in 1978 went from Gothenburg to Oslo with the CHRISTIAN RADICH taking second place. The course of the year showed clearly that the cadets did not choose the sail training ship for an exciting or romantic experience. Half of the students were hired onto merchant ships within 14 days after the end of the term. The large number of applications to become a cadet on the ship was not only due to the CHRISTIAN RADICH being the only sail training ship left and therefore the only option for young people seeking a maritime career on merchant ships.

She was also identified with all the romance of sailing due to a very popular TV series shown at that time. The British TV series *The Onedin Line* became extremely popular both in Norway and other countries. It followed a shipping company in England during the transition from sail to steam, including personal aspects pertaining to the people involved. The CHRISITAN RADICH was used in the series that ran for years. In some scenes she operates as a sail steam ship with a lot of smoke pouring out of a dummy funnel rigged for the filming. A number of British sailing ships of wood, however, accounted for the majority of vessel scenes. But it was the magnificent Norwegian bark STATSRAAD LEHMKUL which had the more profound part when she was used as a vignette for the series. In the opening scene she comes sailing into the TV frame, accompanied by an excerpt from the Adagio movement of Khachaturian's Spartacus Ballet suite no. 2, a majestic opening for any TV series. Most TV watchers could not quite distinguish one ship from the other so the CHRISTIAN RADICH was identified as the most important ship by many viewers as they enjoyed the show in their living rooms all over Europe and beyond.

From 1979 to 1980 Østlandets Skoleskip tried a new approach to keep the ship sailing. She would also promote Norwegian products in the U.S. In cooperation with the Norwegian Trade Council and Scandinavian Airlines, the CHRISTIAN RADICH left Norway in August 1979 with 88 new cadets. They worked on their sail training in the Caribbean when the ship visited Bridgetown, Barbados, and Venezuela before the Panama Canal and the Pacific

Ocean. This time they had embarked on a really long voyage. Their first Pacific port of call was Acapulco, followed by a longer stay in Los Angeles and San Francisco.

Finally the ship had arrived in Hollywood. It took 22 years before the movie star appeared in the film city, but what a success it turned out to be! The Los Angeles Harbor constructed new mooring equipment at the newly established Los Angeles Maritime Museum. They got all the attention they could dream of. The harbor was full of people and a 100 piece orchestra played. No one had forgotten the star of the 1950s and more than 10,000 people were aboard the 11 days she was there. The boys experienced trips to Hollywood, Disneyland and many other tourist destinations. The arrival of the CHRISITAN RADICH was considered by the

Boys left, men returned.

management of the museum to boost the start of the Los Angeles Maritime Museum. Today the museum has a large and excellent collection and is one of the most visited maritime museums on the West Coast. A special CHRISTIAN RADICH poster of the ship outside the museum was on sale in the gift shop in honor of the ship that helped get the museum off to such a flying start.

The cadets spent many adventurous days in San Pedro, including a mini cruise to Avalon on Catalina Island and, last but not least, several trips for the boys to the nearby Norwegian Seamen's Church on Beacon Street. There they could eat waffles with strawberry jam and read the latest newspapers from home. The ship continued her voyage north to San Francisco, the famous and infamous, sailors' town of yesteryear. With all her sails set she entered the Golden Gate like thousands of proud sailing ships had done before her. Many of these predecessors never went further. Their crews fled the ships and the city in the search for gold. At one point a whole fleet of abandoned sailing ships lay rotting in the harbor and many of the houses in the main part of the city today stand on the remains of old sailing ships. The last week of November 1979 was officially proclaimed "Christian Radich Week" by the city council of San Francisco. The cadets embarked on a series of new experiences. In addition, they got a taste of the American Christmas spirit and were able to buy Christmas gifts and meet Johnny Cash. San Francisco was the cruise's turning point. Never had the ship been further away from her home port. The distance from Panama to San Francisco is farther than across

Mission completed. Ready for a reception at the City Hall with the mayor at the completion of the two year long mission to the Pacific.

the Atlantic Ocean. The CHRISTIAN RADICH then went south to San Diego for a short layover during Christmas and New Year, while all onboard returned to Norway with Scandinavian Airlines.

After Christmas, 88 new cadets arrived at the naval base in San Diego together with the crew. The ship lifted anchor and headed for the Panama Canal. Her homebound voyage included visits to Mexico, Panama, the Gulf of Mexico and the U.S. East Coast, including stops in Washington, D.C.. The U.S. capital has never been a prominent seaport and the Potomac River was dredged before the CHRISTIAN RADICH's visit. Few other foreign ships would have received such favors from the Americans.

The last stop was Boston. The old British colonial capital celebrated its 350th anniversary only four years after the nation

celebrated its bicentennial. The port city of Boston has always been one of the continent's main gateways. The location, the good harbor and all the sailing ships' visits were the basis for the city's growth. As expected, the shipping industry was the focus of the celebrations. The jubilee had a retrospective look under the motto "The Tall Ships are Back." With the city's own old U.S. Navy frigate CONSTITUTION as the host leading the parade, the sailing ships came back to the city in a magnificent parade. This was seen by over a million people who surrounded the harbor. Fort Independence slope was packed. It invoked an image of a crowded rookery. No one onboard had seen so many people gathered in one place. The pier where the tall ships docked looked like a forest of masts and yards. The influx of people during the days the ships were in Boston Harbor was enormous. The fact that so many nations from around the world had chosen to send their remaining sailing ships all the way to shed luster over their anniversary warmed American hearts and made them very proud. People from all parts of the nation had found their way to Boston. The anniversary was a national celebration of America's history from its humble beginnings to the advanced nation it had become by 1980.

At this time the Sail Training Association for the first time decided that a race would follow the North American route from Boston to Kristiansand in Norway past Fair Isle. They hoped this would compensate for the lack of wind during the last few years' quite unsuccessful races. The notorious 3,000 nautical mile stretch of the Atlantic Ocean between Boston and the Shetland

Islands is known as the windiest part of the Northern Hemisphere. Low pressure and storm centers follow each other like beads on a string, even in summer.

Some argued in 1980 that the CHRISTIAN RADICH was getting too old to participate in a race. The ship's previous experience with the hurricanes made them worried, even though few from those days were still onboard. She had had many challenging sailing experiences but she would be 44 years old before she really got to prove what excellent sailing characteristics were built into her sleek hull and beautiful rig. The German GORCH FOCK, a vessel over twice as large as the CHRISTIAN RADICH, was seen as the very likely winner and her crew looked forward to a stormy voyage. The Germans, eager for a rematch, wanted to finally prove that the CHRISTIAN RADICH was a light weather sail ship. The CHRISTIAN RADICH was the smallest of all starting ships in the race's Class A. The larger ships with longer waterlines could easily beat her top speed. In theory, she was the slowest ship. Onboard the CHRISTIAN RADICH, however, everybody was ready to show once more that they could beat the larger German bark.

The following quote is from the diary of the author, who was one of the crew members during the voyage:

"The old watch record of 44 nautical miles in four hours, made before World War II, is suddenly within reach. She did well then, will she be able to perform better than that in her youth? The answer comes within the watch. She does 46, the next watch 47, another 46, then 47. She finally closes off the day doing 48 nautical miles in four hours, or a nice 12 knot average; quite a

The author is trying to brush up on his navigation skills by shooting the sun with a sextant. Neither captain nor mate use this tool any longer. They have more modern equipment and relax while the sun passes the meridian.

speed! Topgallant sails are furled at midnight. Then we go really fast. Only the royals were given up before that. She continues at the same speed.

It is in the dead of night that races are won, but this requires a skilled, alert and well trained crew who can go to the top of the

masts and to the tip of the yards during the pitch black night and in stormy gusts, taking in and tying down high up and far out over the foaming waves while the ship is working in the sea. The wind keeps increasing; the sea is about to get big. The CHRISTIAN RADICH is overtaken by the first storm center of the trip.

The voyage continues without significant decrease of the sails. The day after it is clear that the ship has beaten the old 24 hour record by a good margin. During the period from the start of the watch at 12 noon until 12 noon the next day, she has sailed 275 nautical miles through the sea with an average speed of 11.5 knots per hour. With the Gulf Stream as an added bonus, she has traveled well over 300 nautical miles towards Europe. The storm center passes, but the wind remains strong. Not long after, a new low pressure system from the west and a new storm is chasing the ship on. Some days the German ship sails much farther than the smaller CHRISTIAN RADICH can ever hope to manage. The GORCH FOCH's long waterline is of great help. The third storm, more than halfway through the race, is violent and all ships are severely challenged. Competitors report sea damages and withdraw from the race. Only our mizzen gaff snaps with a big bang and comes down. We rig the smaller "storm" mizzen sail. The captain and his talented crew are determined to keep up the speed. This takes us back to the old days of hard sailing when sailors let the sails stand until they blew out or the rig came down. Our crew furl the sails as needed and fools the wind again and again. Not one sail is damaged even if we log top speed all the time.

The captain is motivated to lie just south of the others, even though the distance is longer. He wins in a big way when one of the storm centers passes just north of the CHRISTIAN RADICH. Then it is our turn to say goodbye to the other ships. Slowly, but surely, the CHRISTIAN RADICH passes all competitors regardless of class. The GORCH FOCK was way ahead earlier, but is now struggling in headwind and eventually falls 100 nautical miles behind.

The weather is getting rougher. The

Details of ropes and wires. All pass through at one location in the rig.

How the galley staff is able to cook and get food across deck in such weather is still a mystery to me. The barometer falls for a whole day, finally settling down at 980 millibars. The sea becomes rougher and rougher. It is flat out ugly to look at. The top of huge waves break all the way, "He pours" as they say on the coast of Norway. The top part blows off and foam is torn away by the wind. Between the waves' ridges small waves form of which the peaks also break loose and fly off. The air is full of salt water. The visibility is significantly reduced; the horizon is just a short distance in front of the ship, sensed more than seen. The officer inspects the masts and shrouds. The sails are fine. All the wires, turnbuckles and lines are holding the rig together as expected. They pull together. The bow of the ship plows the sea like a snow plow and puts cascades of white sea far away on each side.

But everything comes to an end. So also this violent storm; eventually the low pressure center has passed. The anemometer creeps back to a more normal part of the scale; the worst is over. But the waves that catch up with us are still ugly. Entire mountains of water come rolling. Our ship slides down

anemometer works its way slowly up past 30 knots and continues. At the peak it shows up in the 50s. Several sails are given up and sheathed without the speed decreasing significantly. Sails help less when the ship is pushed too far over and large amounts of sea wash in and out of the drainage ports on the ship's lee side. Finally, she sails only on the lower topsail and jib with the wind gauge oscillating well above 60 knots during gusts and the log swinging around 12 knots as well. "Now we have a hurricane, guys," is the first officer's dry remark, and then he orders eggs and bacon at the watch's end.

a steep hill of water, makes her way across a valley and plows up the back of a new mountain of sea to ride over the top and down again at an impressive speed."

Only two of the Class A tall ships were left in the race. All the others had pulled out, one after the other. It was down to the CHRISTIAN RADICH and the German GORCH FOCK. The two ships left, however, followed each other like shadows across the sea. At the finish line outside Oksøy Lighthouse after midnight the estimated distance was less than 15 nautical miles between the GORCH FOCK and the CHRISTIAN RADICH. This race has gone down in history as one of the classic races. It has many similarities with the most legendary clipper races from the days of the white sails. After crossing an entire ocean and sailing a distance of 3,300 nautical miles where storm followed storm and the ships sailed as hard as the equipment could take, the distance between them at the finish line was so small that they could easily have seen each other, was it not for the morning fog. The race's handicap rule meant that the smaller CHRISTIAN RADICH won by about one day over the German ship.

The CHRISTIAN RADICH set a strong record; a remarkable achievement by a ship of only 662 tons. The passage from Boston to Kristiansand took less than 18 days. It was alleged that only once in the days of sails had a sail ship made the trip faster. As many as 14 watches were traveled faster than the old watch record. In nine days the ship sailed over 200 nautical miles each day. Only two days at the beginning did she gain almost no headway and log less than 100 nautical miles. The voyage in 1980 was named "The Record Race" and added new history to the Sail Training Association and the story of the CHRISTIAN RADICH. The expedition to the Pacific from 1979 to 1980 also set a formidable distance record. From the time the ship left Oslo, turned around in San Francisco and was back in the city, she had sailed a distance totaling 20,748 nautical miles. This is only 852 nautical miles shorter than the Earth's circumference.

After the cadets left the ship following a grand reception at the City Hall of Oslo, the CHRISTIAN RADICH went to Framnæs Shipyard in Sandefjord, and for the first time since 1947 she received a thorough renovation with new masts, new rigging, and repairs to the hull. It was revealed that she suffered from extensive corrosion and the repairs became far more invasive than anticipated. Everything damaged was replaced, but this took time and blew the budget. The interior got an upgrade. The 'tween deck got fixed berths. From now on, girls would also be accepted as cadets. It took until 1983 before the ship could resume the training of cadets, and this time the girls came with.

While the organization's pride was being repaired at Framnæs, Østlandets Skoleskip celebrated its 100th anniversary. The board had decided that an anniversary book about the company and the sail training ships in Norway would be a suitable symbol of their success. It was the good citizens of Christiania that in the 1870s decided that the capital should have a sail training ship and therefore started the sail training ship movement in Norway. After many years of hard work they managed to put the CHRISTIANIA into operation in 1881. The book *Skoleskipene* was published by the Norwegian publisher Gyldendal in 1981, presenting all the sail training ships of Norway. The anniversary was marked by the old STASRAAD LEHMKUHL taking the voyage to Oslo for the launch of the book. It was presented to a joint press corps in the lovely lounge aboard the largest and most beautiful of all the former Norwegian school ships. His Majesty the King of Norway sent a touching greeting. It was reprinted in the book. *Skoleskipene* received extensive press coverage and was elected the Most Beautiful Book of the Year in 1981.

The CHRISTIAN RADICH was incorporated into a new national education program for high schools under the category maritime and culinary programs. She took another voyage across the Atlantic to Quebec in Canada in 1984, and in 1986 she was back in New York for the celebration of the anniversary of the Statue of Liberty. The improvements continued so that the ship was in tip top condition for her 50th anniversary on the 17th of June, 1987. That a sailing ship makes it to 50 is quite unusual. Most barely made it to half that age during the good old days of sail. This anniversary was celebrated with a grand gala performance at the Oslo Concert Hall. A special program

A pamphlet gives information on the ship's many adventures, particulars, and lists her accomplishments in international races. In most of them she placed first.

The bark GORCH FOCH has always been the CHRISTIAN RADICH's main rival.

was put together and representatives from the Norwegian Royal family were present.

From the late 1980s the number of girls onboard increased drastically until about half of the students were girls. Many potential cadets applied and the education program followed the regular school year. Some workshop teaching and theory took place on land at Horten, the rest occurred onboard. From the late fall, the ship sailed south for up to six months; usually to the Azores, Madeira or the Canary Islands with a visit to France or England on the trip home. She was back in Oslo around Easter. The 78 students took their final exams and graduated before midsummer.

In 1992, the 500 year anniversary of Columbus' voyage to the West Indies was celebrated with a race in the discoverer's wake from Cadiz via the Canary Islands to San Juan in Puerto Rico. Once again the CHRISTIAN RADICH took home a first prize in the race. There was also time to visit New York and Boston. She continued to sail incredibly fast when the conditions were right and set a new formidable one watch record of 296 nautical miles. This gives an average speed of 12.33 knots over 24 hours.

The beginning of the 1990s was characterized by great turmoil within the school system in Norway. There was much talk of restructuring; many had opinions and debates in the media and elsewhere about reform plans, the best age for children to start school and pedagogical approaches. All the reforms would improve things that were not as they should be; everything would be so much better, promised the politicians and the bureaucrats. One hundred and thirteen different certificates shrunk to 12. The Reform of 1994 allowed for more classroom instruction and theory for freshmen. The introductory course in maritime disciplines disappeared after 1994. The CHRISTIAN RADICH was once again repurposed, and the full rigged sailing ship was forced into a new system she was not built for. From 1994 to 1998, the ship from Oslo therefore offered a set of preparatory courses for the Maritime College in Vestfold. She was kept sailing and took a couple of trips to the Caribbean. Yet another curriculum plan and class structure at the Maritime College went into effect in the fall of 1998.

Since 1945, some in the industry and others have stubbornly championed the argument that it is nonsense to conduct training on sailing ships for a career onboard motor ships. They forget that the CHRISTIAN RADICH has always had an engine and auxiliary machinery in addition to her sails, and thus has far better range than a motor ship. Training in the use of sails has always been varied and provided solid knowledge of the sea. In 1998, the final victory went to those who opposed training onboard sailing ships. This marked the end of 120 years of sailor education for the merchant marine on sailing ships in Norway. Two old motor vessels took over the training. The rest of the training takes place in schools ashore, which have now assumed responsibility for the training of aspiring sailors.

The end of the era of sail training ships arrived quickly and without any fanfare. No debate or referendum took place. The preparatory course was removed and the CHRISTIAN RADICH was quietly discarded as a sail training ship for the merchant marine when she was 61 years old. The ship had reached retirement age. The nation no longer had use for this sailing ambassador and world famous movie star, despite documented statements and promises from the government. After finishing the semester in the spring of 1998, the CHRISTIAN RADICH suddenly found herself unemployed. Like the other sail training ships she was restructured to become a "cocktail cruise ship" for people willing to pay to experience sailing ship romance. The ship's new owner is Stiftelsen Skoleskipet Christian Radich. Those who sail with her have the title "paying co-sailor." "Onboard you will be sailing, standing at the helm, keeping lookout, and last but not least taking in the experience when 27 sails are set and the ship makes 13 knots," an advertisement in the Norwegian newspaper *Dagbladet* noted. The goal is no longer a career in the merchant marine or a naval career. In this respect, Norway is left behind by nations who use their sailing ships as cadet training vessels for young people, paid for by their government. Having young cadets onboard is a prerequisite for further participation in the Tall Ships' Race. This requirement is fulfilled by inviting young people to participate at a discount or even for free, just to be allowed to sail with the Sail Training Association.

Norway's last three sailing training vessels were acquired in order to promote recruitment and increase the quality of new seafarers. Today the CHRISTIAN RADICH is used for parties, seminars, and light sailing for people with money who want to experience something new and the ship still participates in the yearly Tall Ship Race around the ports of Europe together with many new vessels from many countries.

A ship with square sails is a complicated instrument which requires knowledge of sailing. What about the safety of everyone onboard and for these fine old vessels when they sail with a minimum of skilled sailors? The majority of the new "crew" may be more or less unfit to perform the relatively harsh physical labor and skilled work required aloft

136

It took 21 years after the filming of *Windjammer* before the ship finally showed up in the city where the movie was made. It gave a real boost to the newly started Los Angeles Maritime Museum.

Los Angeles Maritime Museum
San Pedro, California

and on deck in tough situations or during a race. There have been situations where over 30 highly trained 17 to 18 year olds with six months' experience onboard are dead tired and exhausted at the end of their watches. In the days of sailing ships, a crew of 18 experienced sailors was considered a minimum for a full merchant rigged ship. Safety requirements may in the future discontinue the use of the old sail training ships for pleasure cruises in international waters due to the lack of a sufficient number of experienced sailors.

When the CHRISTIANIA was retired at the turn of the Nineteenth Century a few visionaries tried to salvage the ship. This was long before the preservation of old ships became common. She was from the U.S. and had been Norwegian for only about 20 years. Norwegians should have long since learned to understand that the CHRISTIAN RADICH is a treasure which Norway must save, protect, and preserve. The nation should immediately commence building a beautiful home in Oslo Harbor for the CHRISTIAN RADICH like Stockholm has done with the VASA, or like the KON TIKI received after Thor Heyerdahl drifted with the balsa raft to Polynesia in 101 days, one of the shortest active lifespans of any craft.

Norwegian authorities have always had an ambivalent relationship to the merchant marine. Control and taxation of ships and sailors have been issues regularly debated in the Parliament for years. Even more peculiar is that in the list of 218 preserved and protected ships in the Cultural Heritage Conservation Plan for Norwegian Vessels from 2010 to 2017, the CHRISTIAN RADICH, along with some of the nation's oldest and most valuable icons from an era long gone, are not included.

There are reasons to argue that the CHRISTIAN RADICH has been the foremost ambassador for Norway abroad for 60 years. The ship has been an important carrier of the tradition of the days of white sails and a nice vessel for the presentation of Norwegian youth in training. Few learning tools can surpass a sailing ship when it comes to understanding the forces that surround a vessel at sea and the teamwork that is required. This is knowledge for life, even for those who subsequently change their occupation from seafarer to landlubber.

The CHRISTIAN RADICH was created with respect for the forces of nature, and to exploit and cooperate with them. She is a passive user of the elements. Hull, masts, rigging and sails and handling of lines, ropes and pulleys with pure muscle power do not pollute. This is the way people have sailed since Leif Eriksson was in Vinland more than a thousand years ago. The voyage went between the continents with the wind and the sea as helpful aids. This is how our ancestors built the world we live in today. The sailing vessels were the most important prerequisite for this development and expantion.

Time and again, sailing youth on the CHRISTIAN RADICH outperformed cadets from other countries and returned home with the coveted trophy. Many times the ship was used in media and received starring roles in film and television. She helped museums get started and inspired nations to build their own sailing ships.

Books were written about her and she was often featured in the media. The CHRISTIAN RADICH became a living legend at home and abroad. Everyone wanted to see and if possible come onboard when she called on ports during a cruise. She set an example, she was "The Windjammer" and she promoted products, tourism and Norwegian culture abroad.

Few memories of the past stimulate the imagination like sailing ships. They tied the continents together then and today connects our own time to the past. The symbolism the CHRISTIAN RADICH represents becomes even more important because so few old sailing ships have survived. Sadly, Norway's last Cape Horner, the bark LINGARD, was sold for scrap by the Norwegian Maritime Museum after she was fully restored. Only the sail training ships remain, representing the tradition back to the days of sailing ships when hundreds of Norwegian merchant vessels plied the Seven Seas.

Today's owner has provided these photos of "The Old Lady" as she looks today. She still sails on exciting voyages in Norwegian waters and abroad.

The LANCING, in 1917, under full sails by Læsø, Kattegat. The four mast ship is on a voyage between Denmark and America. With all her record voyages, she provided the perfect finale to the era of white sails.

Lancing
-The Speeding Legend of Sail

The LANCING is truly a ship for the record books. The memory of this storied ship, which consistently made record breaking passages and steadily profitable voyages for her owners, has faded from our consciousness because of a simple problem of translation. Most of the LANCING's documentation is in Norwegian, while the most well read histories of this era of shipping are written in English. This is a presentation of her career. The ship's accomplishments will not be forgotten.

The most famous voyages during the age of sail were done by packet and clipper ships between the U.S. and Europe, from New York to San Francisco, by British clipper ships on their yearly tea runs from China to England, and also the grain races to Europe, first from San Francisco then from Australia. These voyages sometimes took place with many speedy windjammers that started sailing about the same time, but these are only the best known examples of speedy voyages on world trading routes.

Individual crossings were, however, the most common. A speedy voyage generated a lot of interest and was published in the newspapers. This could give the ship a bonus and the captain honor, while a ship that used far too many days led to great worries and sometimes penalties if she ever arrived.

PEREIRE was a French pioneer in the Atlantic mail and passenger service. The ship operated the route between Le Havre and New York in her early years.

Famous sailing ships and some of their captains belonged to the windjammer hall of fame; for example the American clipper ships FLYING CLOUD, ANDREW JACKSON, JAMES BAINES, RED JACKET, LIGHTNING, and the British tea clipper ships ARIEL and THERMOPYLÆ, just to mention a few. These ships include a small group of vessels constructed for speed and manned by a large crew, holding many of the classic speed records. Some of the wool and immigrant ships going to and from Australia and New Zealand were "wet" ships and should be in the same exclusive club, as should some of the big iron and steel built windjammers from the latter days of sail. Giant windjammers like POTOSI, PREUSSEN, FRANCE and MOSHULU could undertake extremely fast voyages due to their long water lines and enormous rigging. One of these large sailing ships was different from all others and belonged in a class of her own.

The four mast full rigged ship LANCING has a unique history. There are several reasons why this ship should be known as one of the fastest sailing vessels ever. One of the things that makes this ship so unique is that she started sailing record breaking voyages when she was well past her prime. It was Norwegian captains and crews that really helped her reach her potential. The history of the LANCING is therefore also the history of excellent seamanship from the captain down to the deckhand.

It is counterintuitive that sailing vessels become faster with age. The large American clipper ships built of wood were constructed for maximum speed. They had a large crew and made most of

"When Sail Beats Steam" became a famed motif for posters and paintings. The LANCING was known for overtaking slower passenger steamers and cargo ships over and again on the high sea.

the record breaking voyages during their early years. Hardly any managed to reach top speed when they became ten years of age, if they survived that long. This goes for modern sail racing vessels as well. They are usually replaced after a few years of competition as new and faster boats are constructed. Even iron and steel built

142

windjammers from the latter days of sail became slower with age. There are, however, special reasons why the LANCING became such a legend and performed best well past her prime. The ship's history and differences in seamanship must be analyzed in order to understand this.

That the LANCING had the ability to reach great speed was obvious, but she was never put to the test before she became Norwegian, even if some writers have misinterpreted old records and moved some of her record breaking voyages back in time.

Many windjammer captains would not seek record breaking runs even if they knew they had, or suspected they had, a speedy ship. It was their job to take the ship and its cargo safely across in due time and without any damages to the ship and its cargo. The size of the crew was also a challenge towards the end of the age of sail. It was kept at a minimum. Seamen jumping ship in port and a shortage of well educated able bodied seamen with the needed knowledge of sailing ships and the work aloft were common challenges.

A few captains, however, had a special ability to give the ship and its rigging a maximum drive at any time and at the same time avoid damage of sails, rig and the ship itself. It was those virtuosos within their trade who put the ship to the test and made record breaking voyages when wind and weather were cooperating. One point is of utmost importance. To make an exceptional passage is possible if the wind blows with perfect velocity throughout a voyage. But that never happens and if it does blow hard, the sea will eventually become ugly with enormous waves which threaten to cripple any ship. It is therefore imperative that consistent performance on various trade routes around the world, with different captains and over years, should be considered before determining the faster sailing vessel.

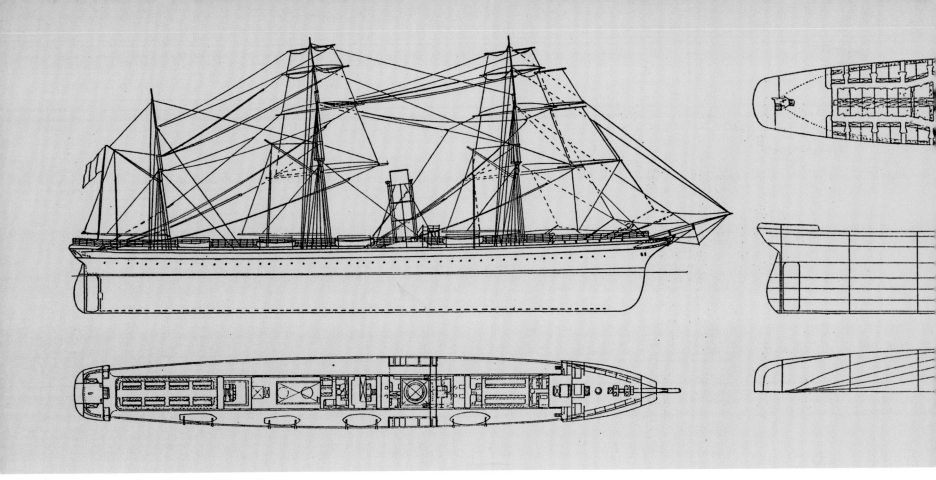

The reason that the LANCING has not been included among the world's greatest sailing ships is that her accomplishments were primarily detailed in Norwegian. The leading nations in regard to research on fast sailing ships were the U.S. and Great Britain. Therefore, research on this topic has not included much of the Norwegian material. In addition, the LANCING was originally French, built as a sail steam ship back in 1865. After she was converted to a sailing ship in Great Britain, her British captains and crew never seemed to get her up to speed. For these reasons,

the LANCING has been the strange "stepchild" when it comes to fame and honor in the world of sails.

After Captain Nils Bull Melsom discovered what he could squeeze out of this almost 40 year old sailing vessel, it became important to record exact speed, based on accurate chronometer measured time and a newly calibrated towing log. Captain Melsom once recorded in his logbooks that the ship did 20 knots per hour for two consecutive hours in a four hour watch where he had a sailed distance of 76 nautical miles. The average speed for this watch of

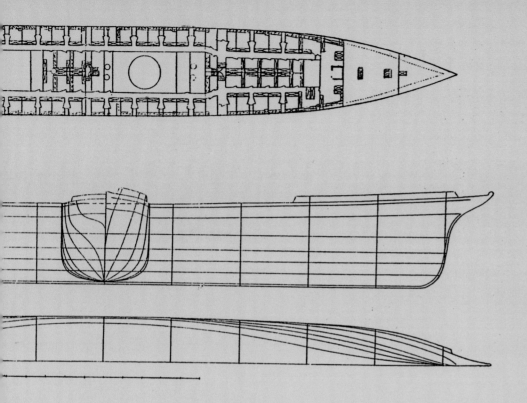

The Atlantic steamer PEREIRE was designed by Sir William Pearce and built in Glasgow, Scotland in 1865 at Napier & Sons.

four hours was 19 knots! Logbooks that still exist show that the LANCING over and again held an average speed of well over 15 knots on a 24 hour run. This happened in the Twentieth Century when the measurements of speed were much more accurate than earlier.

What was so unique about the LANCING was that she kept on sailing record breaking voyages when the weather conditions were favorable and the captains let her make a speedy passage. Captain Oscar Olufsen was a mate on the LANCING under Captain Melsom for many years. He turned out to be just as good as his master in handling the sails of the ship. While under his command in 1916, the LANCING sailed from the AMBROSE LIGHTSHIP outside New York to Muckle Flugga on Shetland in 12 days and 21 hours. The crossing of the Atlantic from Cape Race to the northern tip of Shetland was accomplished in an unbelievable six days and 18 hours. At that point in time the LANCING was 51 years old.

The LANCING has had a history not unlike a fairytale since she was new. The ship was built in 1865 of iron by Robert Naiper &

"First Sight of Land," oil on canvas, by Henry Bacon, 1877.
Painted after several sketches he made onboard the PEREIRE.

Sons at Glasgow as the steamer PEREIRE for French America Line, just four years after the company was established with paddle steamers on the Trans-Atlantic run. The same company later owned the famous ocean liners NORMANDIE and FRANCE; the FRANCE was later to become the famed blue cruise ship the NORWAY. The PEREIRE was originally intended as a paddle steamer, but the drawings were changed to propulsion by screw during her construction. The PEREIRE and her sister ship became the prototype of the new type of Atlantic passenger steamers. Like

The painter got the inspiration for this painting from the shipboard life onboard the luxurious steamer. Travel across the Atlantic by steam became common in the late 1860s and during the 1870s. A new trend in ocean transport was that the mail steamers carried passengers both ways, not just immigrants to America. The mast is the main holding point in any vessel. Its prominent size indicates that sails were still in use on steamers. Saving fuel by using the wind was not new. The mast later helped the LANCING gain world fame.

The well dressed young lady is not an immigrant longing for a better life in the new world, excited to see land, but rather a first class passenger traveling the other way. During the late 1800s, this became so common that some Europeans gave those women the nickname "dollar princesses." It started with the PEREIRE and continued well into the Twentieth Century. Young ladies from wealthy families were often sent to Europe to get educated, perhaps visit relatives, and hopefully find a nice and handsome European "prince" during the stay abroad. Clearly Bacon tried to paint excitement, longing and great expectations into this beautiful painting.

other steamers of her era she was given sails and rigged as a three mast bark. The engine was small and not very powerful compared to the ship's size. To obtain proper speed, the ship was built with an easy driven hull with a block coefficient far lower than an ordinary sailing ship of her time period.

This feature was quite common for first generation sail steam ships. The PEREIRE was 371 feet long and only 43 feet wide, with a draught of almost 39 feet. These dimensions made for a long and narrow hull. With a length to beam ratio of 8.5:1 she was more than anything like an enormous Viking longship or *drakkar*. Her displacement was 5,217 tons and she measured 3,018 gross tons. The engine was 1,250 horsepower and the trial run showed that the PEREIRE could do 15 knots. She was licensed to carry 284 first class passengers, with 104 in second class, and 30 in third class. Her first crossing from Le Havre to New York in 1866 took nine days and four hours.

The passenger steamer PEREIRE received lots of publicity. Emperor Napoleon III came onboard. The ship was said to be especially well constructed and the most successful mail and passenger steamer of that time. She also proved to be very seaworthy. With an average cruising speed of 13 knots she was considered the fastest steamer across the Atlantic, even better than Cunard's CHINA, the ship that held the speed record between New York and Great Britain. The introduction of the Blue Ribbon for the fastest passenger steamer across the Atlantic came after the time of the PEREIRE. Much later a French newspaper, on the

The main deck of the LANCING looking aft with the officers cabins to the right. They used to be the stateroom for the first class passengers on the PEREIRE. They were still intact when the ship was broken up.

editorial page, noted that it was difficult to believe that this proud ship would manage to do a far better top speed in her old days without the aid of a steam engine.

The same summer the PEREIRE was built a group of French intellectuals met in Paris to plan an international monument of liberty. However, the plan did not materialize under Emperor

The passenger steamer PEREIRE after rebuilding. With her two smokestacks she eventually became a well known emigrant ship, bound for America.

Napoleon III's autocratic regime. But in 1871 the 37 year old artist Frederic Auguste Bartholdi was sent to New York on the PEREIRE to present the idea to the American people. It is said the he did not have any specific drawings or location for such a monument, only a small terra cotta model of what it should look like. When the PEREIRE approached New York Harbor, Bartholdi was on deck looking towards the city. He then got a vision of a great goddess with a torch in one hand as a welcome to the land of freedom and possibility for all the oppressed people of the old world. Bartholdi quickly made a sketch, got his painting gear and made a drawing of a Statue of Liberty with Lower Manhattan in the background. The first draft of the Statue of Liberty was very similar to the giant statue that later was erected on Liberty Island. Not until 1884 would the statue be unveiled. When the LANCING later approached New York on one of several such trips, no one onboard would know that it was on her deck that the ultimate symbol of the free world was conceived.

The PEREIRE was the luxury liner of her time, where the rich and famous from the old world would travel across the Atlantic in ultimate comfort, while all the emigrants she later carried down in the steerage compartments would travel one way to freedom. The world's first famous science fiction writer Jules Verne was a passenger and used the PEREIRE in the introduction chapter of his most famous novel *Twenty Thousand Leagues under the Sea*. The PEREIRE was the QUEEN MARY of her day, but times change. When the PEREIRE was 15 years old she caught fire and was deliberately

When LANCING sailed by the Statue of Liberty on one of her many voyages to New York, nobody knew that it was on her deck Bartholdi stood in 1871 when he looked towards the city. He envisioned a giant goddess wishing all Europe's poor and oppressed welcome to the Land of Opportunity. When she was newly erected and the first of the wonders of the New World, the Statue of Liberty was not green, but shining like a bronze goddess should shine. Maybe she needs a good polish?

sunk by a torpedo to extinguish the fire. This was done in order to save the ship. She was repaired and got two funnels and continued her passenger service, mainly as an emigrant ship until 1887, when she was wrecked and written off. The wreck was sold to Great Britian. Salvage operations were long and costly. After salvage she was towed to Blyth for docking and conversion into a cargo ship. The engine and boiler room were removed.

She was entered into Lloyd's Register in 1889 as the four masted full rigged ship LANCING under British flag. Canadian and Norwegian interests were also behind her. The LANCING became a cargo carrying windjammer of 2,785 gross tons. Her measures were the same and show that the hull was not altered externally since new in 1865. She was given three new masts of steel. The PEREIRE's foremast became the jiggermast and she was given a very short bowsprit which became her singnature. Her overall length was 405 feet. Ballast tanks were installed where the engine and boiler had been. She also got a pump room along with a boiler and steam winches on deck. The five watertight bulkheads were kept. This was highly unusual for a cargo sail ship and added immensely to her strength. Instead of a big hold almost the entire length of the ship, the LANCING had three separate cargo holds and a 'tween deck. The ship was given 24 square sails, nine staysails and a mizzen. The LANCING was classed 1A by Lloyd's of London.

Under survey for her class renewal in Greenock when she was 54 years old, an elderly surveyor came on board. He had been with Lloyd's as a young apprentice, and was onboard when the

149

The full rigged ship LANCING, previously called PEREIRE, became a legend. The slim hull, tall rig and Norwegian seamanship contributed to her becoming a world champion on the ocean.

steamer PEREIRE was built in 1865. He told that Lloyd's considered the LANCING one of the world's wonders. She had never had any negative comments in her files. Her folder was clean just as it was when she was certified for service. He stated flat out that she could sail another 50 years. Lloyds' never had remarks on anything including general condition and maintenance. This correlates with research on and recent knowledge of early steamships built of ship quality wrought iron that have been well maintained. They are among the most lasting constructions that were ever made for a saline environment.

The LANCING's voyages during her early years under British ownership are well documented. Her departures and arrivals suggest that she was not driven hard or that she was any "Greyhound of the Seas." A few short recordings seem to indicate that she was always a speedy vessel. She easily left the pilot boat doing 14 knots behind, sailing into New York under Captain Hatfield. The pilot was highly surprised and asked for her speed. The captain replied that he had no log and could not tell the speed. From existing material the conclusion seems to be in line with Basil Lubbock's statement of the LANCING's ability to sail well: "With her great length and heavy yards she was not an easy ship to handle, and the Norwegians certainly seemed to have got the hang of her better than her British officers as I can find no specially good passages under the Red Ensign."

The LANCING had several owners from different countries during the 1800s. From 1888 A. E. Kinnaer of London had her.

After that Johan Bryde of Sandefjord, Norway became the owner. Bryde, involved in the whaling industry, has even given his name to a whale species that he helped identify, namely the Bryde's whale. In 1896 her title was transferred to Frank Ross of Quebec. Norwegian interests were still involved and the LANCING was transferred back to Norway while lying in San Francisco in 1901. The new owners were Lancing Ltd., with Johan Johansen & Co., Lysaker, with Christiania as her home port.

The LANCING sailed as a tramp sail ship around the world. Her cargo could be grain, flour, corn, linseed, coal, nickel ore, raw iron, phosphate, oil products, or case oil as well as many types of wood and lumber, sawmill products, spool wood, and other wooden objects for the textile industry. In 1896 while laid up in Sausalito waiting for a cargo of grain for Europe, she was chartered by a group of adventurers hunting for Inca treasures in Peru. On January 1st, 1897 the LANCING sailed for Callao and continued to Sydney for cargo before returning to San Francisco in time to pick up grain for London. To hunt for the legendary Inca gold was all treasure hunters' big dream in those days.

Just after the turn of the century in 1901 and at an age of 36, the life of the LANCING changed drastically. A period with good freight rates for tramp sailing ships started at the same time. This resulted in good money for the company. The LANCING also got her fair share. She was dry docked frequently, cleaned and repainted if needed. Sails and rig were renewed regularly. She had several sets of good sails for all the oceans of the world. LANCING sailed world wide during the duration of World War I and did very well financially. At the end of the war in 1918 Magnus Melsom became the owner. Then in 1920 Melsom & Melsom became her final owners. The following details were the reason the Melsoms became attached to this ship.

Captain S. B. Johnsen was her first master under full Norwegian ownership from 1901 to 1903. Then, in 1903, Nils Bull Melsom became her captain and

Nils Bull Melsom, captain of the LANCING.

with him things changed drastically. He must have been an extraordinary seaman and master who understood the strength and ability of this ship and how she could be sailed. The first two things he did were to install a new towing log and purchase a new chronometer of the best quality. From 1903 the LANCING embarked on a long series of extraordinarily swift passages. Over the next two decades she never experienced damage to her sails or rigging even if Captain Melsom and his followers made her sail as never before. They had a completely different and tougher way

The unusually sharp lines become prominent when the LANCING is seen from the bow while in dry dock. The photo reveals that the ship was built to sail very fast. Norwegian seamen showed the world how this ship should be handled.

of running her before the wind. Speedy turnaround made for even greater profit. Officers and ship owners were happy, but for her crew this meant backbreaking labor. Even if they later could boast to other sailors that they had done record breaking runs in the LANCING, many fled the ship at the first opportunity.

Captain Bull Melsom was the LANCING's captain for more than 11 years. After that, his regular mate, Oscar Olufsen, became her master. He had even relieved his captain on several prior occasions. It is in the period from 1903 on that the LANCING is recorded to have done a long series of unbelievably swift watches, outstanding 24 hour sailings noon to noon, and record breaking fast voyages from port to port. Over the following 20 years the ship sailed a series of very good runs, indicating that she must have been one of the speediest cargo carrying sailing ships of all time. This happened during the twilight of sail. It is therefore tempting to put the record straight that the last days of white sails were not necessarily a time of sadness when once proud ships rusted and rotted away. The LANCING, the last of her class, made the close of an era a grand finale anybody could be proud of.

There are many examples of impressive runs. Captain Stenstrup has worked through the LANCING's many existing logbooks and he summarized his work in a booklet published by the Norwegian Maritime Museum before World War II. It is time to analyze the LANCING material once more and update these documents. Records show that four of her Norwegian captains sailed the ship well over 300 nautical miles on a 24 hour run. They also had several four hour watches each with an average speed well in excess of 14 knots. Here is a short summary of some of captain Melsom's recorded passages:

In 1904 the LANCING sailed from Saint John, New Brunswick to Melbourne in 79 days, averaging 18 knots during many watches en route. In 1908 she sailed from Horten to Melbourne in 74 days using only 64 days out from Land's End to Melbourne on the same voyage. In 1909 Captain Melsom took LANCING from New York to Tusket Wedge, Nova Scotia in four days, and in 1910 from Cape Chat in the St. Lawrence River to Ardrossan, Scotland in 14 days. In 1911 she sailed from Montevideo to New Caledonia in 44 days, and in 1913 from La Plata to New Caledonia in 58 days and the next year from Rio to New Caledonia in 69 days.

An article published in *Shib-o-Hoy* magazine in the 1930s corroborates Captain Melsom's recordings of LANCING's speed according to her propeller log. Captain Krøeber commanded a four masted bark deeply laden with grain from Australia to Europe. At the latitude of the Falkland Islands and in gale to storm force winds he was proud to do 13 knots on her lower topsails; indeed, any captain would have been proud of such an achievement. He then discovered a ship coming up from dead astern and on the same course, also deeply laden: "It was a large four masted full rigged ship, and she carried all her top gallant sails! She must have logged a speed of at least 18 knots and was a fantastic sight! She passed us like a lightning rod and made us appear standing still with our 13 knots. We barely managed to exchange greetings and signal letters. She was the LANCING of Christiania!" The whole event was unbelievable according to Captain Krøeber; it was an experience he would never forget.

Captain Olufsen only got to command the LANCING for a few years. On September 16th 1918, he fell overboard aft by the logline and was lost. Captain Olufsen's best 24 hours was 366 nautical miles with 72 miles on his best watch. That is an average speed of 18 knots. Speed like this is only obtainable with exceptionally fast sailing vessels when the wind is steady. His best crossings include sailing from New York to the Shetland Islands in 1916 in 12 days and 21 hours. The LANCING only used six days and 18 hours across the Atlantic from off Cape Race to the northern tip of Shetland. During that time the LANCING sailed 2,071 nautical miles. That is an average speed of 12.3 knots for the crossing and is the fastest Atlantic crossing ever with a sailing ship. On top of that, the return trip from Denmark's SKAGEN REV lightship to Halifax was completed in 20 days and 16 hours with a recorded speed of 16 knots one day and the following recording the next day: "Calm the whole watch, no recorded speed, sails given up." A voyage with a crossing of the Atlantic Ocean both ways and including the North Sea in a mere 27 days is an outstanding achievement. As if that was not enough, this happened during World War I and the LANCING was stopped and boarded by British warships for inspection and run-through of her papers both ways before she could continue her voyage. After arriving in America and before the return trip she loaded spool wood in Canada and returned to

The captain and his men, lined up for a photographer in Australia. The back of this picture reads: "LANCING's record breaking voyage from Horten, Norway to Melbourne in 74 days in 1908." Captain Melsom is in the center middle row with First Mate Oscar Olufsen to the right. On September 16th, 1918, as the ship's captain, Oscar Olufsen fell overboard and drowned.

Glasgow in 15 days sharp, from the time she discharged her pilot in Canada until the new pilot came aboard in Scotland, one hour before arriving in port.

The North Atlantic is difficult to sail with a good speed both ways as the ship might hit head wind from the low pressure systems coming from America. It is the long haul down "The Roaring Forties" that gives a steady push in the right direction for days and weeks on end. According to her logbooks, from these voyages it gives us the right to proclaim that LANCING under optimal conditions was able to obtain a speed of 20 knots. That

happened over a two hour period on a watch that recorded an average of 19 knots, with Melsom as master and Olufsen as mate. They must have been a perfect team to get the best speed out of the LANCING's long and narrow hull.

From 1919 until 1922 P. T. Pedersen held command. Like her previous captains he also did more than 300 nautical miles in 24 hours and commanded watches of more than 14 knots. He took the LANCING from Cape Chat, Canada to Ardrossan, Scotland in 16 days in 1919. The same year she managed to sail from New York to Aarhus, Denmark in 24 days and in 1921 had a new voyage from Cape Chat to Ardrossan in 16 days. It was in June of that year she could have been lost. With a full cargo from St. Lawrence to Scotland in fog and at a speed of about five knots, she collided with a big iceberg. She struck the iceberg with the bow and port side, and remained fastened to the iceberg for about half an hour as her yards were jammed into the ice. The entire crew took to the lifeboats expecting her to go down. When she finally broke loose from the ice the crew managed to get onboard to monitor her cargo holds for water. She was dry and the captain and crew got her under sail anew and continued the voyage. She had sustained damages to the upper hull, one mast, some yards and the rigging. The LANCING limped into port in Scotland 17 days out, and was checked by divers and declared safe and sound. With the TITANIC disaster in recent memory, no one could believe that such a large windjammer could escape from an impact with a big iceberg and

Finally home! Not all sailing ships returned to their home port. Here we see the LANCING in Bjørvika in front of the Akershus Castle in Christiania, repainted and well presented for the occasion.

The LANCING sailed all over the world. She was in San Francisco seven times, in New York six times, and undertook ten voyages to Australia. She was in South America, Africa, India and the Far East many times. Only once did she return to her home port. That was before Christmas in 1907. She arrived in Christiania (later Oslo) from Greenock on December 19th and stayed until March of 1908. Then she left Horten for Melbourne and arrived there after 74 days of record-breaking sailing. Ten years later she arrived in Kristiansand and stayed for five days. On May 25th, 1917 she left Norway for the last time.

A clean picture of the LANCING at anchor in Australia. A very impressive scene, showing of one of the greatest windjammers of all time.

not go down. One argument could be that the TITANIC was made of steel, which gets brittle in low temperatures with compromised riveting. The wrought iron hull of the LANCING, however, was softer and could take such impacts easier by giving way, much like a fender. Though the main difference must have been the TITANIC's greater mass and speed upon impact.

A. Larsen was the LANCING's captain in 1922 and 1923. He did one run from Cape Chat to Ardrossan in 15 days in 1923. That spring was difficult with much ice on the east coast of Canada and the LANCING was stuck in the ice for eight hours before breaking loose. Unlike power driven ships, sailing ships have small chances of negotiating ice as it often breaks loose and drifts, like the ship itself, with the wind. Finally, in 1924 Captain P. Hansen took her on two runs from Canada to Scotland and managed 58 nautical miles on his best watch. Towards the end of that year the LANCING was sold to breakers in Italy. The last entry in her logbook is dated Ardrossan, December 6th, 1924. She was sailed and towed to Genoa by a skeleton crew, later to be moved to Savona where she was broken up in 1925. She was then 60 years old. This legend of a sailing ship from the time of sail and steam did a series of runs around Cape Horn. She deserves to be remembered as one of the most successful and speediest sailing cargo ships of all time.

A good ship like the LANCING needs a knowledgeable captain who knows what his ship can take, along with good officers and crew. The LANCING was a ship in the latter days of sail and had the required 28 men onboard most of the time. This crew consisted

The deck of the LANCING taken from atop the old first class stateroom aft shows the length of her deck towards the forcastle and three of her four masts.

of the captain, two mates, two bosuns, a timber man, sail maker, steward, cook, donkey man, 11 able bodied seamen, six ordinary seamen, and one deckhand. Two bosuns and 18 men were required for her day to day sailing, rig work and maintenance. The cook and the second mate went aloft if required, while the first mate would handle the lines on deck with the captain aft at the helm. The LANCING was hampered by a lack of professional sailors. Besides continued recording of her hourly progress under way, the logbooks are full of notes about problems with the crew in port. Drunkenness, fights, and disease were common, and deserting crewmembers added additional challenges. Especially in North

and South America and Australia did sailors disappear, seeking adventures ashore. Sometimes the captain had to sign on sailors from steam who had been ashore long enough and were broke. To sail on the LANCING with her heavy yards and big sails must have been very demanding and exhausting work. Even so, sailors around the world talked about her. She was a famous ship among mariners in those days.

The LANCING became a living legend around the world. Stories of how she had overtaken steamships with ease and offered the traditional line for a tow were so many that posters with the motif were made, showing a big four mast full rigged ship in the dusk or daylight speeding by a big ocean liner with a lot of lit portholes. Some passengers and emigrants experienced such events during the last days of sail and told stories about events like these. Able bodied seamen that had sailed on her never missed an opportunity to brag about a record-breaking voyage and how they left a slower steamer behind. The back breaking work was forgotten. As a young ordinary seaman in 1921, Alan Villiers heard about her and traveled on other ships trying to find her and sign on. He mentions this in his books and regrets that he never was able to intercept the LANCING before she was broken up.

In the British Isles she was often in the news. They had built her as the steamer PEREIRE and converted her to the speediest ship they knew of, and her final sortie was met with great sorrow. She was the last of her kind to have her full classification with Lloyd's. She was a good and legendary ship. Some were saddened that no one could manage to save her for the future. After word got out that she was sold to breakers the papers really made it a story. On Christmas Eve of 1924 the *Glasgow Herald* had a picture and an article on her that ended with a two line poem: "Out of the bay you may sail away, but never out of 'our hearts'."

The same article concluded that when the day comes for the complete history of the era of white sails, then the beautiful and 405 foot long, four mast full rigged ship named the LANCING with her towering masts and her many record breaking voyages will be remembered and get a place among the best sailing vessels the world has ever seen. The paper even mentions paintings depicting her in steady wind and with all her sails set, speeding past big power driven passenger liners.

The LANCING must have been one of the speediest windjammers in the world. It was her Norwegian captains and crews that really made her sail up to speed. Once the LANCING did an average speed of 18 knots over a period of 72 consecutive hours, or 432 nautical miles in 24 hours, in "The Roaring Forties" under the command of Captain Bull Melsom. Over and again she sailed well over 400 nautical miles in 24 hours. That was witnessed and recorded. Watches when she reached an average of 18 and 19 knots were common. Such speed by sails should give the LANCING a place among the fastest sailing vessels ever. This honor can only be earned by many passages over years as the wind is always unpredictable and only occasionally will make a ship run at extreme speed from port to port.

Built in 1865, she was 60 years old when broken up. This was the legend that closed off a thousand years of ocean crossings under sail. It started with Leif Eriksson and other fellow Norwegians sailing to America. She was the last of the big sailing ships to hold international certificates and insurance to transport cargo around the world. The years that followed the turn of the Twentieth Century became the last period of big sailing ships in world wide trades. Bigger and better steamers, the opening of the Panama Canal, and other events made ships with sails disappear even faster. When the LANCING was sent to the breakers, the age of sail had come to its conclusion even if some ships in special trades made it possible to hang in there a while longer.

One could definitely argue that the age of sail concluded in 1925 and that the LANCING of Christiania made the perfect finale to the thousand year long era where sail was used to cross the oceans of the world. For two generations she had first steamed and then sailed the Seven Seas. In her youth as a steamer she would have held a blue ribbon. As a full rigged ship she did even better with sails alone. The LANCING was the last four mast fully rigged windjammer to hold a full classification with Lloyd's Register of London.

The great painting of the LANCING on the cover of this book
(with general information on page 2) has no visible signature.
But on the back, in the lower left-hand corner, is a signature
with possibly a two-digit year underneath.

No one has so far been able to interpret what it depicts. We
hope readers of this book can help find the answer.

The LINGARD, under full sails, painted by Geoff Hunt. This painting adorns the cover of George Kåhre's book on the Åland ships. The image is inspired by a famous photo where the LINGARD negotiates a tow from a tug boat off Southend-on-Sea. This famous photograph is reproduced elsewhere in this book, as well as in many others. The painting is a mirrored image showing the LINGARD on its way out to sea.

Lingard
-Saved, Restored and Scrapped

The history of the sailing ship LINGARD is a story of proud Norwegian maritime history and shameful cultural heritage. Enthusiasts had brought home and fully restored the ship. It became the main attraction at an exposition in 1938. After World War II, with all loans fully paid off, the LINGARD and the enthusiasts' cash holdings were donated to the Norwegian Maritime Museum. The museum sold the ship immediately. It was broken up and the museum kept all the money!

The bark LINGARD was "Norway's last sailing ship of the Seven Seas" and one of the few steel hulled sailing vessels for worldwide trading built in Norway. The ship was in 1936 brought back to Norway and painstakingly restored by old seafarers and maritime history buffs. They were pioneers in saving a representative of the ships that helped transform Norway from a poor agricultural country to one of the major seafaring nations of the world. The LINGARD was the nation's collective memory

Many postcards with the LINGARD as the main motif were printed during the *Vi Kan* exposition in Oslo, 1938. This shows an overview of the area with the roller coaster and the Norwegian memorial ship LINGARD.

161

This shows ship designer Randulf Hansen's line drawing and deck plan as well as the rigging of the LINGARD.

of Norway's proud maritime heritage. The ship became the main attraction during the celebrated *Vi Kan* (We Can) exhibition in Oslo in 1938.

The deep tragedy of this case is that while the sailors and other hard working enthusiasts showed responsibility, the Norwegian cultural institutions, as well as the government, failed miserably. Even if many years have passed since the ship was broken up in 1949, museums around the world still cannot comprehend how an important maritime nation like Norway could do something like this.

Several generations after the LINGARD was broken up, it is time to recap the ship's long and exciting life and history. We must ask why the ship, after a full restoration in which people all over Norway contributed and also after having been the main attraction at a national exposition, was sent to the scrap yard without any public institutions trying to prevent such stupidity from happening.

The steel bark LINGARD was built at a time when the international shipping community realized that the long and glorious era of sailing ships was coming to an end. Thousands of sailing ships in international trade were gradually being replaced by steam ships. The best, newest and most modern square rigged ships were able to hold on for a while longer, due to modernization of the rig and various rationings onboard, smaller crews, less and simpler food, longer voyages, and lower pay. Sailors worked on "slave contracts" according to legendary union leader Andrew Furuseth, who later received the nickname *Abraham Lincoln of the Sea*. Ill-treated seamen sailed big beautiful ships worldwide in the hunt for cargo. They took wheat from California around Cape Horn to Europe, coal for the steamers, timber to Australia and New Zealand, nitrates, guano, dyewood and firewood; a cargo which no steamer with any self-respect would accept.

In the 1890s it was still possible to commission a well built ship, and Fevig Jernskibsbyggeri of Fjære in Norway had built eight barks over two years. In the fall of 1892 their order books were empty, and the shipyard decided to build hull no. 9 on speculation in order to keep the business going. It would be the fourth sister ship to ships no. 1, 6 and 8 which were all bark rigged vessels of about 1,000 tons, built after the same drawings. Towards the end of 1892 the keel to Norway's last major sailing ship built of steel was laid down. Shipyard director Randulf Hansen was responsible for the construction, and a model of hull no. 9 achieved a gold medal and very nice reviews at the exhibit in Skien in 1893. The famous constructor of FRAM, Colin Archer, was the head of the jury. The ship was launched on June 1st, 1893 and was named LINGARD. It was rigged as a bark with three masts, measuring 216 by 34 by 18 feet, and with 1,040 net register tons. The name LINGARD was an old spelling of the name Lyngør, an archipelago in the southern part of Norway.

Randulf Hansen was the leading Norwegian designer of large sailing ships of iron and steel. He also designed the bark SKOMVÆR, built by Laxevaag Skibsbyggeri in 1890 for Gunnar Knudsen in Porsgrunn. SKOMVÆR was a very famous sail ship, said to be the largest ever built in Norway. Several of the other ships Hansen designed sailed very well, and it is reasonable to suggest that the LINGARD could make good speed under favorable conditions.

An interesting aspect pertaining to the LINGARD is that she came to be the very last square rigged cargo ship built in Norway. The price was 200,000 Norwegian kroner for the entire ship, everything included. The ownership arrangements were untraditional in that the yard paid for the construction up front. General Manager B. A. Olsen of Lyngør then paid more than half of the cost and became the owner of the company Skibsaktieselskapet Lingard. Ship owner H. J. Stangebye took over the rest of the shipyard's shares.

In July of 1893 the LINGARD was completed at the shipyard and the ship was towed to Kristiansand where pits and props for the coal mines in Wales were loaded. She arrived in Cardiff after about 11 days, a very good passage over the North Sea and the English Channel during the summer with light weather. The crew of 17 were signed on in Norway and consisted of Captain Christian O. Bernt, two officers, a carpenter, a sail maker, a steward, a mess boy, four able bodied seamen, four ordinary seamen and two deckhands. Later, under Finnish flag, the crew was reduced to 14, and without

The new steel bark LINGARD as it appeared in 1893 with the Norwegian-Swedish Union flag on the main mast and the British ensign on the fore top, showing she is ready for her maiden voyage to the British Isles. Many proud sailing ships had ties to the south coast of Norway, but few large ships of iron or steel were ever built in the country.

any able bodied seamen onboard. The crew seemed far too light for a bark of more than 1,000 tons.

From England, the LINGARD continued her voyages to distant destinations. First, she sailed to Para (which is now Belem on the Amazon River), then Barbados and to Savannah in the U.S. with a return trip to the Baltic Sea. The LINGARD then continued in overseas trade to Buenos Aires in South America, Australia, New Zealand, South and East Africa and North America with many voyages to Europe in between. The LINGARD passed Cape Horn and the southern tip of Africa, and struggled through the doldrums and crossed the equator, both southbound and northbound.

She was a real deep water sailing ship which went on long voyages to known and unknown places all over the world. Around the turn of the century the LINGARD took some voyages from the Gulf of Bothnia and the Baltic Sea with lumber to Australia via Cape Town. The ship stayed for long periods in the Southern Hemisphere. In subsequent years there were many voyages across the Atlantic between Europe and South and North America, southern Argentina and the U.S., with side trips to South Africa and Australia. It was challenging for the 17 men onboard in that it could go months between each port. In 1899 the LINGARD went from Fremantle in Western Australia on March 11th and arrived in London on July 2nd, after 113 days out. Two years later she left Melbourne on June 28th, passed Falmouth on November 5th and arrived in Antwerp on November 8th, 1901. That voyage took 133 days. Apart from quick trips back to the home port Lyngør for provisions and meetings with the ship's owners when it was possible, the LINGARD did not go to Norway for freight until she went to Moss in 1905 and again in 1908.

The crew of the LINGARD, as in so many other sailing ships in those days, experienced hardships and deprivation that often resulted in poor health. On long voyages the food consisted of poor quality salted meat, ship's biscuits infested with small bugs, and stale, bad tasting water. Scurvy was a common disease for those who sailed for extensive periods of time. The hull was brown with rust topside and heavy with marine growth below the waterline, which slowed the ship down. During periods of inclement bad weather, the lack of sleep was a challenge. Crewmembers off duty were called on to save sails or help with tasks that required all hands. After a challenging voyage it often happened that the hard earned wages disappeared in the first port. All these were common experiences for seafarers onboard the sailing ships.

But there were also exciting experiences for those onboard. Seamen on the LINGARD met exotic looking women in foreign ports. They experienced tropical nights on deck in January while those at home were suffering through a cold and dark Norwegian winter. They observed the stars and anchored by tropical islands and were excited when local boys and girls swam out to the ship. The men experienced foreign countries unlike anything they had ever seen before and saw things that nobody at home had any idea about in those days. This was also part of the a sailors' life that now is woven into the mythical story of the days of white sails. The deep water sailors brought home camphor wood chests, exotic souvenirs and silk dresses for their mothers or girlfriends. Most people in Norway did not travel outside of their home towns, and few had seen such artifacts from around the world.

Quiet days with little or no wind and tropical heat were replaced

The LINGARD in 1914 under tow in Rotterdam, painted gray with rust on her hull after a long trip across the Atlantic from Haiti. The tugboat aft is the DELFSHAVEN.

165

A stylish photo of the LINGARD as the WATHARA of Port Adelaide in San Francisco Bay. The Australian flag is waving proudly from the mizzen gaff.

by tumultuous voyages with small sails in cold weather around Cape Horn, in "The Roaring Forties", in the North Sea or crossing the North Atlantic in the winter. But after challenging days they experienced quiet times during warm summer days when they could catch sharks and fish for the galley and get fresh food. Some were catching albatrosses by hanging out a triangle with bait in the wake of the ship, and letting the big, beautiful birds walk around on the deck before they were released. Superstitious sailors did not want to kill an albatross; they were said to carry the souls of dead sailors.

Sudden downpours cleaned the vessel, provided fresh drinking water and gave the men the chance for a quick shower. They enjoyed accordion music and dancing on deck as well as baptism ceremonies when crossing the equator. Skilled sailors taught the younger ones knots, macramé or scrimshaw work, or made walking sticks from the vertebrae of sharks or beautiful decorative items of old hemp. Some built model ships and some hazing also happened.

As usual during the days of sail, the LINGARD faced many problems and experienced perilous voyages. This is well documented. The ship sustained damages at sea. Captain Steenstrup collected newspaper clippings on some of the LINGARD's incidents. Here are a few of the remarks in the news:

Lyngør, Norway, May 13th, 1897:
"Bark LINGARD, from Savannah to St. Petersburg with resin. Captain and two of the crew sick and had to leave the vessel."

Boston, Massachusetts, June 24th, 1904:

"Norwegian bark LINGARD from Buenos Aires reports: Lost lower topgallant sail, and the cargo shifted in a hurricane off Bermuda."

St. John, New Brunswick, August 4th, 1904:

"The Norwegian bark LINGARD that ran aground in the Petite Passage is now on the slipway in Yarmouth, Nova Scotia. Repairs will take one week. "

Thorshavn, the Faroe Islands, January 6th, 1915:

"Bark LINGARD, which has been given shelter here, must probably be towed to a Norwegian or English harbor for repairs. The ship has lost all her best sails; the steering wheel is broken and it has sustained several other damages. The load consists of 476 standard pieces of lumber. The LINGARD is on a voyage from Sundsvall (Sweden) to Melbourne (Australia) and sailed from Lyngør on December 11th."

The LINGARD was towed to Stavanger for repairs and was there from February to May, 1915. The crew had to unload the lumber and had trouble getting it all back onboard. A considerable quantity was left behind when the locals failed to load as well as the longshoremen in the Gulf of Bothnia. The ship set sail for Australia on May 11th and arrived on September 11th after a four month long voyage out.

In the meantime the LINGARD had been sold to Wilfred J. Wardle & Co. in Port Adelaide, Australia. Wardle died in November of 1917, and Frank Amos Tirco then took ownership of the vessel. The LINGARD was renamed WATHARA, and during World War I she carried cargo between Australia, South Africa and the Pacific Coast of North and South America, with several trips between Sydney and San Francisco with the legendary Finlay J. Murchison as captain. These trips brought handsome profits to the company. Shipments would usually be wheat, motor oil, lumber and general cargo. The trip from Port Adelaide to London, which lasted 130 days in the spring of 1919 with rabbit skin and general cargo, brought in a net

The captain, to the left, with his wife and child onboard the WATHARA. The ship bell at the top right on the aft railing is today located at the Norwegian Maritime Museum.

The memorial bark LINGARD was a favorite subject for photographers as she sailed through Øresund with all sails set and at a good speed in 1927.

profit of nearly 12,000 British pounds, or twice what the ship was purchased for four years earlier. Old LINGARD sailed outside the actual war zone in the worst years of World War I. Many Norwegian ships, both sail and steam, were sunk by German U-boats, some with the loss of their entire crews.

After the rabbit skins were unloaded in London the WATHARA was sold to England in 1919. The buyer was James Bell & Co., Hereford Shipping Company. They were headquartered in Hull. She retained her WATHARA name, got Hull as her home port and continued in overseas trade, including from Gothenburg to Durban with 495 standard boards and planks, and from Durban with 1,530 tons of coal to Argentina. Other voyages took her between North Europe, Mauritius and Australia with timber and coal, and 1,576 tons of nitrates in bags on the return from Tocopilla in Chile and around Cape Horn to Hull.

She arrived in Avonmouth in September 1921 and was laid up. The ship stayed there for over a year. In the summer of 1922 the price had dropped so much that Alf Monsen in Tønsberg bought her. Old LINGARD regained the Norwegian flag and got Tønsberg as her new home port, but kept her new name. She still had the highest class in both Lloyd's Register and in the Norwegian Veritas. Freights for the last sailing ships that were still in good condition became harder and harder to find. Insurance became a problem. In 1922 the WATHARA only took a short run from Cardiff to Turku where she again was taken out of commission. For Alf Monsen and his partners in Wathara, Inc. there was little money to be made.

Most sailing ships had already been broken up, and on ships in international traffic the crew rarely got to admire a square rigged ship under full sails on the high seas anymore. These ships belonged to the past and those left received much deserved attention.

The following year was better. The ship embarked on a world cruise for the last time and used all of 1924 and more on the trip around Africa and home again via Australia and South America and Cape Horn; the route of today's Around the World Race. The WATHARA arrived in Hull on February 27th, 1925, discharged her cargo and was sold to Gustaf Erikson in Mariehamn on the Åland Islands for 2,200 British pounds. She then got a Finnish flag. Gustaf Erikson was known to change ships' names back to their original, and WATHARA regained her old name LINGARD. Erikson made a bargain with the LINGARD. The ship gave him many years of good sailing and strong earnings.

The Panama Canal that opened in 1915 had eliminated sailings from California via Cape Horn to Europe. The invention of chemical fertilizers caused the large fertilizer ships to lose business. The depression after World War I sent almost all of them to the buoys. There was no longer any work for the old sailing ships. Ship breakers did very well scrapping the white swans that rust and rain had discolored. By the entrance to the wrecking company Stavanger Skibsopphugning, dozens of figureheads piled up. Most of the beautiful wooden figures that had sailed around the world ended up as firewood. After 1925, many of the square rigged ships that were still able to sail were found in a few specific ports. In San

Francisco as well as an in Mariehamn on the Åland Islands there were still sailing ships laid up. Alaska Packers' big "Star Fleet" was eventually sold for scrap and towed from San Francisco to Japan to become iron for the armaments industry, as part of Japan's War against the U.S. and its allies. The oldest and least expensive the STAR OF INDIA was sold to San Diego.

Gustaf Erikson became famous because he was able to make money off of old sailing vessels in a declining market, charging freight rates that no one else could beat. He was self insured and capitalized on his team of skilled sailing ship captains. He hired capable professionals to-be at nominal wages because they lacked the required sailing experience to get their officer's license. The last batch of large and beautiful sailing ships got a reprieve and once more got underway by sail. The Åland Islands became their home port. Annual races carrying wheat from Australia to Northern Europe were the last remnants of the famous earlier clipper ship

Newspaper clippings from when the LINGARD was towed into Gothenburg after the collision with steamer GERD in November of 1935. Photos explain better than words the violence of the impact. The ship was not leaking, testifying to the sturdy construction of a good and well maintained ship. The steamer GERD was 3,000 tons, several times larger than the LINGARD, but was lost with all of her 21 hands.

voyages from China to London with tea.

The LINGARD did not take part in these races. The vessel was too small, but Gustaf Erikson had other assignments for her. She participated in the dyewood trade between Haiti and Jamaica in the Caribbean to Northern Europe, especially Le Havre. Loading ports were often in open bays with primitive infrastructure. They were barely marked on the charts. The LINGARD loaded while at anchor. Branches and roots of logwood and dyewood were full of thorns, bends and growths. They had to be cut and cleaved on deck before they could be stowed in the hull. The ship had to absorb the cost of this. The wood that was taken onboard was often infested by lizards, caterpillars, frogs, small snakes and scorpions. Some snakes were poisonous, and the scorpions were dangerous. They crawled around on the deck. The indigenous people taught the sailors how to remove scorpions from their bodies by blowing on them. It was hot, and the strong local Jamaican rum was cheap and popular among the sailors. Boys and girls swam out to the ship, perhaps out of curiosity or maybe in the hope of receiving small gifts. If the sailors threw a coin into the water where it was not too deep and one could see the bottom, the youngsters dove down after it and did not stop until one of them came up with the prize, waving it triumphantly to everyone on deck. It is told by the sailors that girls more often than boys would surface proudly showing off the coin.

During 1927 the ship was gradually moved into the firewood trade from the Baltic Sea to England. Throughout 1928 and 1929 the LINGARD took in wood for England on both the Swedish and Finnish side of the Gulf of Bothnia. Erikson had a number of medium sized vessels in this trade, and the LINGARD was regarded as his best and fastest ship for moving firewood.

It was during such a trip to London with firewood that a photographer who was onboard a ship off the mouth of the Thames was able to take the world famous photograph of a tug approaching a sailing ship under full sail to negotiate about the price of a possible tow up the Thames. The sailing ship in this picture is good old LINGARD on her way coming in from the sea. It is told that a skilled sailing ship captain did not take the first offer, but let the tug captain understand that he intended to sail his ship all the way if the wind was agreeable. In this way experienced commanders could drive tug skippers to despair. The tug boat men had to go far down in price before the ship captains would agree to do business with them. But once the price had been agreed upon, it was always paid even if the agreement was through the megaphone and not based on a written contract.

Skilled, brave captains with a cohesive crew were sometimes able to sail a ship like the LINGARD into port without the help of a tug, using only sails and anchors. Independence was always important to previous generations of sail ship captains. Before help from a tug became common, the sailing ships had to fend for themselves. But then the ships had larger crews and a simpler rig, and they were usually smaller. If the winds were not cooperating, the ships had to anchor and use the skiff for towing.

Before the ice settled for the winter, the LINGARD was laid up in Mariehamn Harbor in Åland. The following spring she was rigged anew for a new season under sail. Between trips to England with firewood the LINGARD made occasional trips to the West Indies for dyewood. In January of 1934 she returned from London and was laid up. The economically challenging 1930s affected everyone. The ship was laid up for one and a half years. It was not until July of 1935 that she was chartered for a new trip with firewood to England. On the 10th of October, 1935 she took onboard a full load of firewood in Hernøsand. The LINGARD was going to London. This was to become her last voyage under sail.

After midnight in the Kattegat on a northwesterly course east of Læsø, the LINGARD collided with a steamer. The date was November 2nd, 1935. The LINGARD was maintaining the required steady course, and made eight knots with all sails set. The side lanterns were checked and burned clear, the carpenter was at the helm and the crew was ordered to move aft. The

Fully loaded with a large deck cargo of wood and with all her sails set, the LINGARD is on her way to London. The year is 1930. A steam tug from Southend-on-Sea is in place to try to negotiate the tow up the river Thames. This photo is known around the world and has been used in many contexts. It is one of the last classic photos of a cargo wind ship approaching port with all her sails still pulling.

LINGARD's bow hit the steamer on the port side, and the collision was so violent that the jib boom broke off and was thrown onto the deck. The top foremast broke, and there was major damage to the rigging. A gaping hole in the forepeak meant that it was full of water. The steamship was severely damaged on one side. In the fresh breeze the ships quickly moved away from each other. The LINGARD's rudder did not work, and she drifted in a north easterly direction with the currents and the wind. Everybody put on lifebelts and got the lifeboats ready, but the hold was checked and reported all dry. A tug arrived with the daylight and towed the LINGARD into Gothenburg. The steamship it collided with was the GERD and belonged to the company Sveabolaget. It went down, and nobody survived. After this tragic incident the LINGARD was seized, and there was a trial to determine if the captain of the LINGARD was to blame. The case went all the way to the Swedish Supreme Court in which the captain was acquitted. The ship was finally released and the cargo was discharged. LINGARD's owner was self insured and the ship was sold to the breakers. The buyer was the shipbreaking company Stavanger Skibsopphugning in Norway.

Gustaf Erikson and his captains did the world a favor in that they preserved some of the last of the proud and magnificent sailing ships. In addition, Erickson provided work for young people who understood this and were interested in sailing. Among this new generation of sailors who wanted to sail around the world in a real sailing ship were Englishmen, Americans and Australians and others who did not understand Finnish-Swedish, but were willing to expand their knowledge and experience. Several of these crewmembers later became world renowned authors and ship preservationists. People with good handheld film cameras mustered so they could document these unique voyages. They created maritime film classics. All this generated a lot of interest in preserving the last square rigged ships. Several countries eventually secured their historic vessels from the ships in the Åland Islands and those which still remained in San Francisco. The U.S. and Norway were among the first to do so, and with that set precedence for other countries to follow.

The Norwegian Sail Ship Club had explored whether to buy the LINGARD so she could become a Norwegian memorial ship. A bank in Oslo funded the endeavor, and ownership of the LINGARD was transferred from the wreckers to the club, who paid the scrap price. It was obvious that Norway should have a memory of Norwegian shipping from the time that nation conquered the oceans of the world. The LINGARD was a beautiful and worthy ship that Norway could show off with pride. The editor of the magazine *Skib-o-Hoi*, former sailor and writer Fred A. Fredhøi was the person primarily responsible for the LINGARD being rescued, taken to Oslo and restored after the serious damage from the collision with the GERD. Funds were raised from the people of Norway. They sold certificates, and even His Majesty the King and the Crown Prince

173

supported the fundraising efforts. People all over the country pitched in to save the LINGARD. Many old sailors lined up to help as volunteers on the ship.

March 21st, 1936 was a fantastic day for maritime interests in Norway. It felt like May 17th, Norway's Constitution Day, in Drøbak when the ship was towed by. All school children were given time off and stood on the pier with their Norwegian flags. Oscarsborg Fortress saluted the flag and got a reply from the ship's mizzen mast. It was luckily still in one piece after the collision. The LINGARD was greeted in Oslo by many representatives from broadcasting and newspapers when the ship arrived in Pipervika. The LINGARD was called a monument honoring the brave men from the days of the white sails on the Seven Seas. She still had her crippled bow that was to be repaired.

The ship cost 24,500 Norwegian kroner, and was delivered in Oslo by the breakers. The effort, zeal and enthusiasm of volunteers led to the LINGARD's hull quickly being repaired. The rig was reinstated and renewed as needed. She was cleaned and painted; from a distance she looked brand new. The total investment was 70,000 Norwegian kroner, a considerable sum of money at that time. The LINGARD was administered by the Norwegian Sail Ship Club with Fredhøi as chairman. The agreement was that when the ship was free of debt, it would be given to the Norwegian Maritime Museum to be preserved for future generations as *Norges Minneskute* (Norway's Memorial Sailing Ship).

The LINGARD was moored by the Hjortnes Pier in Oslo. A sign with "Norway's Memorial Ship LINGARD" told the story of how she had been saved with the help of the club. She was the last Norwegian built square rigged ship. The admission fee was nominal, and visitors were served coffee. There were monkeys in a cage on the foredeck in addition to other memorabilia from the ship's sailing days on the high seas.

The preservation of LINGARD happened during the greatest major depression of the 1900s, which makes this endeavor even more impressive. In retrospect we know that Norway has never before or after experienced such challenging economic times. The saving of the LINGARD was one of the few positive events that inspired, pointed forward and showed an optimistic attitude to counter all the negative things that happened. The ship's solid jib boom became a symbol that pointed forward toward the future.

Two years later, the LINGARD became the main and most visible attraction during the optimistic *Vi Kan* exhibition which opened on May 12th, 1938. "The knife that cuts through chaos" was the motto of the exhibition. It was held to celebrate the Oslo Trade and Industry Association's 100th anniversary. The intentions of the exhibition went far beyond this, however. It was in reality a major national exhibition that focused on four themes: Shipping, whaling, heavy industry and tourism. The exhibition area in Frognerkilen was 1,200 meters long and covered a large area by the water in Oslo Harbor. There were opera and theater performances as well as sailing competitions. A picture of the bark LINGARD was used in foreign newspapers to promote the exhibition internationally. The LINGARD never got more attention than during the *Vi Kan* exhibition in 1938. Thousands of postcards with "Norway's Memorial Ship" were mailed from Oslo. They went around the world just like the ship LINGARD once did. The ship was booked for a memorial voyage along the coast with Admiral Børresen as honorary captain. She was to sail to Stavanger and then continue to Bergen where she was supposed to be the main attraction during an exposition there in 1940.

But less than a year after the exhibition closed, World War II started. On April 9th, 1940 Norway was attacked by Germany and the country was occupied for five long years. It did not take long before the Germans needed more tonnage for their many activities and facilities along the coast. The LINGARD was clearly visible in Oslo Harbor, and was quickly taken by the Nazis and used for various tasks along the coast. The LINGARD was loaded with materials for fortifications and towed away, came back and was requisitioned for new trips. The cargo was mostly cement, rebar, wood and brick, barbed wire, ammunition and other types of cargo. Fredhøy tried to protest, but to little avail. The ship was rigged down. Fredhøy finally managed to pry the ship away from the Germans and hid her in a strait by Nøtterø. There she rested quietly until the war was over.

Of course it was a battered and reduced LINGARD that was towed to Oslo, but those representing the Norwegian Sail Ship Club knew what to do. The LINGARD was chartered to the National Grain Corporation and became a granary moored by Sjursøya with a

Postcards of the memorial ship LINGARD, alone and abandoned during the winter of 1938 to 1939 in Oslo with snow in the rig and on the deck.

security guard onboard. At the same time a new rig was raised, and she was carefully checked out. The contract with the National Grain Corporation secured money to pay off all loans. Norway's memorial ship stayed by Sjursøya through the winter and earned good money. The last page in the last deck log for the LINGARD describes the two weeks leading up to January 17th, 1946, when the grain was unloaded and the hold was cleaned before the last watchman left. His last notes state that the Maritime Museum has taken over the ship and that the keys were handed over.

On behalf of the Norwegian people the owners gave the three masted bark LINGARD to the Norwegian Maritime Museum for preservation and future protection according to their objective on handing over the ship when it was debt free. This was a mutual agreement both parties had had 10 years to think through, revise and prepare for. In addition to this magnificent gift a large amount of cash was included. Fred A. Fredhøi and the Norwegian Sail Ship Club were well prepared and kept their part of the 1936 agreement. All the loans had been paid off, and the ship was debt free. The LINGARD was intact and in working order and was even loaded with grain for a whole winter, but needed a lot of tender loving care and repairs after the Germans' use and five years of inadequate maintenance. The LINGARD had been damaged along with everything else the Germans had used in Norway. "Rebuild!" was the spirit and the motto when the war ended in 1945. The shared national goal was to rebuild every part of the country as quickly as possible. The parliament and the government showed the way. This pertained to all sectors and all parts of society. Damages due to the occupation were taken care of, one by one. The museum took ownership of Norway's memorial ship LINGARD at the very end of 1945.

The nice words spoken in connection with the transfer became bitter pills to swallow for all those who had worked for, supported and sympathized with the LINGARD for more than 10 years. The bomb exploded less than two months later. Long articles with pictures and headlines such as "The LINGARD Cannot Be Preserved for Posterity," and "Norwegian Maritime Museum Is Going to Sell the Vessel to Use the Funds for Other Very Interesting Purposes" were published. On February 27th, 1946 the newspaper *Norges Handels & Sjøfartstidende* revealed the truth: Director Vogt stated

that it would be too expensive to repair the ship, and since the Norwegian Maritime Museum received a gift with no obligations, he regarded it as a matter of course that the museum was going to sell her. A bid had been received, and the director's statement suggests that the museum needed the money the sale would bring in for new plans that he would not reveal at that time. In addition, Vogt noted, they would ensure that "everything of interest" from the ship would be saved. The museum had a booklet with all the historical information and data, "so that maritime historians can obtain or even seek out all desired information at any time deemed appropriate."

The truth is that the material on the LINGARD found at the aforementioned institution does not meet today's historians' requirements, although there are a lot of newspaper clippings and other documents. Museums around the world have contributed significant data and photographs for this book's story of the ship. The reason that there is quite a lot of information on the LINGARD in many countries is that the ship had sailed under four national flags. Also, she sailed for so long after other ships were broken up and had been preserved as a national memorial ship until the Norwegian Maritime Museum took ownership.

The world took, for these same reasons, a passive but watchful part in the drama that would unfold after the newspaper articles were published. The news hit like a bomb. The first reaction came from donors, Fred A. Fredhøi and the organization that had facilitated the preservation of the LINGARD. They were absolutely shocked and let the newspapers know. The main argument was of course that the *Norges Minneskute* was given to the museum to be preserved. None of the stakeholders had imagined that selling the ship was an option, or as Fredhøi stated, "We could have managed that ourselves." Worse than that was when allegations surfaced that one of the museum's representatives in the committee charged with receiving the ship had negotiated the sale of the ship before it was taken over and thus decived the owners.

Both sides went into the trenches, and the battle was long and very bitter. The museum said that they would like to give the gift back, but they did not follow through on this. Fredhøi and his men said they would not say yes to receiving the ship back. It had been given to the museum for preservation. The club members had done their part, but were willing to continue to support the ship and suggested soliciting help from volunteers across the country. They also shared advice regarding how to prioritize the use of the existing means. The agreement with the National Grain Corporation could maybe be extended. The "club" stated that one should take one step at a time in the restoration of the ship rather than get caught up in discussing a total estimate, noting that it would be too expensive.

The Norwegian Maritime Museum would least of all receive help from their bitter enemies in this case. Funds Fredhøi personally had invested in the ship were to be returned. To illustrate how bitter the battle was, it may be mentioned that the museum's representative turned up at Fredhøi's office to return the check of 8,654.58 Norwegian kroner, equivalent to the amount Fredhøi had transferred when the ship was given to the museum. The funds should have been used to start the restoration. Fredhøi said that he personally had not contributed more than 6,000 Norwegian kroner and asked for that amount to be refunded. The incident ended with the museum keeping the entire amount. During the fine speeches at the reopening of the museum in July 1946 the LINGARD and the gift from the Norwegian Sail Ship Club was not mentioned at all, something that Fredhøi and the other invited guests found very offensive.

The LINGARD was sold in 1946 and taken to Moss to become a lifting pontoon for the ship salvaging company Norsk Bjergningskompagnie. The downrigging started after the museum had first secured some selected objects from the ship, including a bit of stern decoration, and the small charthouse steering wheel and pump. The LINGARD herself still proved to be quite tenacious. The floating solid hull represented a significant value and had an aura as a national monument and museum relic. Newspaper articles revealed that most of the people who were surveyed thought the ship should be preserved, although some went so far in the other direction as to say that she never should have been built. In addition, there was growing international interest in this somewhat peculiar maritime battle which took place in Norway. The LINGARD was widely known as a beautiful and very good ship and was marketed abroad as a memorial ship. For newspapers and especially magazines with a maritime focus, this was a major story.

They kept writing about how the LINGARD case was progressing.

In her rather reduced condition but with considerable inflation the ship's value increased, and the LINGARD was bought and sold several times over the next two years. According to the Norwegian newspaper *Dagbladet* she was in Bergen on June 3rd, 1948. The newspaper was critical to the Maritime Museum's role in this case, noting that the public was entitled to a straightforward explanation. The newspaper discussed how people outside of the maritime sector were able to make money on the LINGARD. One example was an avid race horse player who took out large loans secured in the ship to continue his betting. Stavanger Skibsopphugning bought the ship for the second time, and the LINGARD's final journey was a tow from Bergen to Stavanger in September of 1948. Norway's newspaper agency ensured wide press coverage. Breakers started the dismantling of her in the spring of 1949. But the company was ordered to reimburse the large bank loans related to the ship. The LINGARD likely did not yield the scrapping company much.

Norway's memorial ship the LINGARD was 56 years old. Compared to many of today's cargo sail ships of steel that are still preserved around the world, she was a young lady. One example is Stockholm's full rigged ship AF CHAPMAN. It was built in England of iron five years prior to the LINGARD and is slightly bigger, and was Norwegian for a while before being sold to Sweden. She is today considered one of Sweden's best kept historic sailing ships, even if the VIKING in Gothenburg is bigger and younger. The LINGARD was Norway's only maritime memorial. She was a Cape Horner and a worthy representative of the final days of sail on the Seven Seas, Norway's national pride and its maritime cultural heritage.

The LINGARD case is what a later director of the Norwegian Maritime Museum referred to as the darkest chapter in the museum's history. What happened to the LINGARD is a good example of private citizens taking responsibility and acting when public institutions do not pay attention. There are several similar examples pertaining to maritime history in Norway. The famous Oseberg Viking ship find was rescued by a Swede. The sail steamship HANSTEEN was also saved by dedicated individuals when the official Norway chose to look the other way. The cargo ship the HESTMANDEN was likewise saved by devoted persons.

The new sad story is that the last escort trawler from World War II, the T-276 CAILIFF, saved as BORGENES, was broken up in 2012 with government approval. It was restored for millions in the 1990s. Surveys showed a good hull and the engine and boiler was intact. Unfortunately, there was no funds, no museum or no good will to keep this historic ship as a museum piece in one of the world's most prosperous countries.

After keeping the LINGARD preserved for ten years during very challenging times in the country's history, it is odd that those who most of all should have done something and could have saved the LINGARD did not step up to the plate. The Norwegian cabinet headed by Prime Minister Einar Gerhardsen accomplished a lot, and the focus was on rebuilding. It showed very poor judgment in some regards. One example is the treatment of the Norwegian foreign fleet, what it stood for during the war, the war sailors and the lack of refund after the war. The treatment of seamen and the government's attitudes towards shipping and Norway's maritime cultural heritage in the first decade after the war is a sad and little known part of Norway's recent history, probably because this is an embarrassment for a great seafaring nation. The coastal nation of Norway has always been a nautical country since before the time of the Vikings, the first known navigators to conquer the Atlantic Ocean and beyond.

It took decades before the authorities in Norway began to see the sailors and the merchant fleet as anything else than a revenue generator. The LINGARD was as much of a national scandal as when the World War II secret Nortraship fund belonging to the seamen sailing during the war was confiscated by the government. The war veteran sailors were eventually somewhat compensated, but this happened far too late as many of them had already passed away or settled in other countries. The miserable treatment of Norwegian war veteran sailors and irresponsible actions related to the country's maritime cultural heritage can never give back what is gone. Ships and lives have been lost forever.

A long time has passed since the LINGARD was broken up. Norway should not wait any longer to make a contribution that makes a difference by at least preserving the ships still left, by including them in museums. The Twentieth Century was the century when Norway was one of the world's major seafaring nations. No Norwegian ships that sailed the Seven Seas has survived, not a single liner or major tanker has been preserved. Not even a museum for the oldest iron built ships in Norway exists. These relics from the Industrial Revolution are left abandoned outside to deteriorate with no proper care during the long and harsh winters. They are older than the Eiffel Tower in Paris, which is so well preserved that its original iron has not been replaced.

A name plate of unknown origin and location.

The FRAM, ready for departure from Oslo on its maiden
expedition in 1893 with Fridtjof Nansen as the leader.

Fram
-The Most Famous Ship

The FRAM was made immortal by the famous Norwegian polar explorers Nansen, Sverdrup and Amundsen. The ship was received with enthusiasm in all ports where she appeared. Of the three explorers Sverdrup was the only one who really contributed to preserving the ship as a Norwegian cultural heritage icon. Today, the Fram Museum at Bygdøynes is one of Norway's major tourist attractions.

The second half of the 1800s was a period when ideas from colonial times were extended to all corners of the world. There were still vast areas where nobody, regardless of ethnic origin, had been, but where some daredevils had tried to venture. Finding the Northwest Passage was the most famous of these quests, as it would shorten the voyage from Europe to East Asia by thousands of miles. The areas near the poles consist of immense ice masses, with extreme low temperatures and winds, ice, and inhospitable land. A winter with no sunlight would hamper intruders.

The mass production of iron created an industrial revolution of steam engines, railways, bridges and ships. Due to advances in education and research, as well as new inventions, the main focus became to conquer the Arctic and the Antarctic and plant national flags on the North and the South Pole. The result was an international "race" to discover and claim land, and to help complete the world map. Several nations were involved in the goals for the polar regions with varying success. Tragedies were common; the hunt for the North West Passage clamed numerous lives over very many years. Many realized early on that Norway with its harsh winter climate had residents who were better prepared for success in the battle against cold temperatures, storms, ice and darkness than people from other countries.

Fridtjof Nansen's skiing expedition across Greenland's inland glaciers in 1888 was a tremendous inspiration to all Norwegian people and increased the interest in taking part in the conquest of new lands. Nansen himself was a pioneer in this field. He had early decided to try to reach the North Pole and shared these

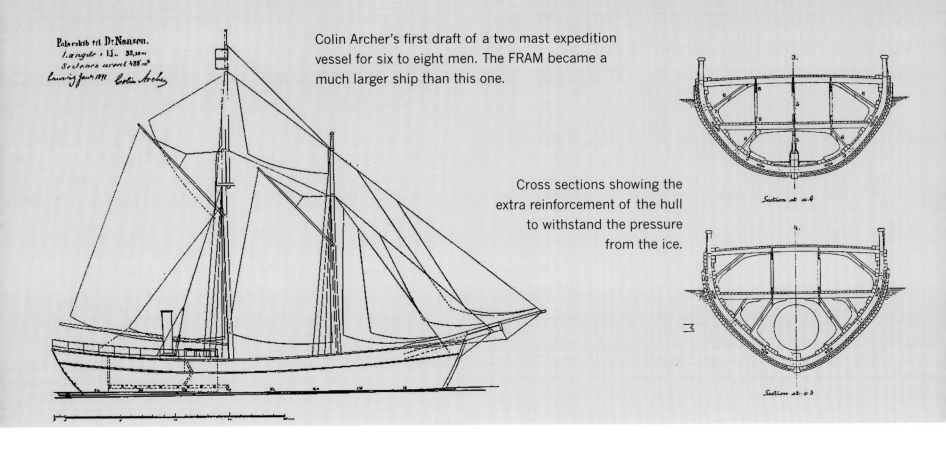

Polarskib til D.Nansen.
Længde i ll. 33,₀₀ₘ
Seilareal 435m²
Lauving Janv. 1891 Colin Archer

Colin Archer's first draft of a two mast expedition vessel for six to eight men. The FRAM became a much larger ship than this one.

Cross sections showing the extra reinforcement of the hull to withstand the pressure from the ice.

Section at a b

Section at c d

plans with Otto Sverdrup, who wanted to join him. Nansen had a full university education and had obtained a doctoral degree in zoology. He was 27 years old when he skied across Greenland with five others, including Sverdrup who Nansen knew from before. Sverdrup was seven years older than Nansen, had a full maritime officer's education, and had worked onboard sail and steamships since his early teens. The challenging journey across Greenland's icecap made them friends for life.

Manmade objects identified as coming from Eastern Siberia and Alaska had from time to time washed ashore along the east coast of Greenland. When identifiable objects from De Long's tragic JEANNETTE expedition which started from San Francisco in 1879 appeared in Greenland, Nansen believed that they were carried there with an ocean current flowing across the Arctic Ocean. If there was no land there, this current could carry a ship all the way to the North Pole. The only problem was that the JEANETTE was

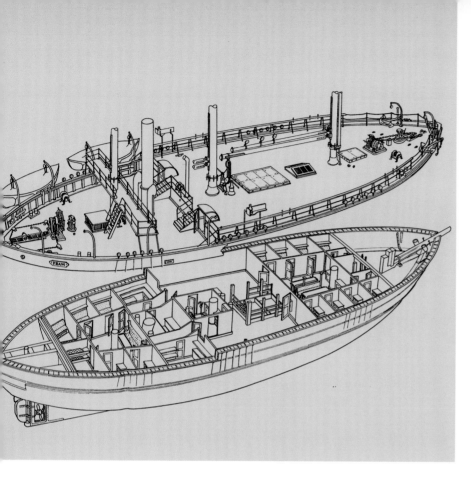

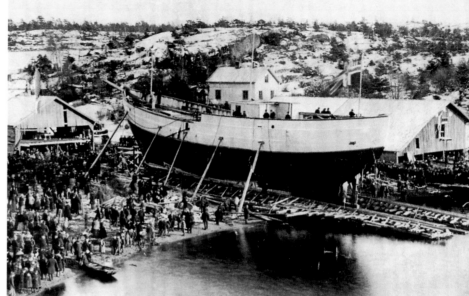

Pictures from the launching of the FRAM in 1892.

smashed to pieces by the crushing pack ice even though her hull had been heavily reinforced.

In 1890 Nansen submitted a detailed plan to the Norwegian Geographical Society regarding a national expedition to the North Pole. With the aid of ocean currents, a specially designed research and observation platform could be taken with the flow of the ice from a starting point north of the New Siberian Islands to the seas east of Greenland, with the help of the moving ice. The

The three mast steam schooner just after her launch outside Larvik.

Expedition leader
Fridtjof Nansen.

main challenge with the plan was to build a vessel that was strong enough to withstand the enormous pressure of the ice. Nansen needed a ship, as strong as possible and large enough to keep 12 men for five years with room for stores, supplies, fuel, equipment and sear parts. The design specifics called for a ship with sloped sides so that the pack ice would not crush the ship like it had the JEANNETTE, but rather, that her sloped sides would cause her to be pushed out of the ice.

Such a ship would need internal reinforcements to withstand the sustained pressure from the ice. Nansen put special emphasis on the research aspects of the expedition, though reaching the North Pole was the main goal. He was not alone in his quest. The plan created a lot of debate. National patriotism prevailed. The Norwegian Parliament appropriated the needed funds for Nansen to build the ship and equip the expedition.

Colin Archer was known as an outstanding boat builder. He had created new boat prototypes. But he was not a sail ship builder. He did not believe that he could build the ship Nansen wanted. Nansen therefore visited Colin Archer in Larvik and brought Captain Sverdrup along in hopes of getting Archer to change his

mind. Sverdrup promised to assist Archer in building the ship. It worked. Colin Archer produced sketches, drawings and several models of the ship Nansen hoped would survive lengthy and challening operations in the ice.

Elm for the keel arrived from Scotland and in August of 1891 construction began. Many new solutions were discussed and decided upon. Knees, side supports, ribs and trimmings as well as several layers of outer skin, topped by a protective "ice skin" of zinc coated steel sheets, were added for extra protection and

The FRAM, ready for departure from Oslo, with Fridtjof Nansen as the leader.

strength. Using a new type of sealant was a difficult choice.

The ship leaked heavily after the launch which indicated that not everything went according to plan. The steam engine and boiler was ordered at the Aker Shipyard in Christiania. Captain Sverdrup and Colin Archer agreed to give the ship three masts and a schooner rig in which the sails would not reduce the draft and thereby impair the machinery's efficiency. It is important to remember that a ship with machinery was perceived as a power driven vessel with the support of sails. At that time machine propulsion was of such a tremendous advantage that all sailing ships with engines in fact were motor ships, or auxiliary sailing vessels, as they were called back then. Only sailing ships without engines were genuine sailing ships.

The launching was awaited with great excitement. The polar ship was not just any vessel, but a world prototype. She was also double ended like a Viking ship. Finally Norway too would participate in the race to reach the North Pole. The launching took place on the 26th of October, 1892. The weather was good. Steamships took spectators out to Rekkevik by Larvik for the launch. Mrs. Eva Nansen had the honor of breaking the champagne bottle with the words "FRAM is your name!" The word "fram" means "forward" in Norwegian and was an appropriate name for a ship that wanted to go where no one had been. A party followed with speeches and congratulatory telegrams. Norway had already had a sail-steam ship with the same name and a pioneering purpose. Little has so far been known about this.

The first FRAM was built by Charlottenlund shipyard near Trondheim 25 years prior and was, like Nansen's ship, a prototype. A newspaper article from 1868 presents this first FRAM: "We could not be happier to greet this first attempt to use steam power in servicing the fisheries and hope that good results will bring more of the same." The first FRAM had a steam engine and schooner rig and could carry 200 barrels in her hold. Only two years old, the first FRAM was on loan to the government and used as a mail steam ship in Finnmark. The FRAM returned to Trondheim with the rescued crew from the steamer TRAFIK, built in Trondheim in 1856 as Norway's first local steamer to be contracted by common folk, originally as the paddle steamer INHERRED. She was lost in the Kara Sea in the Arctic in 1870. This was a story from the Arctic Ocean the 16 year old Otto Sverdrup knew and could have shared with Nansen. It is the author's opinion that it was Otto Sverdrup who knew of this previous FRAM. Long before Nansen's FRAM embarked on her first voyage in 1893, steamers and sailing vessels had sailed the Arctic Ocean and ventured deep into the Kara Sea east of Novaya Zemlya. The GJØA was such a ship before Amundsen purchased her. Significant trade took place in this area 20 years before Nansen's FRAM sailed the same waters on his voyage to the North Pole. By that time the first FRAM had been deleted from the ships' registry, and the new ship built by Colin Archer could thus use the name.

After launching, the new FRAM was towed to Oslo where the masts, rigging and machinery were installed at the Aker Shipyard.

The steam engine had 220 indicated horsepower. The propeller had to be twin bladed so it could be hoisted up on deck as needed to avoid being crushed by the ice. The rudder was likewise placed in a well and could also be taken on deck to avoid being destroyed. Several spare propellers were provided. Nansen's plan was to bring scientists along on the expedition. Despite his best efforts he did not succeeded. It is still true that people with advanced academic degrees prefer to do research behind their desks rather than enduring seasickness to experience new approaches to test maritime theories in practice. This and more is highlighted in the book *Viking to Victorian*. No one with a university education wished to participate except for the medical doctor. This was in stark contrast to the nation's commoners. Many people with different backgrounds applied to join the expedition. Nansen's old friend Otto Sverdrup was from a distinguished family of public servants and had a full maritime education. He had also been the captain of a steamship. He was the ship owner's inspector during construction and a shoe-in as captain of the FRAM. Nansen chose the other ten participants.

FRAM was designed as a sailing ship without a forecastle. Nansen abolished the class society; all participants lived behind the mast. There were four one man cabins with entrances from a small lounge in the rear section of the ship. Expedition leader Nansen stayed in the first cabin on the starboard side with the "scientist" and mate Lieutenant Scott Hansen in the next. Captain Sverdrup's cabin was located far forward to port with the doctor

186

in the next cabin. Behind the lounge there were two four man cabins with a stairwell between. This is where the rest of the crew lived. The men had to sign a loyalty statement to Nansen. They were prepared for the possibility of an uncertain outcome. Despite strong public funding Nansen was short of money. Before their departure, good friends came to the rescue so that Nansen could start his expedition debt free. The loading of equipment for the next five years was a carefully organized task. What they needed had to be available at any time. Coal for the steam boiler and fuel for heat and light took up a lot of space. They planned to make a refueling stop in Siberia. Extra wood, lumber and barrels became

The crew of the FRAM had to utilize skis in the 1890s, long before skiing became a world sport.

deck cargo. Before her departure the FRAM was heavily laden.

On Midsummer Eve in 1893 the FRAM was ready for departure. The next day she left from Christiania Harbor. The first stop was the city of Horten to pick up ammunition and signal guns from the Norwegian Navy. She then went to Rekkevik where two large and six smaller boats were taken onboard. The largest were equipped to take the whole crew home if the FRAM was lost. The expedition was met by gale force winds in the Skagerrak. Those who were seamen were well aware that the ship's hull shape would lead to excessive movement in bad weather. The FRAM lived up to these expectations and rolled heavily, taking a lot of water on deck. This led to the loss of much of the deck cargo. Nansen therefore needed to visit Bergen. It was in this city that he, as a young man, made big plans for achievements in the ploar regions. The subsequent voyage north along the coast was akin to a parade as they were met by many cheering onlookers. The FRAM went to Beian at Ørlandet on the central coast of Norway where Captain Sverdrup joined to take command of his new ship. It took a whole month before the ship arrived in Vardø far northeast in Norway, where the city gave a resounding farewell party. Nansen was at this time worried that the expedition had too little time to reach the starting point in the east. The FRAM had to get there by crossing the open sea. While people were asleep, he roused the lookout. Before the people of Vardø were awake, the FRAM had departed. Norway seemed to sink in the sea behind them. The date was the 22nd of July, 1893.

The FRAM became an observation and research platform after being stuck in the ice at about 80 degrees north. The ice drift had begun.

The FRAM's arrival in Christiania on September 9th, 1896, was a celebration like no other. The ship can be seen approaching, behind the ship mast to the right with persons atop.

Homecoming. The streets from the pier to the Royal Palace were packed with people. They hailed Nansen and his men. The journey to the Royal Palace was a victory parade.

The participants of the FRAM expedition with Nansen.

They met a belt of old drift ice that FRAM easily steamed through. In Kharborova by Jugor they took onboard dogs and struggled on, slowly, using machine or sail power depending on the weather. The charts did not match the terrain. They encountered sea where they should have seen land. In September, the ice opened up and they passed Cape Chelyuskin, the northern most point on the Eurasian continent, at good speed and in open sea. The course was set north towards the pack ice north of the New Siberian Islands. They moved fast towards the northeast with clear skies and snow clad mountains to starboard, just as Nansen had hoped. On the 22nd of September FRAM met the ice edge at 79 degrees north latitude and 133 degrees east longitude. The FRAM was moored in the ice, and the drift towards the North Pole could start. From now on the movement of the ice would determine where they would go.

The winter came quickly. Soon there was thick ice everywhere. The dogs and the forge were moved onto the ice. The FRAM was transformed from a ship into a stationary research and accommodation unit. The windmill to power the generator for electric light was installed anew. In 1893 it was a sensation to have electric lights onboard a ship. It had worked perfectly on trial runs while the ship was still in Oslo. However, the Arctic cold contributed to the turbine's malfunction; FRAM could thus contribute to the body of knowledge regarding electricity and cold weather. At this time, the light bulb was a new technology. The power unit simply did not work in the cold. The kerosene lamps had to take over. Meanwhile, scientific work continued around the clock. All were excited to see if the FRAM moved towards the North Pole. The doctor studied how extreme cold and constant darkness affected the body. All the men were in excellent health thus far.

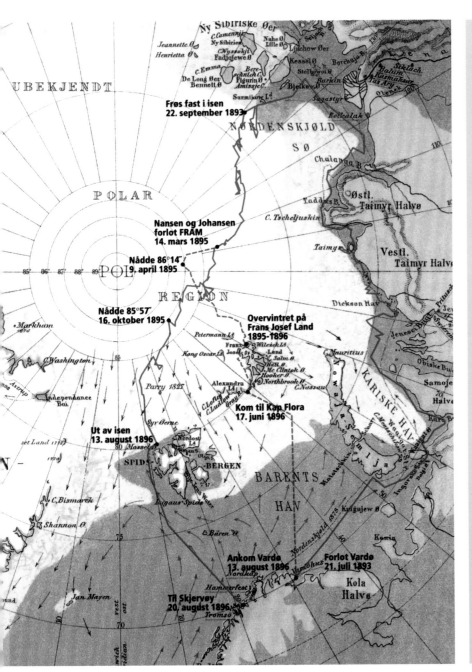

Dramatic breaks in the routine came with the pressure of the pack ice, which made small mountains of ice, standing on end as if attacking the hull of the FRAM. The noise was deafening, with all kinds of sounds. The ship shook, heeled a little and, just as designed, was pushed upward and out of the ice's grip. Everyone was impressed with the FRAM. Her movement in the ice was worse near the open sea and when the moon was full. The forces of nature were in power.

Their progress towards the North Pole was slow and this bothered Nansen. But all the scientific work went well, apart for the depth soundings; they just could not find the bottom. The JEANNETTE expedition had recorded shallow water not far from where they were, and Nansen expected to find a shallow sea, perhaps with land to the north, land he would very much have liked to find. But their sounding line had problems reaching the bottom. Finally the crew managed to splice a long enough line and found the bottom about 10,000 feet. This discovery at the time was a sensation. A number of other observations were taken continuously. The FRAM drifted back and forth to some degree, but more in a westerly direction than towards the North Pole. Although they passed 80 degrees north during the first year, their movement north went very slowly.

In October of the second year the FRAM passed 82 degrees north. Nansen realized that if he was to reach the North Pole he would have to use the dogs. No one had ever traveled this way or even been close to their current location before. Nansen elected Hjalmar Johansen to join him in a push for the pole. On the 14th of March 1895 they left the ship with the dogs heading north. The FRAM at this point lay at 84 degrees north, approximately 360 nautical miles from the North Pole. After their departure, the ice sent Nansen and Johansen off in the wrong direction and they had to overcome massive pressure ridges. It was a backbreaking experience to move forward towards the Pole. They fought against a most hostile environment. At 86 degrees, 14 minutes north Nansen decided to turn around and head home. At that time they were less than 240 nautical miles from the North Pole. Nobody had ever been this far north before. Using ice floes as vantage points, Nansen and Johansen could see no mountains or other evidence of land, only an endless expanse of ice.

Nansen and Johansen's attempt to reach the North Pole in 1895 is one of the greatest achievements in the history of the Arctic. They brought food for barely 100 days and had to turn back to reach Frantz Josef Land before the last boat left the islands. The return trip was a struggle between life and death. The weather was horrid. The ice opened up and was often covered by surface water. The kayaks leaked and the men were constantly wet. To increase the pace they left most of the equipment behind. There was enough wild game for both them and the few dogs they had left. August came. The days had become a lot shorter when they finally saw the mountains in the distance. Between them lay the ice edge. They had to cross the open water in their kayaks. The men reached the shores of Frantz Josef Land on the 15th of August and continued along the west coast. They spotted no vessels and they were uncertain where they were because their watches had stopped. There was only one solution: To prepare for a new winter in the Arctic ice and snow, this time on a barren island. They chose a good location, and built a stone hut with driftwood and walrus hide for roof. The fauna was diverse. Polar bears and walruses became their basic food for the winter. Nansen used what the native people of Greenland had taught him. Together he and Johansen survived the nine month long winter in a frozen wilderness where most others would surely have perished. The fact that they avoided contracting scurvy during the winter of 1895 to 1896 was a miracle. In May 1896 they started on a new journey which took them back to an area where trappers and hunters would come by ship from time to time during the summer in search of Arctic prey. Nansen and Johansen finally met such a ship and were saved. That the two managed to make it back to civilization, virtually without equipment and provisions, testifies to iron will, high intelligence, and a certain degree of luck.

The FRAM continued her ice drift with Otto Sverdrup as the expedition leader. The ship remained at around 83 degrees north for a while before she began to move south. In the spring of 1896 she approached the waters north of Spitsbergen. The ice opened up and the struggle to break free began. They used explosives to no avail. The men onboard assumed that Nansen and Johansen were back home in Norway if everything had gone well, and they worked hard to get their ship loose. It was not until the 13th of August that the FRAM was out in the open sea and headed south. By Spitsbergen they met several ships. The VIRGO lay at anchor at Danskeøya. The Swedish explorer Andree would try to reach the pole in the balloon EAGLE. They got to see the balloon house and were given a briefing. Andre's balloon flight ended in tragedy. After midnight on the 20th of August 1897, the FRAM anchored by Skjervøy in Northern Norway. Sverdrup was rowed ashore to send telegrams. He had to wake up the telegraph operator. No telegram was sent. Instead, Sverdrup was told that Nansen and Johansen had arrived in Vardø the week before. The captain ran out of the house and down to the dingy and was rowed back to the FRAM as fast as possible to let everybody know that Nansen had returned. Then it was off to shore again to report that the FRAM also had arrived in Norway.

The entire expedition was reunited

Expedition leader and Captain Otto Sverdrup.

192

in Tromsø after 17 months away from each other. There, the captain ordered the ship cleaned. He hired 20 maids to get this accomplished. The FRAM received a thorough cleaning; she smelled clean below deck. Her decks, brass fittings, rig and hull, both inside and outside, were polished. Shortly thereafter FRAM began her celebratory voyage south along the coast. Nothing like this had ever happened in Norway before. Cities and towns fought over the privilege to get a visit from the FRAM and the heroes of the Arctic Ocean; explorers who had been further north than anybody at that time. Norwegian patriotism saw a strong resurgence with the FRAM voyage. The larger towns built honorary portals and grandstands. There were torchlight processions and parades; parties and speeches.

Fridtjof Nansen had accomplished what he set out to do and gave pride to the country. He made Norway a nation the world had to reckon with in regard to polar research and the discovery of unknown land. Nansen became a leader in the Norwegian independence movement from Sweden which followed.

At the outlet of the Trondheim Fjord the FRAM was met by 17 steamers which escorted her into the city. There were speeches, singing, dinners, parades, and a gala concert at the Nidaros Cathedral. Twenty thousand people celebrated the polar explorers. The arrival in Bergen was equally impressive. The famous Norwegian composer Edvard Grieg was among the speakers. When Nansen said that the idea of the FRAM expedition was laid at Nordnes in Bergen when he was a young scholar, the cheers would not end.

They were running late, and the FRAM had to continue.

When she sailed up the Christiania Fjord she was escorted by eight naval vessels. In the harbor a host of smaller boats waited. Everyone was out to meet the FRAM. The celebration tour from Tromsø had taken three weeks. The capital thus had ample time to prepare for her return. At the Honnør Pier they had built a pavilion for the guests of honor. Flags adorned the harbor. Along the route up to the Royal Palace there were flags and portals. Shops remained closed and there were swarms of people in the streets with greetings, speeches and much ado. At the palace King Oscar II, Crown Prince Gustav and members of the government waited to greet the heroes. All of them, as well as shipbuilder Archer, were honored. They received Royal recognition and the FRAM medal. A bust of Nansen was made, as well as new music, poems, a Nansen pin, cigars, matches, hats, beer, wine; all bore Nansen and FRAM decorations. In short, the country was in awe of the heroes from the Arctic. The celebrations lasted for several days.

The scientific results of the expedition were extensive, and some of them were surprising. The depth of the Arctic Ocean had not been known before. Furthermore, the expedition members had not seen land masses anywhere, only some islands near Siberia. Theories regarding land in the north now changed to account for the possibility that there could in fact be deep sea across the entire top of the world north of the continents. Samples of animal and plant life were of great value. Temperature measurements over such a long time had never been performed.

May 17th, 1899, Norway's Constitution Day, is being celebrated west of Greenland.

In addition, measurements of sea temperature, salinity and the ship's operations were important. Nansen calculated that there must be an underwater threshold between the Norwegian Sea and the Arctic Ocean. The material was later published in six large volumes under the title, *The Norwegian North Polar Expedition 1893-1896*. This report is considered a classic publication in the field of polar research.

The first FRAM expedition set a new standard for future polar research and opened the world's eyes to new daring challenges. Youngsters dreamed of being like Nansen when they grew up. Many applied for and joined the expeditions to the Arctic as well as the Antarctic. These people were pioneers. In addition, this intrepid spirit and determination was often the direct legacy of whaling and sealing vessels' endeavors and their crews' experiences. Trapping, hunting and fishing had been going on in the north and south polar regions long before anyone sought to conquer the last land and ice masses. Antarctic whaling, in which the Norwegians played an important part, would later play a crucial role for the FRAM. Important national expeditions were paid for with profits from whaling. Lars Christensen deserves to be remembered as an important pioneer along with the big three: Fridtjof Nansen, Otto Sverdrup and Roald Amundsen. Lars Christensen was in Antarctica

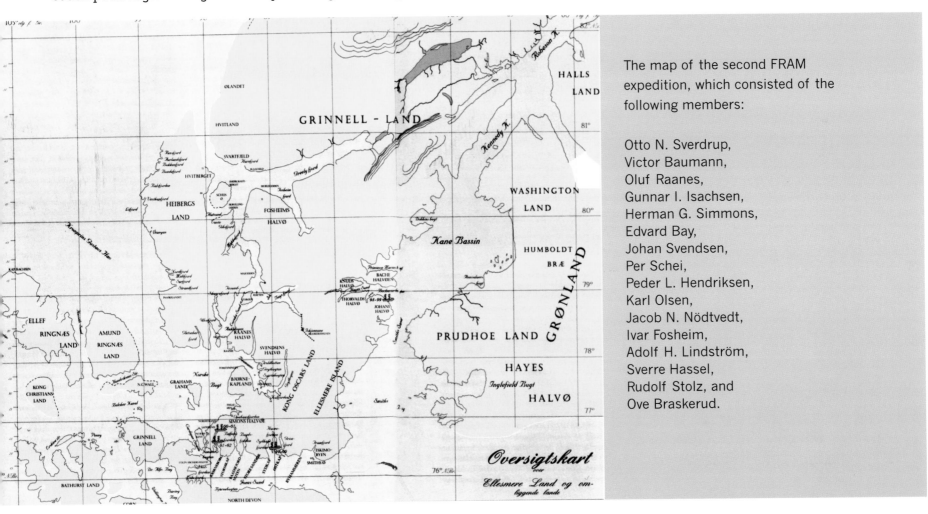

The map of the second FRAM expedition, which consisted of the following members:

Otto N. Sverdrup,
Victor Baumann,
Oluf Raanes,
Gunnar I. Isachsen,
Herman G. Simmons,
Edvard Bay,
Johan Svendsen,
Per Schei,
Peder L. Hendriksen,
Karl Olsen,
Jacob N. Nödtvedt,
Ivar Fosheim,
Adolf H. Lindström,
Sverre Hassel,
Rudolf Stolz, and
Ove Braskerud.

on a whaling ship as a young boy and realized that hunting and research were mutually dependent. Later as a ship owner he had opportunities to contribute to furthering this pioneering spirit and outfitted several new and extended expeditions to Antarctica. Christensen's predecessor Nansen also learned from his peers; he was a skiing champion who copied the native nomads' clothing, food and sleeping arrangement as well as their use of dogs. The dogs were the only reliable means of transportation and a necessity before the aircraft became common. Nansen, Sverdrup and Amundsen fully understood this, and showed the way together with many less famous Norwegians.

The world prototype FRAM had survived where other vessels invariably would have been lost if they became trapped in the pack ice. The FRAM returned to Christiania in practically as good condition as when she left. This inspired many; such a vessel could not be left to decay. Both Nansen and Sverdrup were aware of this. But Nansen had a problem: The scholar and researcher had to write books and work with the results of the voyage they just had completed. In addition, he had his wife Eve and a little daughter, and was also actively involved in the union dispute with Sweden. Captain Sverdrup on the other hand was a sailor and had been on ships practically his entire life. He could write, but this was not his main focus. Both Sverdrup and Nansen were aware of this. Therefore, it was Otto Sverdrup who had to take care of the FRAM's future fate as both the captain and top leader of new expeditions.

The FRAM was taken to Larvik for rebuilding and repair. The low bow that had taken on so much seawater was now covered with a shelter deck over the main deck. This added a lot of extra interior room. Towards the bow there was placed new workshops, research areas, and storage for collected samples. Further aft, a roomy lounge was built between the foremast and main mast, with six cabins outside. Together with the 12 original berths aft this gave the needed space for a larger expedition. Rebuilt behind the main mast there was a spacious galley. Copious amounts of cork were used for insulating the hull sides and ceiling. Light

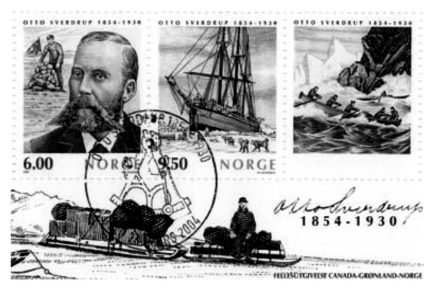

FRAM became Norway's most famous ship. It has been honored over and again through the years. Many stamps have been issued. This is a First Day cover from 2004, comemmorating Otto Sverdrup's birth 150 years earlier.

filtered down through the deck prisms and the skylight over the lounge. Here another good oven was added. Nearly the entire keel of the FRAM lay inside the ship. Similar in this respect to a barge, she could turn very easily. This was a big advantage when she needed to move between ice floes, but the ship was virtually uncontrollable with the wind on the beam and presented great challenges to the helmsman. To remedy this, the ship yard added a protective straw keel about 16 inches deep aft, declining to zero towards the bow of the FRAM. The foremast was too short and was lifted about six feet. Finally, the ship was careened and painted. A few hull planks were replaced. In the autumn of 1897 the FRAM was back on the buoys outside Akershus Castle close to the *skoleskibet* CHRISTIANIA and provisioning began. Groceries and canned goods came from abroad. The rest of the supplies needed for five years were obtained in Norway. Fuel, wood, textiles, tents, expedition equipment, and all the other things they needed were taken onboard during the winter. There were long waiting lists of people who wanted to join the expedition.

Five years after her first voyage started the FRAM left Christiania for the second time for scientific work in unknown regions west of Greenland, today the East Canadian Arctic. This time the quay and the harbor were teeming with people to see her off. The capital of Norway wished the FRAM a safe voyage west to the 1,000 year old Norwegian settler sites in Greenland and further abroad. Once again, the FRAM received a clean sweep of her weather deck during bad weather, but the new shelter deck turned out to be a

blessing. Loose objects moved about, but the ship escaped damage from the sea. North of Godthaab (today Nuuk) they took onboard 70 dogs. The men said goodbye to civilization and set out in a northerly direction. They soon had ice problems. Although there was still a lot left of the Arctic summer, the ice stopped them from proceeding north, so they found a sheltered cove by Ellesmere Island. This became the FRAM's first winter quarters.

The surveying efforts of the uncharted land started immediately, and other scientific work got underway after a while when it became safe to travel the ice. Before the polar night descended over the expedition, they received a famous visitor. Robert E. Peary traveled past in a hurry. He only had time for a brief greeting. He had his winter quarters further north. The American was obsessed with reaching the North Pole and tried for over 20 years. He was determined that Sverdrup should not beat him to it, and moved the base 250 miles to the north. This cost Peary the amputation of several of his toes. Otto Sverdrup however was a sea captain and had no ambitions to reach the pole. He wanted to be near his ship, but enjoyed dog sled expeditions. The winter was used to build a cabin for those who would explore the northern part of Greenland. In the spring natives came to visit. Being a Stone Age people, the FRAM's blacksmith was a shaman to them, and they were very pleased to receive empty tin cans. They were in contact with Peary and his men. But Peary avoided Sverdrup. The American apparently never understood that others had different goals than he had.

The summer of 1899 brought challenging conditions; neither Peary nor Sverdrup was able to get further north. The captain gave up and took the FRAM southward and thereupon to the west. After bad weather with a lot of pitching and rolling, they found good winter quarters in a narrow fjord south of Ellesmere. They named the place Havnefjorden. Before that they had secured an ample winter supply of walrus for dog food and fresh meat for the crew. The fall was used for long sleigh rides and the mapping of new land. Sverdrup took part in these activities. The men experienced illness and death without being able to determine the cause of it. Chef Lindstrøm and botanist Simmons became ill with high fever. The last Christmas of the Nineteenth Century therefore did not go as planned. But with spring came the return of sunlight and the mapping of more of the new country. In May, a fire broke out onboard. Those remaining on the

Ready for a new mission. The motor schooner FRAM outside Roald Amundsen's home at Svartskog, with Amundsen (who also used the FRAM) and his dog Pan in the foreground.

ship had a tough time. It was a close call; they almost lost the ship when the flames came dangerously close to the ship's powder stores and a 50 gallon barrel of flammable liquid.

They said farewell to Havnefjord in August. Sverdrup had given up surveying the north coast of Greenland. To the south, by Devon, there were large masses of ice. Ice conditions were no better than the previous two years and would require them to stay another winter. There were plenty of tasks to the north and west of where they were and Sverdrup decided to go into Jones Sound. They were met by strong currents; at times it seemed as if the FRAM was speeding along sideways. The ship was also for a time stuck in the ice. The captain found good winter quarters with lots of wildlife in the Gåsefjord. There were musk oxen, bears, hares, grouse and fish. Good winter food was secured.

The winter of 1900 to 1901 was stormy. When spring came, Isachsen and Hassel traveled to the major islands in the west which had been discovered the year before. They were named Amund Ringnes Land and Ellef Ringnes Land as thanks for the contributions for equipment for the expedition. The islands were measured and mapped in two months. Baumann and Stolz mapped fjords and land at Norwegian Bay. They found coal and petrified forests. Many fossils were brought onboard. Sverdrup and Schei traveled north. Their route home went along Axel Heiberg Land, which has many bays and fjords. Here they found the remains of settlements, traps and pits. They did not know to whom they might have belonged or the age of the findings. The trip lasted

for 77 days. They came back with a lot of information regarding newly discovered land. The summer of that year was unusually cold. For three weeks after mid-August they tried to get out. There was open water further out, but it was impossible to get there despite their best efforts. Their attempt to get out failed and a new winter was fast approaching. They needed to focus on hunting for food instead.

The spring of 1902 was used for continued research, but also to lay out depots with messages about where they were in case

The ship's new lounge was a great improvement. Kerosene lamps were still in use several years after the failed experimental use of electric light in the cold environment of the Arctic.

rescue expeditions were looking for them. They had not seen natives since the first winter. If they had any luck, the rest of 1902 would be different. The FRAM came loose in July, but did not get out of the fjord before a storm from the north blew the sea free of ice on the 6th of August, and the FRAM could head to Baffin Bay, Greenland, and Norway. Sverdrup took a pilot onboard at an island outside Norway. He took the vessel to Stavanger. The Royal Norwegian Navy vessel HEIMDAL had the honor of towing the FRAM to Christiania. Scott Hansen had been promoted to captain of HEIMDAL. All were invited onboard. Harpooner Hendriksen and Captain Sverdrup felt at home with the second in command from the first FRAM expedition. The return of the FRAM was this time, if possible, even more spectacular. The Akershus cannons fired a 77 shot salute of honor. The streets were filled with people. There were parades, torchlight processions, lunches, and dinners in perpetuity; quite a contrast from months spent eating rancid seal meat. Otto Sverdrup received the Grand Cross of the Order of St. Olav and Peder Hendriksen the King's Gold Medal of Merit. The others received the FRAM Medal.

Otto Sverdrup's FRAM expedition mapped about 58,000 square miles of new land with great precision. Sverdrup took possession of the large islands with Norwegian names on behalf of the King, as had been customary for many centuries. The Norwegian government never followed up with a formal recognition, as was done with the islands and sectors in the Antarctic much later. Otto Sverdrup's claim of land in the north must have been the largest since the Viking era, when the Norse migrated to Iceland, Greenland and used North America for ship building and trading activities. Specimens and written documentation from the expedition were analyzed by a number of researchers. It took a total of 20 years to publish all the material in five large illustrated volumes: *Report of the Second Norwegian Arctic Expedition in the "Fram" 1898-1902*. The Nansen Fund paid for the printing. The work was published shortly before Otto Sverdrup died.

A rare photo of the FRAM with her sails set. The ship is on its way to refuel before heading to Antarctica in 1910.

Roald Amundsen was Fridtjof Nansen's opposite, but they had one thing in common: An affinity for exploring unknown lands in the polar regions. Nansen was a scientist who wanted to set records. He had early made specific plans to conquer both the North and South Pole. Amundsen was a record hunter without an academic education, but with big ambitions. For the ten year younger Amundsen, Nansen was a great role model. After the GJØA's sailing through the Northwest Passage, Amundsen became a famous polar explorer. He then wanted to continue Nansen's

Expedition leader
Roald Amundsen.

work in the Arctic. He wanted to be the first person to set foot on the North Pole.

The FRAM by this time had been laid up in Horten for seven years. Nansen, Sverdrup and others were concerned about this very famous ship; she could not just lie there. After Amundsen's GJØA lecture in London where Nansen was present, Amundsen dared to present to him the idea of an expedition living on the ice. Hopefully the participants could drift with it over the North Pole. Nansen advised against this. His thought was that a new polar exploration with the North Pole as the goal had to start from the Bering Strait. Their talks ended with Nansen agreeing to help Amundsen with a polar expedition starting from Alaska with the FRAM as a base. The plan was presented to the Norwegian Geographic Society on the 10th of November 1908, with the King and Queen of Norway both present at the lecture. The FRAM would be equipped for seven years starting in 1910. Amundsen would undertake a polar drift that he later, during World War I, sought to perform with the MAUD.

The day after the lecture the plan received support by the Royal couple, who contributed 30,000 Norwegian kroner. The snowball started rolling. A national fundraising effort brought in 400,000 Norwegian kroner, but this was far from enough. Nansen suggested a government grant that also would secure the FRAM for the future. The application to the Norwegian *Storting* (Parliament) to borrow the FRAM and in addition get 75,000 Norwegian kroner in support to restore the ship was granted by a large majority of the members of the *Storting*.

The year 1909 was an important year in polar exploration. In September, the world received word that the American Frederick A. Cook had been to the North Pole, and the week after that the news that probably another American, Robert E. Peary, had finally succeeded in reaching the Pole. In January of that year, Britain's Ernest Shackleton got to 88 degrees south when he was forced to turn around and narrowly escaped death. Peary and especially Cook's conquests of the North Pole have been questioned in hindsight because of poor documentation. In 1909 Amundsen had little choice but to trust the news. He also knew that Britain's Robert Scott planned a foray to the South Pole.

Roald Amundsen's secret plan to make his North Pole expedition into a race to reach the South Pole was a gambler's decision. To fool the King and Queen of Norway, Nansen, and the entire Norwegian people was something which would not go unpunished unless the result was 100 percent successful. Even so, critics would say they were deceived. Wintering in the Antarctic required equipment other than what they needed for the ice drift. Amundsen had to find excuses to take things they did not need in the Arctic. Dogs that were to be taken onboard in Alaska were taken onboard before their departure south. They went from Greenland to Copenhagen. Amundsen went there to talk with Cook and ordered 100 Greenland dogs, footwear, fur suits and special equipment. Some were suspicious, but they kept quiet. It was of great help that Peary told the *Daily Mail* newspaper that a race for the South Pole between the U.S. and the United Kingdom would begin about seven months later, and become the most exciting challenge the world had ever seen. Thus, Amundsen's discreet plan to outdo both remained unknown to the world.

In the meantime, the FRAM received a solid overhaul at the Norwegian Navy's Main Yard at Horten. Amundsen had good experience with the oil engine from the GJØA and replaced the steam engine and boiler with a new type 360 horsepower internal combustion engine built by Diesel AB in Stockholm. The type was named Polar. A motor had clear advantages over steam operation. A certificate issued by the Norwegian maritime authorities in May of 1910 still hangs onboard the FRAM. It shows that the FRAM was converted to a motor schooner, measuring 510.82 tons, with a length of 117.7 feet, a breadth of 36 feet and a depth of 16.2 feet. The papers stated that the engine could produce 180 horsepower, that the FRAM's hometown was Horten, that the government was the owner and that Roald Amundsen was the captain.

The start of the expedition had to be postponed due to the work at the yard and the loading of equipment and supplies. This fit perfectly with the timing of arrival during the short Antarctic summer. The original voyage to Alaska for the start of polar drift would require many months of additional sailing, and Amundsen wanted to have plenty of time since his old ship GJØA was still in San Francisco. It would require a long layover and a major celebration in the city that celebrated Amundsen's first achievement of penetrating the Northwest Passage and arriving in San Francisco half a year after the 1906 earthquake. Amundsen was an honorary member of exclusive clubs there and would be expected to participate in the festivities before traveling to Point Barrow and the start of his polar expedition. Not even the most cunning journalists suspected that anything was off, even when a prefabricated house for staying the winter ashore was built in the garden at Svartskog, his home, in the spring of 1910. Amundsen chose to keep a low profile. Those who tried to contact him were told that he was not at home. This happened to Scott when he wanted to meet while he was in town. Amundsen did as Peary did in relation to Sverdrup. He kept the cards close to his chest.

The FRAM was done at the yard in May. She then went to Christiania where the month long loading began. Amundsen himself picked all expedition members except Hjalmar Johansen. Amundsen probably felt that Johansen was Nansen's extended arm. As a naval officer and famous athlete with more experience in the polar regions than himself, as well as being older, he was seen by Amundsen as a threat. Amundsen's attitude towards Johansen later was anything but admirable. Amundsen chose to keep all individuals with formal higher education away from his expedition. Not even a medical doctor was included. The expedition consisted entirely of Norwegians without university degrees. He would take care of scientific work in Antarctica himself.

Before the departure King Haakon and Queen Maud came onboard to wish them a safe journey to the North Pole. After loading the house that was built in Amundsen's garden in Bunnefjorden, the FRAM set out to sea on the 7th of June, 1910, allegedly bound for Cape Horn. The ship was off to a long voyage. Well into the North Sea they had engine trouble and had to return to Bergen. They changed to a lighter diesel oil and the factory's technician, a Swedish man named Sundbeck, joined as chief engineer. Thus, the machine was in order and a Swede came with. When the FRAM left Norway she carried 20 men, 97 dogs and four pigs. The mood onboard was subdued. A select few were initiated into the plan to make a dash for the South Pole; the others, having been left out, felt that something was wrong. On the island of Madeira everybody was informed. Most were taken by surprise when informed that their actual destination was the South Pole in a race against the British and Americans. Amundsen explained everything in detail. As this deception had been a clear breach of the original contract, Amundsen took a roll call. Not a single crewmember backed out; the FRAM was ready for Antarctica.

The ship had already reached the doldrums by the time all this became known in Norway. That the FRAM would continue to perform scientific investigations in the South Atlantic was appreciated by Nansen. He agreed that the South Pole was a reasonable goal because the expedition was already well on its way. After five months the FRAM moored by the Ross Barrier. Equipment for the winter and the dogs were taken ashore and the camp Framheim was built. Nine men were left behind when the FRAM left after a month. Ten men remained onboard.

The FRAM headed west to measure water depths in the Ross Basin, and got as far as 78 degrees, 41 minutes south. This corresponds to 30 miles north of Longyearbyen at Svalbard in the north. This position is about as far south as it is possible to get by sea. The FRAM was thus at that time the ship in the world that had been farthest north and farthest south.

The FRAM continued into the Atlantic. Beset by a hurricane like storm, the ship sailed on just her rig and raced down huge wave crests without getting any water on deck. The FRAM proved to be a very seaworthy vessel and a great sailing ship even though she was always restless and always rolled awfully. The ship sailed through the Drake Passage, passing Cape Horn the wrong way in relation to the original plan, and arrived in the port of Buenos Aires in time for Easter. Don Pedro, an expatriate Norwegian with money, equipped the ship with everything it needed and Captain Nilsen hired four Norwegian sailors for the research expedition.

The FRAM collected 891 water samples from 60 different locations at sea, as well as 190 plankton samples. Halfway to Africa the FRAM crossed her own course from when she was sailing from Norway to Antarctica; the FRAM had thus made a circumnavigation of the globe via Cape Horn and around the Antarctic. A month later the ship arrived at the island of St.

First at the South Pole. Amundsen, to the left, and his team at Polheim. Bjaaland is the photographer. This is the unaltered original copy that the film developer at Hobart, Tasmania kept to himself which surfaced recently.

FRAM at anchor in Hobart, Tasmania after Amundsen had conquered the South Pole.

Helena. The expedition turned around near the African coast and returned from where it came. After the return to Argentina, it was time to sail back to Antarctica, the same way as before, but this time with a significantly lighter ship. The FRAM managed the comparatively impressive feat of reaching ten knots during this voyage. In so doing, she cut out on top of a wave and ended up with her beam to the seas. The sails split and new ones were bent under. This was a "race" the men liked to talk about. Captain Nilsen managed to take the FRAM to a Norwegian whaling station in Kerguelen where they replenished provisions before the trip back to Framheim to pick up the South Pole party.

204

Meanwhile, Amundsen and four others reached the South Pole on the 14th of December, 1911. Staying there for three days, they found the exact location of the South Pole and on it raised Rønne's small tent, Polheim, topped with a modestly sized Norwegian flag before leaving letters for Robert Scott and King Haakon of Norway. The explorers then returned to Framheim as fast as they could. The 2,000 mile return trip was covered in 99 days with an average speed of 20 miles per day. On January 26th they got back and, packing up, waited for the FRAM. She arrived three days later. Their equipment and the remaining 39 dogs were taken onboard. The next day the FRAM set out for the Bay of Whales, easily navigating through the ice before setting sail for Hobart in Tasmania. Naturally the conquest of the South Pole became first page news. Word quickly spread around the world after Amundsen had sent a telegram from Hobart that Norway had won the race to the South Pole in 1911. Once again they sailed to South America via Cape Horn. There the FRAM was supposed to provision and proceed to San Francisco, but this did not happen. The crew was sent back to Norway on leave, while Amundsen relaxed at Don Pedro's home and worked on his book. The FRAM arrived at Buenos Aires in May of 1912 after the ship had sailed 54,400 nautical miles since leaving Christiania in 1910.

For 15 months the FRAM remained in South America, languishing in the heat without needed maintenance. Amundsen sent a message to Captain Nilsen from the U.S. that if the FRAM could go to Cristobal, Colon it could be a test ship for transiting the Panama Canal which had then almost been completed. On the 14th of August 1913 the FRAM left Buenos Aires and reached the Channel Zone at the beginning of October. There the FRAM stayed for almost four months. Amundsen never arrived, and nothing happened. Just before Christmas, Nilsen was told by Amundsen to go back around the Horn again. The FRAM started on her return voyage to Buenos Aires.

After conquering the South Pole it must be noted that Amundsen seemed fairly uncommitted in regard to the FRAM. This contributed to the ship no longer being fit for polar expeditions. The voyage south was stormy. The FRAM had become so overgrown

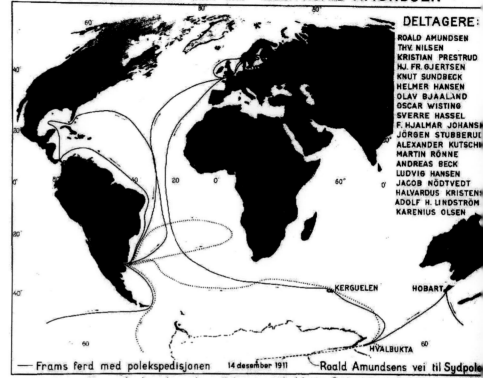

3ᵈⁱᵉ FRAMFERD 1910-1912 Leder: ROALD AMUNDSEN

DELTAGERE:
ROALD AMUNDSEN
THV. NILSEN
KRISTIAN PRESTRUD
HJ. FR. GJERTSEN
KNUT SUNDBECK
HELMER HANSEN
OLAV BJAALAND
OSCAR WISTING
SVERRE HASSEL
F. HJALMAR JOHANSE
JÖRGEN STUBBERUI
ALEXANDER KUTSCHI
MARTIN RÖNNE
ANDREAS BECK
LUDVIG HANSEN
JACOB NÖDTVEDT
HALVARDUS KRISTENS
ADOLF H. LINDSTRÖM
KARENIUS OLSEN

— Frams ferd med polekspedisjonen   14 desember 1911   ⋯⋯ Roald Amundsens vei til Sydpole

The third and final FRAM expedition took Amundsen and his men to the Ross Ice Shelf. There they erected base camp Framheim, from where they proceeded to become the first on the South Pole.
With this, FRAM had sailed further north and south than any other vessel. It also circumnavigated the world during this expedition. FRAM started from Oslo on June 7th, 1910, and returned to Horten on July 16th, 1914. This was the ship's final trip under its own sail, aided by a diesel motor.

"Catch of a Lifetime" Consul Lars Christensen was the main benefactor of the FRAM. He was also a great sportsman.

with barnacles and growth in the tropics that she moved laboriously. The trip back to Montevideo took more than three months. Once there, she was docked and cleaned. Then came the counter orders to go to Horten in Norway. The FRAM arrived on the 16th of July, 1914, less than one month before the opening of the Panama Canal and 18 days after the shot in Sarajevo which sparked Word War I.

The FRAM was in many ways a victim of external circumstances. Amundsen's excuse was that the timing of the departures from South America did not fit with the onset of polar operations, even if months of preparation in San Francisco would be a natural solution to this challenge. Amundsen was in America on a lecture tour and had his hands full with his tasks. He was at that time what we can refer to an A-list celebrity. Even if his English was difficult to understand, he was a popular presenter with a unique visual material never before seen.

The FRAM was discharged after her return, and laid up at the Norwegian Navy's main base. There she remained without much happening. Norway managed to remain neutral during World War I. Amundsen continued with his tasks. Nansen was dissatisfied because Amundsen had broken his promise to continue the expedition north. There were major issues with the FRAM. Surveyors who inspected the vessel found significant rot damage. The long stay in the tropical and subtropical climate without the required care had of course taken its toll. But she was far from condemnable. Extensive repairs were needed. The estimate was for 100,000 kroner and it would take one year at a ship yard.

Amundsen, who constantly sought new goals, had discovered the airplane and concluded that it would be the next generation's most important tool in the exploration and mapping of polar regions. He did, however, need a platform for polar operations, but did not want to invest money in the FRAM which at that time was over 20 years old and in need of significant repair. Instead he put his money into building a new ship, an improved version of the FRAM even more suitable for the crushing forces of the pack ice. This ship became the MAUD.

Early on, some people tried to secure support for preserving the

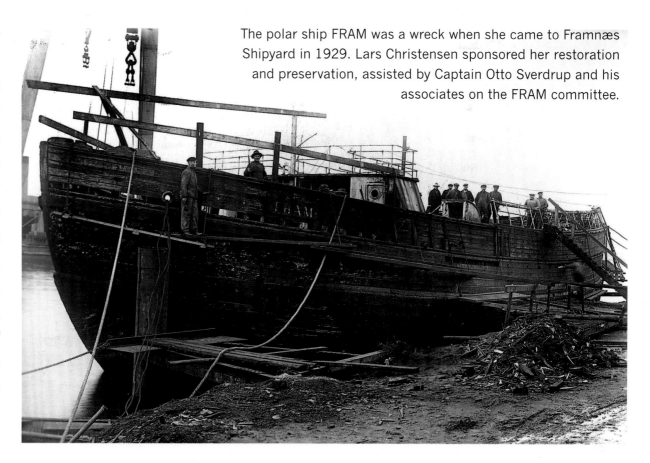

The polar ship FRAM was a wreck when she came to Framnæs Shipyard in 1929. Lars Christensen sponsored her restoration and preservation, assisted by Captain Otto Sverdrup and his associates on the FRAM committee.

FRAM rather than let the ship lie and perish in Horten. As noted in the chapter on MAUD, the authorities chose to let Amundsen help himself to the parts from the FRAM which he needed to equip his new ship. It is no secret that the FRAM was left rather barren after the MAUD was ready to embark on her expedition. The FRAM was Norway's most famous ship and well-known around the world. She was in her time the finest and most advanced vessel the nation ever built for civilian purposes, and a national symbol of the international race to explore the last unknown regions of the world during the end of the Nineteenth Century and beginning of the Twentieth Century. The FRAM belonged to the Norwegian Parliament; it was the Norwegian people's ship. She had been celebrated and admired by communities all along the coast on a number of occasions. This was a ship that made people proud. On top of that, this was a ship that was built differently from all other ships, and for that reason she should be taken care of to show

Was this the steering wheel that took the FRAM on all the expeditions to the north and south? Could it later have served on the MAUD?

everybody the ship's unique characteristics and design solutions.

The ship's expeditions to the north and south polar regions had given her tremendous status. She had also set a whole series of first records. The FRAM had been farthest north and south, sailed around the world and rounded Cape Horn. She had sailed all oceans and survived crushing pack ice and hurricanes. The FRAM had sailed far without engine power and put enormous distances behind her as a steamship and as a motor vessel. It was clear that such a world champion could not just be left to rot. This was, however, exactly what happened. A committee formed in 1917 recommended conservation, but got nowhere. There were no funds

for security and maintenance. One reason might have been the ongoing war. The FRAM committee was dissolved. The ship was lying in Horten without masts, rigging and deck equipment. People got onboard and caused extensive damage. Most of the doors were missing; some were even torn off their hinges and smashed. All her metal fittings were gone. Door locks and hinges had been removed. Vandals had nearly destroyed the FRAM.

Many years passed. Discussions and attempts to do something with the FRAM surfaced from time to time. The newspapers participated in the discussion and printed proposals and presentations. Captain Sverdrup was in favor of conservation. The ship was not completely abandoned but was docked and sealed from time to time, but not protected by a simple roof to keep the rain out. Proposals to preserve parts of the ship were presented. Nansen himself was careful. There was little left of his ship except for the hull, and he suggested building a model instead. This was discouraging to many. Moreover, Amundsen was indifferent. In 1925, old Captain Sverdrup tried again with a well thought out solution. After an inspection onboard he wrote a detailed report, recommending conservation. The conclusion was that the hull was not in much worse condition than what was stated in *Det Norske Veritas'* report from 1914, except for the upper deck. Sverdrup estimated that the total repair cost to bring the FRAM back to seaworthy condition would be more than double the price paid in 1914. He asked for a fairly small amount to repair the FRAM, put the ship on land in Oslo and give her museum status. He was a visionary: The ship was built of wood, and this alone was the main argument for conservation in a time when all the larger tonnage long had been constructed of steel. He prepared detailed solutions on how the FRAM could be secured in a house. This way the FRAM could be preserved for centuries, Otto Sverdrup claimed.

The struggle for FRAM went on. Sverdrup continued to present convincing arguments that all could understand about the uniqueness of this vessel, both nationally and internationally. Moreover, it was government property. Nobody knew this ship better than Sverdrup. Bringing her ashore would prevent her disappearance along with all her glory and fame. The old captain was stubborn and enlisted his good friends. Gradually more people joined the conservation efforts. "FRAM must be saved," became their slogan. A new committee with Otto Sverdrup as chairman was formed, including representatives from several organizations with stakes in the outcome. Sverdrup wrote an article. It was printed in newspapers nationwide. He called the FRAM an historic vessel, a designation that currently is being reintroduced to describe the even older and most original iron ships built in Norway. The three oldest Norwegian iron ships are all older than the FRAM and at least as original as she was, but they have still not been added to the Norwegian government's list of vessels they intend to supply with public conservation support. These iron ships are the largest remains of the industrial revolution in Norway.

In 1929 a departmental committee with a mandate to determine what should be done with the FRAM was appointed. No conservation interests were included. Sverdrup knew that something was wrong and discussed this with Knud Ringnæs. Together with supportive newspaper reporters they went to shipping tycoon Lars Christensen in Sandefjord to ask for help. Christensen confirmed that the Framnæs Shipyard would be willing to pay for the restoration of the FRAM. Prime Minister Mowinckel's help was solicited and the result was that the Sverdrup committee and Framnæs got permission to repair the FRAM with contributions from whalers and Lars Christensen. This was in November of 1929. The FRAM was taken to Framnæs for professional restoration under Captain Sverdrup's leadership. Basically, there were three alternatives for which version of the ship to restore her to. The choice was easy. The FRAM was at her best during the Sverdrup expedition and the drawings from that period were the most complete.

While the restoration was going on, Trondheim planned the large Trøndelag exhibition in 1930, celebrating the city's anniversary and the 900 year anniversary of the historically significant Battle of Stiklestad. This was to be the largest regional exhibit in Norwegian history. The city wanted to get the FRAM to Trondheim as an attraction during the exhibit. On May 19th, 1930, two days after Nansen's funeral, the FRAM was once again ready to leave the yard, and the tow to Trondheim started. Captain Sverdrup was in Sandefjord to bid the newly renovated FRAM farewell. He knew then that the ship had been saved. This was the last time he saw the FRAM. The tow to Trondheim and visits there and along the coast on the return brought in much needed funds and created

The diesel engine Roald Amundsen gave the FRAM in 1909 is the oldest in the world still sitting in the ship it was built for. It was a 360 HP prototype made in Sweden. The model's name was Polar. It served the FRAM and its men very well.

renewed sympathy for conservation. Otto Sverdrup was bedridden in his home in Sandvika. He received regular updates on the FRAM. By the end of the year Otto Sverdrup also passed. He was the last and oldest of the three major FRAM pioneers. Oscar Wisting took the helm. It took a Royal decree on July 19th, 1931 to transfer the ownership of the ship from the government of Norway to the FRAM committee with Lars Christensen as chairman.

Many wanted to acquire land for the FRAM to be brought ashore. It was Sverdrup's idea that the ship should be located in Oslo and so it was. The committee was restructured and became more permanent. This was a big step in the right direction. Funding was the main problem. Besides the contribution from Lars Christensen, only Knud Ringnæs contributed major funding for the project. Ringnæs replaced Christensen as committee chairman in 1933 and completed the financing. The location issue was finally resolved in the fall of 1934 with an offer of free land, compensation and additional money from Bygdøynes across from Oslo Harbor. In March of 1935 the committee accepted the construction company Selmer's offer to build the 16,000 square foot FRAM house for almost 193,000 Norwegian kroner. Finally, things began happening in earnest. The FRAM was towed from Horten. Captain Wisting was responsible. Work on the foundation for hauling up the FRAM was in full swing. She arrived in Oslo on the 6th of May, and on the 10th of July the ship was relocated to where it stands today. An electric motor of just two horsepower pulled the several hundred ton FRAM up the slip, but it took time. The FRAM took about three minutes to advance one inch. This gave the crew full control if something unexpected occurred.

The construction of the A-framed hall was nearly complete by the end of the year. The concrete floor was waterproof, and the sides and walls built of reinforced concrete were laid up past an upper gallery. The 54 foot tall construction consisted of a steel skeleton with wooden beams and a wooden roof with windows. The Building Council demanded a copper roof, and it was financed through a parliamentary grant. Exterior plaster and interior decor were added after some time. The FRAM building's roof covers more than one acre, and 40,000 pounds of copper sheets were used. The windows cover 7,000 square feet. Three miles of wooden beams and 20 miles of roof boards were used. The total length of the galleries was over 500 yards. Once the building was underway, the fundraising increased. Large and small contributions poured in. Norwegian sailors around the world contributed.

At the same time, even more important work took place onboard the FRAM. The engine was returned from Trondheim. Today she is the oldest ship with her internal combustion engine still onboard. Cabins, rooms and furnishings were made anew. Some original items from the time the ship sailed were left, new parts had to be obtained. The original deck equipment was still onboard the MAUD, that had by this time sunk in Arctic Canada. The steering wheel was taken off and sent back to Norway. Some other parts were also restored, while the rest of the deck hardware, masts and rigging were gone. Some ended up on land at Cambridge Bay.

These remains are still in the wreck of the MAUD today.

Oscar Wisting and other expedition members pitched in and helped make things right. Artifacts from the voyages came from those who had participated as well as their descendants. Slowly but surely the FRAM reemerged in her former glory and as we know the ship today. Although a lot of the upper part of the ship and segments of the interior were not there during any of her expeditions, it is still the hull that Colin Archer built in 1893. It is really worth the visit to go below deck and experience the dimensions and the work undertaken with adding large support beams and knees into a ship that needed to withstand colossal ice pressure. The FRAM is the only example Norway has of how a three masted schooner is built. Otto Sverdrup saw this clearly. He claimed firmly that this would be the last chance to preserve the memory of this type of wood ship building for the future. We all owe the captain from Bindalen and Steinkjer our thanks.

For more than a generation many individuals have worked to preserve the last three

The FRAM today, more than 75 years after it went ashore and the house was built over the ship. It is still visited by tourists, researchers, schoolchildren and other visitors from around the world.

representative examples of Norwegian iron shipbuilding, all built before the FRAM was launched. These ships, the HANSTEEN (1866), the OSCARSBORG (1874) and the VÆRDALEN (1891), are the oldest memories of the iron ships our ancestors created. Unlike younger steel vessels, these ships have most of their original hulls intact. This is because iron is vastly superior to steel when it comes to durability. These unique ships are specimens of a bygone era that future researchers can study and new generations admire. Just like the FRAM they still have their largely original hulls, and are older than the FRAM. This is very similar to the resistance and indifference Sverdrup and others experienced in regards to the early FRAM preservation efforts. Has Norway really not progressed since Otto Sverdrup fought for the FRAM? Sverdrup prevailed in the end. The three aforementioned vessels are unique museum artifacts from the Industrial Revolution. Vessels built of iron must become important parts of our maritime heritage. They need a house, just like the FRAM.

The polar ship FRAM's building at Bygdøynes in the low winter sun. It is at this time of year the ship and its surroundings give the feel of the cold adventures the ship undertook. This landmark building and ship museum is one of the highlights of visiting Oslo.

The MAUD at anchor in Christiania Harbor early in 1918, getting ready for the North Pole expedition. The two stacker to the left is Norwegian America Line's BERGENSFJORD.

Maud
-The Queen of the Ice

The MAUD was the world's premier Arctic expedition and research ship of her time. She was a perfect platform for the pioneering scientific studies conducted in the polar regions. The MAUD became the last representative of the golden era of Norwegian exploration. The construction of the MAUD ignited the discussions on the conservation of the FRAM.

Roald Amundsen's dream was always to finish what Nansen had begun with the FRAM expedition in the 1890s. After Amundsen had succeeded in taking the sloop GJØA through the Northwest Passage he became an established polar explorer people took seriously. Shortly after returning from San Francisco Amundsen put forward plans to make an attempt to reach the North Pole by drifting with the ice, starting from the Bering Strait. The American JEANNETTE had started from Alaska in 1881, but was crushed by the ice and sank north of the New Siberian Islands. Artifacts from the ship were found in West Greenland. Hence, they knew that the ice moved with the sea current across the Arctic Ocean. Nansen had shown that this was the case with his FRAM voyage from 1893 to 1896. But he never came near the North Pole, which was the major goal of adventurers at that time. By starting from the east Amundsen hoped to enter the ice at a point which would carry his ship close to the Pole.

Amundsen borrowed and outfitted the FRAM for this purpose. But reports that Peary had reached the North Pole in 1909 thwarted his plans and he chose instead to try to reach the South Pole as number one, which he did in 1911. This outstanding accomplishment led to Amundsen being seen as a world renowned polar explorer. His plan was to use the FRAM in pursuing her old mission to travel across the Arctic Ocean to reach the North Pole. But after the South Pole Amundsen was busy lecturing in the U.S. and writing a book on his conquest. The FRAM was left in South America rather than embarking on the long voyage to Alaska and

Amundsen and Jensen at the slipway shortly before launching.

Christian Jensen's hull no. 1 was launched on June 7th, 1917.

the Bering Strait for Arctic operations right away. Raising funds for this new expedition was also a challenge he had to overcome.

After the South Pole expedition the FRAM was overhauled and outfitted in Buenos Aires. Following Amundsen's orders and after a long wait, the FRAM was sent to Colon in Panama in October of 1913 in hopes of getting through the Panama Canal, which was almost complete at that time. But the canal was only first opened on August 15th, 1914 and the FRAM was therefore stuck in Colon for months. Amundsen finally ordered the ship around South America. The return voyage along the South American coast was a long and slow haul. Upon arrival at Montevideo the FRAM had so much hull growth after many months in the tropics that the ship had to be docked and the expedition had to be postponed. The ship was therefore sent home from South America and arrived in Norway in June 1914. Expedition equipment and supplies were unloaded by the Norwegian Navy and the FRAM's rig dismantled before she was laid up at Horten.

World War I started one month after the FRAM's return to Norway. At the same time surveyors discovered that the 21 year old FRAM was suffering from rot and fungal decay. Thus, Amundsen had to revise his plans. The FRAM was not in good enough shape for a new polar expedition without a major restoration. The war led to economic speculation and inflation. Amundsen got a good deal of money through investments in shipping. He decided to use that money to order a new expedition vessel fit for operations in ice and contacted Christian Jensen, who was at that time one

World War I was in its third year with strict rationing in many countries. The first export license for food from the United States (License No. 1) was issued in August of 1917 and was a clear exception to a total export ban. All the food was to be exported to the North Pole as the paper shows.

The MAUD at Vollen, Asker.

of the most famous boat builders in Norway. Jensen prepared drawings for a polar ship based on Amundsen's request and with the FRAM as a model. Amundsen himself worked a lot with the drawings. They were based on the FRAM's hull shape, but she was made even stronger and more spherical so that the pack ice would not be able to get hold of the ship and crush her; instead pushing her out of the ice.

Christian Jensen had formal training in ship building, in addition to ship design courses and overseas studies in yacht construction. He was a pioneer in his field. Jensen was also a ship building contractor and in 1897 started his own shipyard at Vollen in Asker, close to Christiania, to build yachts for sailing pioneers. Yacht builder Johan Anker joined the company and the shipyard built successful yachts which year after year took home coveted trophies. Christian Jensen wanted to expand his business and started a ship yard at Vollen for the construction of larger ships of wood. Amundsen's new expedition ship for the North Pole became the new shipyard's hull no. 1.

The MAUD has arrived at Tromsø in Northern Norway, the boss has come onboard and the engine is running. Notice the long exhaust pipe along the aft mast.

The contract with the boat builder Christian Jensen was signed and the keel to hull no. 1 was laid down in July 1916. Jensen agreed to build the ship in one year. The cost estimate was 300,000 Norwegian kroner. But already at the time of signing it was clear that the price would have to be adjusted if the war and inflation continued. The cost of procurement of construction materials was a major challenge for Jensen and Amundsen. Prices on the specific type of lumber needed for the construction of the vessel increased dramatically when the seller learned that it was to be used in Amundsen's new expedition ship. Amundsen claimed in retrospect that a more careful, capable and conscientious work than Christian Jensen's construction of MAUD had not been performed in Norway.

While the yard was building the MAUD, Amundsen was struggling to equip the expedition. Much of the canned food from the FRAM in storage in Horten proved to be rotten and could have caused major medical issues for the expedition participants if the FRAM had gotten underway as planned after the South Pole expedition in 1911 to 1912. Via foreign channels Amundsen managed to get an export permit from the U.S. for 292 boxes of American quality canned food, groceries and other provisions. In addition, he needed large supplies of flour, coal and oil. Inventories were low in Norway due to the war. Scientific instruments for a variety of observations and surveys were obtained. The equipment from the FRAM that could still be used was brought from Horten.

Research in the Arctic would be the MAUD expedition's main task. This was the backup option if the voyage across the Arctic Ocean did not go as planned and the North Pole could not be reached. Amundsen understood that his key contribution lay in scientific research. His first expedition with the GJØA started the same way. Much of Roald Amundsen's success on his many polar missions was due to his immaculate planning and preparation regarding equipment, provisions, and his animals and his men. Participants with no scientific education received training and took part in a special navigation course at the local seamen's school. The objective was that if the ship went down and the leaders perished, those left should be sufficiently prepared to find their way home across the ice.

Amundsen, who had had more than enough money when the project started, found himself in financial difficulties. He struggled to fully fund the expedition. The interior and the rigging of the MAUD was a challenge. Amundsen got permission to help himself to fixtures, equipment and rigging from the FRAM. The boat builder Jensen and some of his workers went to Horten and brought back furniture and equipment. Many who saw the FRAM as a national historic treasure protested. They did not want the ship to be dismantled piece by piece. Protests were held and many shared their views in the newspapers. Others believed it was better to utilize the equipment instead of allowing it to be damaged onboard the FRAM that had just been left to rot. A nascent conservation movement was formed, thanks to the new

The lounge onboard the MAUD. Amundsen in the foreground and researcher Harald Sverdrup in the background.

successor to the FRAM and Amundsen's lack of capital needed to fund his MAUD expedition.

Jensen's new ship was launched on June 7th, 1917 after Roald Amundsen had christened the ship. The traditional champagne bottle was missing. Instead, Amundsen used a block of ice out of a bucket. As he hurled it at the ship's bow, he declared: "You are built for the ice and you will spend your best years in the ice and perform your work in the ice. With Her Majesty the Queen's permission, I baptize you MAUD." Maud was the Queen of Norway.

Harald Sverdrup was a promising young oceanographer who came along on the expedition.

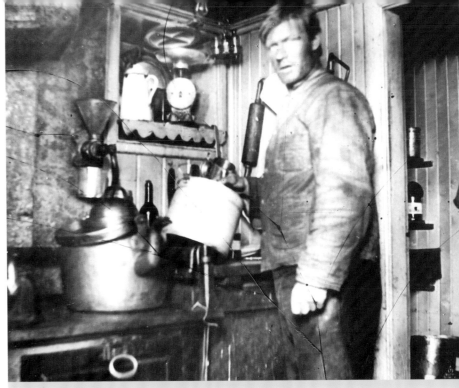

Sailor and Arctic veteran Knudsen in the galley. He vanished in the Arctic the following year.

Many had gathered to see the launching. Builder Christian Jensen and ship owner Amundsen were obviously at the center of attention when the MAUD slipped out into the Christiania Fjord.

The following period was busy with men working on the interior and the rigging of the MAUD. Last but not least, the machinery needed to be mounted. A Bolinder engine, the propeller shaft and the propeller were installed by the Aker Shipyard. As on the FRAM, the rudder and propeller were mounted so they could be hoisted up on deck if it was needed to protect them from the ice. Machinist Sundbeck from the FRAM expedition to the South

Pole signed on and participated in assembling the machinery and finishing the engine room. The ship was at the yard during the summer and fall. Several expedition members arrived. Helmer Hanssen, a veteran expedition member from both the GJØA and the FRAM expeditions, was appointed captain, and Oscar Wisting took over Hanssen's first officer position. Sail maker Rønne came onboard, charged with getting the sails ready. These expedition members, as well as the director of the Swedish Bolinder Motor Company, the pilot, Roald Amundsen and his brother Leon all participated in the trial run on November 8th, 1917. The voyage was successful. The MAUD managed eight knots with a light load.

The next day MAUD went to Horten to fill up on oil. At the same time her crew took off the rest of the bigger items they needed from the FRAM. It is no exaggeration to say that the FRAM was stripped bare. On the way back they paid a courtesy visit to Vollen before the MAUD was moored off the Akershus Castle where so many famous ships have been since the sail training ship CHRISTIANIA was moored there in the 1890s.

The MAUD measured 393 gross tons; 341 under deck and 292 net tons. The ship was given the official measurements with the Norwegian Veritas of 107.1 by 41 by 15.9 feet. She was rigged as a three mast schooner with a sail area of 6,458 square feet. The main engine of 240 horsepower meant that she was classified as a motor ship with sails, or an auxiliary sail ship. The fuel tanks took 120 tons of solar oil.

During the spring the rest of the expedition members, Tessem, Sverdrup, Tønnesen, Knudsen and Rønne, came onboard. They had stayed home over the winter. A great bustle started outside the Akershus Castle with the stowing of provisions to last the next five years. They were sorted and placed in the hold, divided into five equal parts by the estimated annual consumption, and organized so that everything was readily available. A lot was needed for the expedition. When the job was done there was little space left under the deck. The provisions from the U.S. were based on a document signed by the Bureau of Export License and marked for export to the North Pole by the Americans. Amundsen was careful to point out that if any of the provisions ended up in the wrong hands it would put the entire expedition in jeopardy because of strict rationing in Norway due to the war.

Large amounts of oil for the engine and coal for cooking and heating, wood and sheets for the roof, observatory and spare parts of all kinds were also taken onboard. The MAUD could be frozen in the ice for four to five years, maybe more, and replenishment of missing supplies would not be possible. Personal items like clothing and shoes as well as medicine and surgical equipment were also included. Last but not least came the most important items: The scientific equipment, instruments and protocols that would form the basis for the expedition's success. Researcher Harald Ulrik Sverdrup was the scientific leader responsible for the instrumentation. Ready to cast off, the MAUD drew 14.2 feet and was riding significantly higher in the water than the FRAM was when she was ready to set sail. This gave the MAUD a distinct advantage when sailing in waters of unknown depth.

The expedition's budget was exceeded. The construction of the MAUD ended up costing 650,000 Norwegian kroner, which was more than double the estimate from the previous year. Including all the costs of outfitting the expedition, the total ended up being almost one million Norwegian kroner, not including all the equipment, fixtures and rigging from the FRAM. Amundsen received 200,000 Norwegian kroner from the Norwegian government and 150,000 Norwegian kroner from private sponsors. The rest he had to contribute himself. But in 1917, money was easy to come by and many had funds to invest. Help from friends and others made it possible to settle all bills before they departed.

Roald Amundsen was world famous and many wanted to come onboard his fine new ship. It was a smart move to let the ship lie on the buoys during the busy loading period. They had very little time to get everything done, especially the loading and the preparations. Only when the MAUD came back to Vollen and most things were ready for departure did Amundsen allow people onboard. He himself gave an account of the visitors' impressions. The following is a compilation of some information from Roald Amundsen's own description of the MAUD:

The deck was over 40 feet at its widest point and gave the impression of being able to fit "the entire world." "What a deck!" was a common comment. The next surprise was the hold. There were enough provisions for five years. Amundsen noted that he thought the provisions would last for eight years. The hold contained a formidable stock of flour, sugar, tea, coffee, butter, spices and canned goods. These were food items regular people could not buy. Most had very little because of the strict rationing due to the war. All of the supplies onboard the MAUD had come from America and the export permit clearly noted that it was for export to the North Pole.

The visitor's surprise was even greater when they saw how beautiful the lounge was. On the wall hung a large image of the King and Queen of Norway and on the shelf below a silver mug, also a gift from the Royal Family. A stately phonograph, the expedition's main entertainment feature, was placed by the light well to the engine compartment. The other walls were decorated with photographs. The floors were covered with Linoleum and coconut mats. Around the lounge there were ten cabins for the crew with berth and desk, bedding, curtains and drapes. It was up to each man to furnish his own room to his liking. Amundsen's own cabin was furnished and equipped by friends and was presented as a surprise. Amundsen said that he felt like he was on his honeymoon (although Amundsen was never married).

The engine room was unique. Experts agreed that something similar had never been seen. Chief Engineer Sundbeck had put in a central control unit similar to that of modern ships. Nobody had used this before. From the control room he could monitor most of the technical features onboard by pressing the required buttons. In addition to the main engine there was a 15 horsepower Bolinder for winch and windlass and a smaller engine with a Delco generator as well as batteries for electric light. The MAUD expedition was without doubt the best and most well equipped expedition the world had ever seen. Norway has, a century later, yet to build a polar ship with the same qualities as the MAUD. During her stay at Vollen, lifeboats and lumber were taken onboard.

On the 23rd of June, 1917 at 4:00am, while party goers still celebrated Midsummer Eve, the MAUD weighed anchor and sailed out of the harbor which today bears the name Maudbukta in Vollen. The voyage went out the Christiania Fjord from Horten to Bergen, where oceanographer Helland-Hanssen had stored the instruments needed for the oceanographic research. In Tromsø Amundsen boarded and the voyage continued on to Vardø far east in Northern Norway, using the engine for propulsion due to unfavorable winds. War insurance required that the MAUD sailed in the Norwegian zone of neutrality along the coast. Germany had declared unrestricted submarine warfare. Even smaller vessels were in danger of being sunk.

The original plan was to sail via America to Alaska and start where the JEANNETTE was stuck in the ice, but because of the war it was not possible to take this route. The trip east from Vardø was seen as very dangerous. Fishing and hunting vessels had been sunk by the Germans in the same waters they had to transit. Those whose ships had been sunk were left to fend for themselves in open lifeboats in an extremely cold enviroment, often ridden with bad weather.

All onboard the MAUD had been issued thick fur underwear and outerwear. The lifeboats were prepared and flared, ready to be lowered at the first sign of trouble. The MAUD was met with gales and heavy seas in the Barents Sea. Hopefully that meant that the German submarines would be less of a threat. Instead, the men learned a lesson about the MAUD's seaworthiness. The hunch that the ship would not be very seaworthy in open seas was unfortunately confirmed. The MAUD rolled like mad; taking in seawater over both the starboard and port side. She danced around with the wind and the waves. The crew did their best to hang on, and could

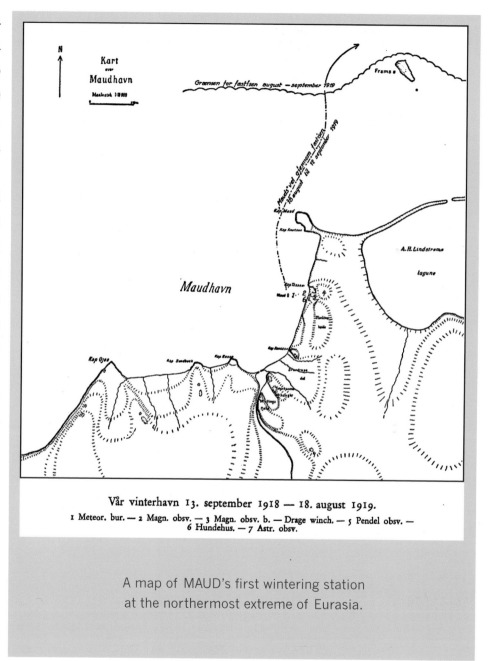

Vår vinterhavn 13. september 1918 — 18. august 1919.
1 Meteor. bur. — 2 Magn. obsv. — 3 Magn. obsv. b. — Drage winch. — 5 Pendel obsv. — 6 Hundehus. — 7 Astr. obsv.

A map of MAUD's first wintering station at the northermost extreme of Eurasia.

In Maudhavn at Cape Chelyuskin with lots of frozen bear meat in the rigging.

The crew shot over 30 bears. Getting this huge bear back to the ship was a five man job.

attest to the MAUD behaving terribly in bad weather. When they tried to sail close-hauled, they ended up going mostly sideways. But with the wind aft, she did quite well. The solution was to use the engine. This helped them make some progress, although the ship received sea damage. The crew had a tough time as all hands were frequently needed on deck.

The entrance to the Kara Sea posed a problem. It was early in the season and the ice was still quite thick. In this situation, the MAUD fulfilled their expectations. The ship worked well in the ice by putting it under her. She could turn on her axis, and came away quite easily if stuck in the ice. Now she behaved like the

polar vessel Amundsen had wanted and this was of course of great importance. She scaled an ice belt smoothly, despite a lot of old and dense ice. On the edge of the ice the sea was very heavy. As she broke free she rolled over so violently that large quantities of ice raged over the deck both to port and starboard. The men joked that they had enough ice for their drinks for the entire summer.

The ice conditions were challenging that year. Winds from the south that could thaw the ice were missing. The edge of the ice was fairly close to land. In an attempt to sail in an opening close to the shore, the MAUD hit some large rocks. The first solid grounding occurred at low tide. The anchor was deployed and it was

Arctic winter, 1920. The temperature is about minus 40 degrees. This was the last western expedition before the Soviet Union became a closed country. News about the Bolshevik Revolution never reached Amundsen in the wastelands of Arctic Siberia.

A sledge expedition, ready to go to Nischne-Kolymsk to secure the late Johan Koren's outstanding bird collection.

fairly easy to get her off on the next high tide. The crew became overly confident. The second time the MAUD hit bottom they did not worry too much. For this they were punished. The crew had to struggle like animals for several days before the MAUD broke free. It took until the 17th of August before the sea finally opened up. In Chaborowa the MAUD met the 10th member of the expedition crew. A young Russian named Gennady Olonkin was signed on as an engine operator and interpreter. He was an asset because he spoke Norwegian well and served as a Russian interpreter when needed. He also proved to be a talented negotiator.

Dikson, the northernmost harbor in Siberia, is located outside the mouth of the river Yenisei, which is open to ship traffic just a few months a year. There Amundsen had placed a repository of solar oil for the rest of the voyage. He also bought Samoyed dogs for exploratory dog sled trips. The dogs were the finest he had ever seen; chalk white with sharp ears. They held their heads high and kept their tails in a nice roll close to their backs.

On the 4th of September, the MAUD left Dikson and the last people they would see for a long time. The continued voyage was also hampered by ice and poor charts. Few expeditions had sailed in these waters before the MAUD. They eventually arrived at the archipelago Severnaya Zemlya, not marked on their charts. The

MAUD had great difficulty continuing her voyage through the ice. They were north of Siberia, and constantly met ice they had to scale. They feared being trapped and taken by the coastal current. Amundsen decided to take winter quarters in a cove at Cape Chelyuskin, the northernmost point on the Eurasian continent.

The MAUD was moored in the ice on the 13th of September, 1918 and the vessel stayed there until August of 1919 before she broke free. During the ship's first year in the ice the expedition's 10 members carried out valuable scientific observation work in a variety of fields. In addition, several parties went out on a number of long sleigh rides and mapped unknown territories and islands beyond. They built solid beacons of rocks at strategic locations with messages inside and named many sites. Few, if any, of these names are in use today. What then was perceived as a big piece of land and called Tsar Nicholas II's land was later surveyed. The area turned out to consist of several larger and smaller islands. The larger were soon renamed in good Soviet tradition: Bolshevik, October Revolution, Komsomolets and Pioneer; geographical names reflecting a country's history. Foreign explorers were passed over in silence in this regard.

Their winter quarter at Maudhavn was a convenient location because they were not able to continue on that year. They had hoped to get as far east as they could in order to drift across the Arctic Ocean and thus save a year. Difficult weather and ice conditions stopped their plans. The crew did well through a very cold polar winter with temperatures down to minus 40 degrees

Roald Amundsen signed this portrait at Chelyuskin, February 10th, 1919. The notes are praising the day when the sun returns. In translation: *Welcome to you, you blessed day. Of night we have had enough.*

Farenheit. Amundsen, however, was unfortunate. He fell down from the railing and landed on the ice, ending up with complicated fractures of the shoulder as a result. Later he suffered carbon dioxide poisoning and thereafter was attacked by a female polar bear with cubs, but managed to get back onboard with a nasty bite in the leg. Polar bears were otherwise popular. The crew often hunted bears and the collection of polar bear skins became formidable. The meat ended up in the rig. Polar bear meat was considered delicious food among both people and dogs.

Before the MAUD left Maudhavn, it was decided that two of the participants would return to Norway with all the valuable specimens and data the MAUD expedition had collected, 50

Sled riders from MAUD arrive at a nomad camp in Eastern Siberia.

pounds total, rather than bringing this with them out into the Arctic Ocean. Tessem and Knudsen would wait in a cabin on land until the ice had settled in September, and then continue to Dikson via the depots that had been left by Otto Sverdrup's search party with the ECLIPSE during 1914 and 1915, in which Knudsen participated. Amundsen's problem was that he had to give up reaching the North Pole by dogsled. The remaining crew members were needed for safe passage with the MAUD across the Arctic Ocean. After his shoulder injury Amundsen understood that the goal was unattainable unless the ice with the MAUD drifted in the right direction and came close to the Pole.

But Roald Amundsen was not a man who gave up reaching the goal he had set for himself. During his lecture tours in America, he got acquainted with flying, the latest technical achievement of the times. He immediately saw that this could make polar research easier in the future and explored this opportunity. He learned to fly. On the 11th of June, 1914, flying license no. 1 was printed in Norway. Polar explorer Roald Amundsen became Norway's first certified pilot, and he went on to introduce aircraft to the Arctic.

Leaving Maudhavn became a long and difficult endeavor. The men struggled for weeks. While the MAUD was a good icebreaker, taking on very thick old ice, that was too much for her. The new ice was starting to settle before they finally got out into the open sea. Tessem and Knudsen kept coming back onboard to help out during these weeks. They waved goodbye for the last time two days before the ship broke free on September 15th, 1919. This

Amundsen feeds the polar bear cub Marie, which he tried to tame so she could pull a sledge. The experiment did not turn out well, and the bear was put to sleep. The MAUD can be seen in the background to the right.

Sledges being prepared for yet another trip.

was the last time these two crew members were seen alive. What happened to Tessem and Knudsen was long one of the Arctic Ocean's unsolved mysteries. The men were experienced polar explorers and the trip to Dikson with sledge and five dogs was not particularly challenging. Rescue expeditions were sent out. Several years later they found the remains of a man a few miles from Dikson's weather station. His pocket watch had a long inscription including the name Peter L. Tessem, and inside a ring *Din Pauline* (Your Pauline) had been engraved. It belonged to Tessem. Other items were found, among them waterproof packages addressed

to Carnegie, Washington, D.C. and Leon Amundsen, Christiania. Knudsen was never found. He probably drowned.

The MAUD continued her dangerous voyage in the area east of Taymyr. The charts did not match the terrain, and the water was shallow in some places with only a few feet under her keel. But there was some open water outside the mouth of the river Lena. The MAUD headed for the New Siberian Islands. There she reached open waters. The land falls off towards the southeast and the MAUD continued, but the winter was coming and new ice grew. It was clear that the expedition would not get any further that year.

On the 25th of September they met the natives for the first time since leaving Dikson over a year earlier. Their new winter camp was at the island of Ayon. If glacier ice broke off and took them out to sea and in a northerly direction, Amundsen believed that the ice in the Arctic Ocean would lead them over the North Pole. This did not happen. The MAUD froze in and was stuck. The indigenous Chukchi were technologically primitive, but were very knowledgeable in regard to dog sledding. They had a large team of dogs harnessed as is done today and sat in the sled with a lot of warm clothes. Small shouts helped the lead dog find the way. They iced the skis to make the sledge slide better and could do many more miles than anybody else. Amundsen was highly impressed with their beautiful dogs and their musher technique.

During the winter more mushers arrived with large fish, reindeer, new dogs and several large and flawless mammoth teeth; seven feet long and weighing 90 pounds. They wanted to trade goods. Sverdrup traveled with the natives to live with them and learn these nomads' survival techniques. Amundsen sent an expedition with Captain Hanssen as leader to Nome, Alaska with mail and telegrams, a trip that took approximately five months. Wisting and Tønnesen joined him. The last four, Amundsen, Sundbeck, Rønne and Olonkin, remained onboard the MAUD to take care of the ship and make observations. Natives arrived and settled close by. They helped move wood from a bay full of driftwood. The wood was used for heating. The coal they had brought along remained untouched. Incoming messages indicated troubled times. The supply ships for trading posts in the East Siberian Sea did not arrive. Ice conditions were to blame. People were starving, and flour and tea were highly regarded barter items. Nobody wanted Russian rubles. There were rumors about Bolsheviks killing and also plundering the fur storage at the trading posts.

A trader reported that the war ended in November the year before with the total defeat of Germany. Peace was celebrated with a party and flag hoisting onboard the MAUD on December 5th, 1919. News of the murder of the Tsar family in 1918 had

Sail maker Rønne has braided Turk's head knots on two solid mammoth teeth. Remains of mammoths were seen sticking out of the permafrost in Siberia.

not yet reached Siberia. With only four expedition members left, Amundsen himself became the cook. On expeditions, especially in the Arctic, food is important. He noted that the American rations were very durable. Dried and canned fruits from California were very much appreciated, and fish balls from Trondhjem Canning were the finest he had eaten.

The MAUD became a popular gathering place for people in the area. They came and went throughout the winter. Many settled. The welcoming atmosphere onboard the MAUD tempted many to stay. An expedition from the east brought a letter from Hanssen, telling about poor weather and that Tønnesen had disappeared twice, the last time for three days. He suffered from frostbite and was sent with a Russian to get a ride south for the summer. Amundsen himself had medical problems. He had chest pains and tried to take it easy. In May Sverdrup returned with lots of scientific material, and a month later Hanssen and Wisting came back. Captain Hanssen was exhausted. He had traveled 1,750 miles under very difficult conditions and had suffered a lot. It proved impossible to get across the Bering Strait to Nome.

In June of 1920, before the ice broke up, the men were informed that Amundsen had decided to sail to Nome and that those who wanted to could leave. Hanssen, who had sailed with Amundsen since the GJØA in 1904, stated that he wanted to go home. Amundsen also expressed disappointment that the expedition had not been more successful in regards to the primary goal of drifting with the MAUD to the North Pole.

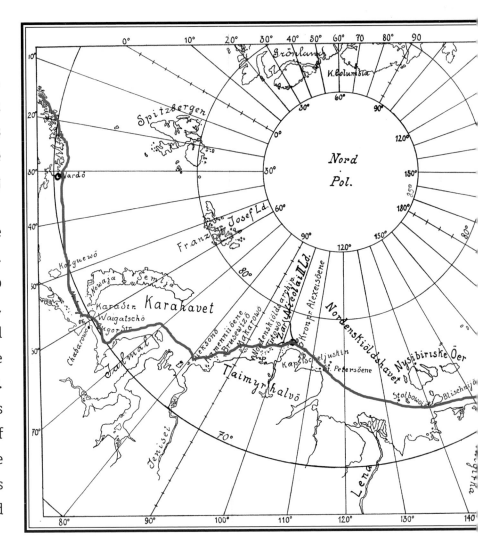

The MAUD came loose in July and fought her way eastward. During a storm, they found shelter in a bay where there were four schooners from Nome at anchor. A fifth was blown ashore. All were manned by Scandinavians. From them they received accurate charts. They had arrived at Sledge Island, not far from Nome, Alaska. With modesty Amundsen noted that after having sailed the Northeast Passage now, as well as the Northwest Passage in

ORDOSTPASSASJEN

KART OVER

MAUDS FERD 1918—1920

A map of the MAUD's first journey from Vardø, Norway to Nome in the years 1918 to 1920.

1906, he was the first person who had completed sailing around the Arctic. The Norwegian flag was first around the Arctic Ocean! A tug with a Norwegian captain arrived and Amundsen decided to hitchhike with him the last stretch to arrive anonymously and send telegrams without being disturbed. Hanssen followed later with the MAUD.

Sundbeck and Rønne followed Hanssen and signed off at Nome to their leader's disappointment. The crew onboard the MAUD replenished what they needed, and set out again to seek the ice without a machinist and with too small a crew under Captain Wisting's command. Amundsen, Sverdrup and the Russian Olonkin came with. This voyage was almost an intermezzo and indicates something about the leader's stubbornness. It is difficult to understand why he left on this mission, trying to sail to the North Pole with only four persons, even

if he had basic supplies for many more. For Harald Sverdrup and the scientific part of the MAUD's expedition, however, this gave an opportunity to continue valuable scientific research. It seems like Amundsen, on his earlier expeditions, had a strained relationship with scholars. Earlier he had not brought any, not even a medical doctor on the South Pole expedition. Amundsen and the scientists finally came to terms. This, however, did not come about without friction. During the first winter of the MAUD expedition, Amundsen and Sverdrup had serious disagreements.

The MAUD back in Nome in 1922, well loaded and ready to continue on her Arctic explorations. Never has a ship been better built and equipped to challenge the brutal forces of the pack ice.

The MAUD in dock in Seattle in 1921. Amundsen is inspecting the ship's propeller.

On the bridge of the MAUD. The steering wheel in the picture has 12 pegs. It has not surfaced as of yet. The FRAM today has an eight-peg wheel.

Open water in between the ice is typical for the short Arctic summer.

Sverdrup corrected Amundsen when he was obviously mistaken, whereupon Amundsen went into a fit, accusing Sverdrup of always trying to criticize him. He was so upset that he refused to have anything to do with Sverdrup. The scientist understood that this could not continue for years, and reached out to Amundsen. They were able to settle their differences. After that incident, Amundsen accepted and respected scientists more so than before.

The polar explorer does not even include the MAUD's experiences from the winter of 1920 to 1921 in his book *Roald Amundsens opdagelsesreiser*.

The MAUD got stuck in the ice near Cape Serdtse-Kamen, a little east of the Bering Strait. Interaction with the native East Siberians was an important activity during this winter. In addition, Sverdrup continued all his observations and measurements of ocean currents, which he had worked on since the start of the MAUD expedition. The material was later incorporated into extensive reports. Sverdrup also wrote about the indigenous people's way of life; their customs and beliefs. A section on spouse swapping is often referred to: When two Chukchi men are good friends they swap women. They often visit each other so that each man has two women, and the women have two men. Triple alliances occur when none of them are siblings.

In the summer of 1920 the MAUD escaped the ice. The ship had to go to Seattle for repairs. The MAUD's propeller and shaft had been damaged. They returned to Nome, where Amundsen left the ship. Captain Wisting managed the feat of sailing the MAUD all the way from Nome to Seattle with one Norwegian, one Russian and six native boys. In Seattle the MAUD was docked and repaired. Sverdrup and Wisting were in the U.S. to prepare for a new expedition. Wisting oversaw repairs and the replenishment of equipment. The use of shipboard radio had become fairly common. The MAUD now had radio contact with the outside world. The ship was the first vessel in the pack ice that had a radio station. Sverdrup went to the Carnegie Institution and the Smithsonian to analyze his collected data and get new instruments.

Aviation pioneer Amundsen turned 50 years old in 1922. He had had his own aircraft since 1914 and was determined to introduce airplanes for polar mapping. The war stopped this endeavor and he built the MAUD. In 1921, he was ready to equip the MAUD with an airplane. Roald Amundsen understood better than all that if the vast areas north of the continents should be explored and new islands discovered, this had to be done from the air.

The area had never been explored and could contain islands and areas of land. The stay in Maudhavn showed tall mountains to the north, at that time called Tsar Nicholas II Land. It was not until 1931, three years after Amundsen's death, that the airship GRAF ZEPPELIN flew over the Severnaya Zemlya and reported seeing at least two major and several smaller islands. American researchers at the time believed there was a big land mass in the Arctic Ocean, while Sverdrup's oceanographic measurements onboard the MAUD

MAUD in open sea, heavy laden with crates on deck containing two airplanes for survey in the Arctic.

led him to the conclusion that there must be deep waters in the North Pole Basin.

While the MAUD was being equipped, Amundsen obtained two additional aircraft pilots and mustered additional crew. Around the same time a Junkers monoplane had set a world record with 27 hours in the air. This was the type of plane he needed to explore the Arctic. It could be brought onboard the MAUD and taken to Point Barrow, and from there flown over the North Pole, landing at Spitsbergen. Amundsen planned to fly his Junkers plane from New York to Seattle, but the engine stopped over Pennsylvania and the plane was totally destroyed during the emergency landing. A new plane was obtained and sent by train to Seattle. It arrived in boxes when the MAUD was ready to leave. At the same time the Curtiss airplane factory had lent the expedition a smaller airplane for reconnaissance. Hence, they now had two aircraft.

On the 3rd of July, 1922 the MAUD left Seattle on her third voyage with a full crew and two aircraft onboard. The ship was adorned with flags, and the dock and surrounding streets were packed with people who wanted to see them off. The fact that new technology would be used to explore the last unknown areas in the northern hemisphere became big news. The plan was to bring the larger Junkers aircraft to Point Barrow to then fly to

Sverdrup collected a large number of artifacts from the indigenous people of East Siberia.

Sverdrup's tidal gauge, one of the many important instruments the expedition had. It was read many times a day and the results recorded.

The first flight ever to take off from drifting ice was done in this airplane; a Curtiss Oriole painted in Norwegian colors.

Spitsbergen. Unfortunately, nothing went according to the plan. The ice stopped the MAUD. The pilots Omdal and Amundsen and two assistants went ashore at Wainwright, Alaska while the MAUD started her polar drift. Amundsen's party had to spend the winter there. In May 1923, the W34 Junkers was made ready for flight and they undertook a test flight. But the airframe broke during landing and they crashed. It was not possible to repair the airplane so it was abandoned.

The party aboard the MAUD had more luck with the small double-decker. Pilot Odd Dahl and observer and navigator Oscar Wisting were able to fly several times in 1923, gaining valuable experience in taking off from, flying over, and landing on ice. The first trip lasted for 45 minutes. It revealed that landing in white landscapes with little contrast is difficult. Blocks of ice and snow drifts are invisible from the air. The compass was useless. A week later they flew again. They were so far out that they barely saw the MAUD, and returned after an hour.

Later they had to build a new runway when there was water on the ice. The takeoff was filmed; the plane lifted too early and fell into a puddle of water. The pilot turned off the engine. The plane skidded across a pressure ridge and stopped. The lower wing and the undercarriage were damaged but were repaired. Two weeks later they tried a new takeoff. The start went well, but suddenly the engine malfunctioned and the plane crashed into a pressure ridge. The propeller broke and the plane was so damaged that it could not be repaired.

These where the first two planes that flew in the Arctic. The takeoff from the MAUD was the first from drifting ice, and also the first flight where a ship in the ice was used as a base. They gained valuable experiences which were of great value to later flights. The drifting ice environment was something completely new to pilots. A Curtiss Oriole plane with skis was considered useless on the ice.

The MAUD's continued drift started out in a promising manner. The ship held a course well north of the New Siberian Islands. But developments during 1923 showed that this did not turn out to be the way to the North Pole. The MAUD continued running back and forth and in circles. The main direction was westward, but closer to Siberia than the JEANNETTE. Towards the end of the year Captain Wisting found it most likely that they would use four to six years and that the MAUD would be following a similar route that the FRAM had taken.

The expedition also had sad experiences. In May of 1923 engineer Syvertsen died of meningitis and was buried at sea. The flights ended in failure. Only two bears were shot that year. For many months they did not have any of their radio calls answered. This was the first time someone tried to maintain radio contact from the Arctic ice. Communication with the outside world was not to be taken for granted even if the transmitter and the receiver were working properly.

The groundbreaking scientific work led by Sverdrup with Malmgren and Dahl as new assistants continued unabated, however. Sverdrup focused on basic research. The analysis of the data from

THE ONLY SEATTLE PAPER OWNED AND OPERATED BY SEATTLE MEN

The Seattle Daily Times

ASSOCIATED PRESS. UNITED PRESS. NEW YORK TIMES-CHICAGO TRIBUNE SERVICE. PHILADELPHIA PUBLIC LEDGER SERVICE.

PRICE, TEN CENTS

SEATTLE, WASHINGTON, SUNDAY MORNING, JUNE 4, 1922.

EIGHT PARTS—90 PAGES.

FINAL EDITION

Times Whistle Signals | Call Main-o 300

Three Long Blasts—Emergency signal will indicate the occurrence of a sensational news event.

For information desired.

ALL THE NEWS THA'S FIT TO PRINT

Amundsen Polar Expedition Heads for Arctic
Grim Icepack Waits to Embrace Norse Ship

U.S. military forces were impressed with the Arctic aviation pioneer.

The Seattle piers were packed with people when the MAUD left.

Capt. Roald Amundsen.

—Color cartoon by Roth.

Army, Navy And Marines Bid Godspeed

Seattle Says Good-bye to Hardy Explorers Who Will Attempt to Drift Across Great Boreal Basin.

CHEERED by thousands while the scepticious June sun cast golden radiance over the whole thrilling scene, the Amundsen Polar expedition, beginning her long journey back to the Arctic Ocean, sailed away yesterday...

(Continued on Page Seven.)

THE SEATTLE DAILY TIMES, SUNDAY MORNING, JUNE 4, 1922.   7

IN QUEST OF GREAT UNKNOWN

COPIES OF THE SEATTLE DAILY TIMES COVERING LAST YEAR, FOR MEN ISOLATED IN THE ARCTIC.

TRUCK-LOAD OF WHITE COLLIES

"JOLLY" AND MATE HANSEN

AMUNDSEN ALLOWS CROWD TO FOLLOW HIS AUTO INTO THE DOCK

Scenes at Departure of Maud.

Amundsen Expedition Sets Sail for North

Seattle Says Good-Bye to Hardy Norsemen Who Will Attempt to Drift Across Vast Arctic Basin.

Crew of Maud Carries Its Own Garden Into Great Unknown

Pilot Roald Amundsen made headlines in the summer of 1922.

The Seattle Daily Times

ANOTHER SPLENDID STORY
By WILLIAM ALLEN WHITE
Will Appear in
NEXT SUNDAY'S TIMES

SCHOONER MAUD MADE READY FOR HER PERILOUS TRIP INTO ICEPACK

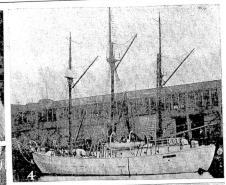

FINAL PREPARATIONS MADE FOR AMUNDSEN NORTH POLE EXPEDITION—Yesterday, with the thermometer at 59 degrees, the crew of the Schooner Maud completed preparations in Seattle harbor for the North Polar expedition with hundreds of interested spectators watching. 1—Capt. Roald Amundsen on the upper deck of the Maud, superintending the loading of the two airplanes to be used for the first time in the Arctic regions. 2—H. H. Hammer, president of the Universal Shipping & Trading Company and business manager for Captain Amundsen in the United States. 3—"Bollie," the fierce Eskimo husky dog, who guards the Maud. 4—The schooner, showing the busy members of the crew aboard. 5—Capt. Oscar Wisting, who stood alongside of Captain Amundsen on the South Pole and is the only member of the South Polar expedition besides Captain Amundsen who will make the North Pole voyage. 6—O. Hanson, the Maud's strong man, who carries a ship master's license but who, like the other captains aboard, is doing the work of a sailor. 7—Dr. H. U. Sverdrup, one of the most famous scientists in Norway, who has charge of the scientific work of the expedition. 8—Dr. F. Malmgren, another scientist. 9—Part of the crowd yesterday watching the loading of the big airplanes on board the Maud. 10—In this photograph are shown the three Eskimos who are rejoicing at the prospects of their return home. They are, from left to right, Yorak, Rota and Attatua. They were picked up by Captain Amundsen during his last voyage to the North. They will not form a part of the regular crew when the Maud starts drifting to the Polar regions.

People in Seattle were full of expectation upon
Amundsen's departure for the North Pole.

...ud in the Harbor of Seattle, Just Before the Start of the Five-... Everything Goes as Planned, Will Carry the Little Ship Over... the North Pole

the three MAUD expeditions represents some of the finest Arctic research in several regards. Sverdrup launched many theories that later were confirmed. He was one of the world's leading marine scientists, and later became the director of Scripps Oceanography Institute in La Jolla for many years.

Christmas Eve 1922 in the pack ice, the fifth Christmas onboard the MAUD. From left: Olonkin, Dahl with Sverdrup in front, Malmgren, Wisting and Kakot standing. (Hansen and Syvertsen are missing from this image).

Radio operator Olonkin finally got connected with the outside world in December. A number of telegrams went both ways and Christmas was celebrated in the traditional Norwegian way with Christmas decor and an exquisite dinner. Christmas gifts were exchanged, and Christmas telegrams read. Greetings came from many in Norway and America. The following arrived from the President of the United States:

CAPTAIN SS MAUD STOP THE COMPLIMENTS OF THE CHRISTMAS SEASON FROM THE AMERICAN PEOPLE TO THE OFFICERS AND CREW OF THE MAUD WITH SINCERE HOPE FOR A SUCCESSFUL EXPEDITION STOP CALVIN COOLIDGE STOP

The year 1924 started quietly. Captain Wisting realized that the course that the ice was drifting would not lead them towards the Pole. Next year they would probably be near the place where the FRAM started from. Back in Norway Amundsen also realized this. That the MAUD for long periods of time was without radio contact, and that the ship's airplanes had been wrecked, must have contributed to the decision to call off the expedition. What is surprising is that Amundsen chose to do this at Nome. The return trip back to Norway would probably have required another winter as the MAUD had to pass Cape Chelyuskin. But the route west to the open water in the Kara Sea and Dikson was better known and no further than Alaska. The current brought the ship westward anyway. Going east also required a winter like the first time.

We know that Amundsen was working with new and very different plans. He was determined, even obsessed with reaching the North Pole and finding land if it was there. It is reasonable to assume that he doubted that Peary had been to the Pole. Peary lacked accurate instruments and solid evidence, and had made the return trip far too quickly.

All the men aboard the MAUD were sad to receive a telegram on the 17th of February asking them to return to Nome if possible. Sverdrup took it very hard and wrote this in his journal. For himself, and especially for Captain Wisting, who had been with Amundsen since his voyage to the South Pole, to turn back was difficult to accept. The expedition had a great ship, the best leader, and everything they needed for further passage and collection of research materials. Regardless, they moved slowly homeward. Sverdrup wanted to continue the oceanographic measurements and his magnetic and meteorological observations. No additional expenses would be incurred if they continued.

Amundsen was supportive of, but not well informed about or educated in, scientific research. He realized that investment in research would be needed to finance the MAUD. But when the ship had no hope of coming close to the Pole, aircraft had to be used. He had also connected with new sponsors who invested in Amundsen as a discoverer, not as a researcher. Money for new adventures and media coverage existed, but not for the MAUD.

Amazingly enough Wisting and his crew managed to pry the MAUD loose from the ice. But before this happened the ship experienced several episodes of encroaching pack ice. Large ice floes were frozen vertically against the ship and led to the MAUD not being lifted as

she was designed to be. On one occasion the pressure of the ice became very dangerous, but thankfully it eventually decreased and the MAUD was able to continue.

The ice opened up and the search for open water began. On August 9th she came loose from the ice. Thus began the struggle to find open water to the west of the New Siberian Islands. They headed south before the MAUD could turn east. They only managed to

Harald Ulrik Sverdrup was in charge of the scientific part of the MAUD expeditions. He stayed onboard throughout MAUD's research voyages.

get about half way to the Bering Strait before they had to seek a new winter harbor at a location that Amundsen later decided to name Firsøyleøya (Four Column Island) due to this island's granite pillars. The expedition spent the winter in a similar manner as before. Natives came to visit. Some wanted to barter food and other supplies. The researchers continued their observations. The rest of the crew resorted to model building, listening to music, viewing films and reading books over and again through the dark and long polar night. A very nice model of the MAUD was built that winter. It is now displayed at the Fram Museum in Oslo.

In the middle of July 1925 the MAUD came loose and left her

winter quarters, only to get stuck again several times. In August the situation became better. The ship reached the Bering Strait and the open sea. On August 22nd, 1925 the MAUD arrived at Nome. Much needed to be arranged and cleared. Amundsen was not able to pay his debt. American creditors made claims. They had no sentimental feelings for this noble ship or Roald Amundsen. The MAUD was sent to Seattle, arriving there on the 5th of October without the slightest form of festivity. This was in stark contrast to the departure from Seattle. Scientific achievements of great importance do not always make the front page of the newspapers.

The MAUD was eight years old when she was taken as collateral for 8,784 U.S. dollars. Amundsen lacked money and the MAUD was

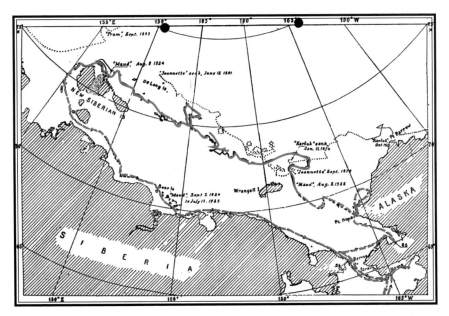

A map of the MAUD expedition from 1922 to 1925 trying to reach the North Pole through an ice drift.

sold at an auction in Seattle in December 1925. No Norwegians showed any interest in the ship. The research vessel specifically built for Arctic exploration was purchased by the trading company Hudson's Bay Company for 40,000 U.S. dollars. They intended to use the ship for transport to the company's stations in Canada's Arctic. The ship was renamed the BAYMAUD and towed to Vancouver in February of 1926. The keel and the rudder base were repaired and the engine overhauled. The trial trip took place on May 25th, 1926 after which the vessel was equipped with supplies for trading posts along the north coast of Canada. The cargo consisted of building materials, lamp oil, canned food, alcohol, coffee, tea and tobacco. A month later the ship was ready to leave and left Vancouver under Captain Foellmer. The BAYMAUD visited the Herschel and Baillie stations and continued on to deliver supplies to several places in Coronation Gulf. From there the ship continued to Victoria Island with material needed to build a new Hudson's Bay Company station. Materials were taken on land and housing construction began. The captain did not like the exposed mooring location and continued to Bernard Harbor for the winter.

In late July of 1927 BAYMAUD broke out of the ice and continued west to the River Kent to disassemble the Hudson's Bay Company outpost there. The material was taken onboard and they continued the journey to Cambridge Bay, a bay on the south side of Victoria Island in Arctic Canada, where a new trading post was being established to serve the Inuit people. Houses were erected on the site. The harbor was good and the Hudson's Bay Company decided that the BAYMAUD would be left there when she proved too big and deep for the shallow waters at some stations. Smaller and lighter ships were better suited. Captain Foellmer made sure the ship was safely moored before he disembarked on the 9th of August, 1927. He travelled south onboard a smaller Hudson's Bay Company ship.

The BAYMAUD was in the following years used as an onsite workshop, warehouse and radio station. The MAUD's radio was now charged with being a weather station in Arctic Canada. Twice a day the weather forecast from Cambridge Bay was sent from BAYMAUD. This was the first regular winter weather reports from the Northwest Passage.

The Canadian Mounted Police's surveillance ship ST. ROCH, the design of which was inspired by the MAUD, visited the BAYMAUD for the first time in 1928 when the ship was new. The mate was Henry Larsen from the Norwegian archipelago of Valer. He was from the same part of the county as Roald Amundsen. Larsen stated that it was sad to see Amundsen's great ship lying there as a floating radio station. Larsen became the captain of the ST. ROCHE and mastered the ship for many years. He followed in Amundsen's footsteps and became the first to take a ship through the Northwest Passage from west to east, and later returned westwards, following the path of the first ship to do this, Amundsen's GJØA. The ST. ROCHE

Hudson's Bay Company's coat of arms. The company did not take good care of the MAUD.

is now a museum ship in Vancouver similar to the FRAM in Oslo.

Hudson's Bay Trading Company had no use for the BAYMAUD anymore and the beautiful, rock solid ship stayed put. In 1930 there was a leak along the propeller shaft that became so large that it was dangerous. The company asked that she be put up on land for continued use as a radio station and warehouse. "It has no value to us," the company noted. The BAYMAUD finally sank in 1931.

Things of value that could be salvaged were taken off during 1931 and 1932. The great deck house became a house on land. In 1935 the masts and deck disappeared; all that was left was the hull and some deck equipment. The vandalizing continued; what could be used as firewood or of other value vanished. The aft part was blown up to get to the FRAM's old fuel tanks. The ice later pulled the wreck out and onto its side.

The MAUD wreck lay like this for years. Preservationists in Norway were interested in saving the MAUD and taking her remains to Norway for reconstruction. The 1990s was the great decade of nostalgia around the MAUD. People inspected the wreckage. There was a debate between those who wanted, and those who did not want, to save the wreck. There were discussions in the newspapers. At the same time the maritime museum in Vancouver sent an expedition to document the wreck of the BAYMAUD. James

Delgado of The Vancouver Museum released a report. Newspaper commentaries and other efforts in Norway went nowhere. The pitiful remains of Roald Amundsen's great ship are still in Cambridge Bay. There is now a renewed effort to get her home.

The world has never quite grasped that the MAUD accomplished at least as much as the legendary FRAM. During her three expeditions, ground breaking work was conducted in many areas and there were many first records that will stand forever. Long after the MAUD ceased to sail, scientists continued to analyze the data acquired onboard the MAUD. One example is their research which during World War II prevented countless soldiers from losing their lives during amphibious landings. This knowledge began with Harald Sverdrup's research onboard the MAUD.

The BAYMAUD sank in Canada's Arctic in 1931, with Roald Amundsen's old MAUD pennant atop of the main mast.

The MAUD's windlass was still in place onboard the wreck of the BAYMAUD in 1996.

The wreck of the MAUD, near Cambridge Bay, Victoria Island. There are plans underway for transporting her back to Vollen where she was built.

Roald Amundsen's dream was to stand on the North Pole. The MAUD was a ship far more famous for her scientific contributions than as a base for adventurers. Until our time the MAUD suffered from the explorer syndrome. Amundsen himself likely contributed to this. Despite his accomplishment on being the first to sail around the world north of all continents and all his many other first records, he felt that he failed in his primary goal with the MAUD: To reach the North Pole through the use of a ship, thus fulfilling Fridtjof Nansen's old dream. Amundsen never did experience standing on the North Pole, his greatest dream since boyhood.

The polar ship MAUD had her best years in the Northeast Passage.

Oddly enough, she ended her days in the Northwest Passage, where the ship was not originally intended to play any role whatsoever. The finest ship built for Arctic research did not only spend her best years in the ice, as Amundsen announced during the ship's launching ceremony. She stayed in the ice until the end of her days. The remains of this magnificent ship still rest in shallow waters in Cambridge Bay, frozen in ice much of the year as she was during her first seasons in the Arctic. Her best years were spent under the Norwegian flag exploring the Arctic. During all her time under the British and Canadian flag the ship did not function as the research and expedition vessel she was meant to be.

BIBLIOGRAPHY, OTHER SOURCES, ILLUSTRATION CREDITS

BOOKS, ARTICLES, NEWSPAPER CLIPPINGS

Albion, R.G.: *Square Riggers on Schedule* (Princeton, 1938)

Allan. J. W.: Gjoa's Fantastic Voyage, *American Boating,* October Issue
  (Centerville, 1971)

Amundsen, R.: *Nordvestpassagen, beretningen om Gjøa-ekspedisjonen*
  (Kristiania, 1903-07)

Amundsen, R.: *Oppdagelsesreiser Nordvestpassasjen,* Bind 1 (Oslo, 1928)

Amundsen, R.: *Roald Amundsens oppdagelsesreiser,* Bind 3 og 4 (Oslo, 1942)

Anderson, J.: *The Last Survivors in Sail* (London 1933, rev. 1948)

Anderson, R.: *White Star* (Prescott, 1964)

Anuta, M. J.: *Ships of Our Ancestors* (Baltimore, 1993)

Arnesen, O: *Fram. Hele Norges skute* (Oslo, 1942)

Baker, W. A.: The Gjoa, *American Neptune,* Vol. 12, No. 1 (Salem, 1952)

Barr, W.: The Last Journey of Peter and Paul Knutsen Tessem 1919,
  Arctic Vol. 36, No. 4

Bass, G. F.: *A History of Seafaring, Based on Underwater Archaeology* (New York, 1972)

Bass, G. F.: *Archaeology Under Water* (New York & London 1966)

Blichfeldt, P. C.: Polarskuta Maud, *Asker Museum* (Asker, 2002)

Bockstoce, J. R.: *Whales, Ice and Men* (Seattle, 1986)

Bonsor, N. R. P.: *North Atlantic Seaway,* Vol. 2 (Jersey, Channel Island, 1978)

Bureau of Architecture, Dept. of Public Works, City of San Francisco: Specifications
for Repairs and Preservation, ship Gjoa (San Francisco, 1939; 1948; 1961)

Boulter, G. E.: First to Sail the Northwest Passage, *Ships and the Sea,*
  Vol. 7. No. 1 (1957)

Brown, T. P.: Amundsen and the Gjøa, *The Time Card* (1950)

Chapelle, H. I.: *The Search for Speed under Sail 1700-1855* (New York, 1967)
  pp. 360, 371, 874

Chase, M. E.: *Donald McKay and the Clipper Ships* (Boston 1959) pp. 33, apx.

Clark, A. H.: *Epitome of Famous American Clipper Ships* (New York, 1910) p 270

Colton, J. F.: *Last of the Square Rigged Ships* (New York, 1937)

Craig, G.: *Boy Aloft* (Hampshire, 1971)

Cutler, C. C.: *Five Hundred Sailing Records of American Built Ships* (Mystic, 1952)

Cutler, C. C.: *Greyhounds of the Sea* (New York, 1930)

Cutler, C. C.: *Queens of the Western Oceans* (Annapolis, 1961) pp. 323, 332, 372, 563

Daily Commercial News: April 17, 1930; mai 10, 1939; mai 19, 1939; mai 16, 1949.

Daniel, K.: *Otto Sverdrups liv* (Oslo, 1934)

Delgado, J. P.: *Made for the Ice* (Vancouver, 1997)

Eilertsen, A.: The End of an Era in Polar Expedition, *The Norseman* (Oslo, 1989)

Enger, R.: An Account of the Gjoa, *San Francisco Life* 15: 7-10, May
  (San Francisco, 1947)

Engvig, O. T.: Anniversary Booklet, *Christian Radich 1937-1987* (Oslo, 1987)

Engvig, O. T.: *Gamle Dampen* (Trondheim, 2008)

Engvig, O. T.: Lancing, A Ship for the Record, *Sea History No. 124* (Peekskill, 2008)

Engvig, O. T.: *Skoleskipene* (Oslo, 1981)

Engvig, O. T.: *Shipping and Culture* (San Francisco, 1997)

Fairburn, W. A.: *Merchant Sail 1-6* (Lovell Maine, 1945-1955)
  pp. 1125, 1529, 1562, 1669, 2085, 2311, 2947

Falconer, J.: *Sail & Steam* (Boston 1993)

Filice, F. P.: Biography of the Gjoa, *Pacific Discovery 5/6* (San Francisco, 1962)

Fredhøy, F. A.: (ed.): Magazine; *Skip-O-Hoi* (Oslo, 1930-1937)

Howe, O. & Matthews, T: *American Clipper Ships* (Salem, 1926)

Huntford, R.: *The Amundsen Photographs* (New York, 1987)

Hurst, A. A.: *Square Riggers - The Final Epoch 1921-1958* (Sussex, 1972)

Ingstad, H. and A. S.: *The Viking Discovery of America* (New York, 2001)

Judson, C. I.: *Donald McKay* (New York, 1943)

Kåhre, G.: *The Last Tall Ships: Gustaf Erikson and the Aland Sailing Fleet 1872-1947*
  (Mariehamn, New York 1948, 1977)

Komiteen til bevaring av polarskipet Fram: *Polarskipet FRAM* (Oslo, 1958)

Krag, E.: The Famous Sloop Gjøa, *Pacific Marine Review No. 4* (1949)

Larsen, N. A.: *Fra Krigens Tid 1807-1814, Den norske marine 1814* (Christiania, 1878)

Lindquist, L.: Through the Northwest Passage under Sail, *Motor Boating and Sailing,*
  no. 132 (New York, 1973) pp. 51-53, 112-116

Lloyds Register Supplement, 1923-25

Lloyds Register, 1894-1924

Lubbock, B.: *The Colonial Clippers* (Glasgow, 1924)

Lubbock, B.: *The Last of the Windjammers,* Vol. 2 (Glasgow, 1929)

Lubbock, B.: *Coolie Ships and Oil Sailors* (Boston, 1935)

Lund, K.: *SvaneSang* (Odense, 1956)

Lyman, L.: *Log Chips,* August 1950, Vol. 2, No. 1 (Washington DC, 1950)

Lyman, L.: *Log Chips,* July 1952, Vol. 3, No. 1 (Washington DC, 1952)

MacGregor, D. R.: *Fast Sailing Ships* (Watford, 1973)

MacGregor, D. R.: *Clipper Ships* (Watford, 1979)

Marthinsen, T.O.: (ed) Sjømennenes Minnehall gjennom 70 år, *Minnehallen*
  (Larvik, 1996)

McKay, R. C.: *Some Famous Sailing Ships* (New York, 1928)

Moen, S.: Kgl. norske marines fartøyer, *Hefte 14, Marinemuseet* (Horten, 1991)

Nansen, F.: *FRAM over Polhavet* (Christiania, 1897)

Nansen, L. H.: *Nansen og verden* (Oslo, 1955)

National Geographic Magazine: A Modern Viking, January (Washington DC, 1906)

Nerhus, H.: *Gjøa, vår verdenskjente minneskute* (Oslo, 1980)

Nordisk Tidende: May 9, 1939; August 31, 1939

Norges Handels- og Sjøfartstidene: January 16, 1939; March 13, 1939; May 13, 1939; August 15, 1939

Oakland Tribune: February 21, 1937; November 12, 1939

Oldham, W. J.: *The Ismay Line* (Liverpool, 1961)

Palo Alto Times: September 4, 1969

Parsons, R.: *Sail in the South* (Adelaide, 1975)

Pearse, R.: *The Last of a Glorious Era* (London, 1934)

Records of the American and Foreign Shipping (Houston, 1901-1913)

Robinson, J.: *The Sailing Ships of New England,* Ser. II (Salem, 1924) p. 26

Sacramento Bee: May 7, 1972

San Francisco Call Bulletin: May 12, 1939; May 20, 1949

San Francisco Chamber of Commerce, Bay Region: The Gallant Gjoa, 12 (San Francisco, 1961)

San Francisco Chronicle: April 11, 1906; October 20, 1906; March 1, 1906; March 2, 1908; June 10, 1909; June 17, 1909; July 6, 1909; August 8, 1909; May 29, 1911; July 17, 1911; February 20, 1921; September 6, 1927; November 11, 1928; September 18, 1932; April 19, 1933; May 31, 1934; July 1, 1934; June 12, 1934; January 21, 1939; April 16, 1939; April 27, 1939; April 28, 1939; April 29, 1939; May 5, 1939; May 7, 1939; May 9, 1939; May 10, 1939; June 7, 1939; December 25, 1939; January 23, 1940; January 24, 1940; July 3, 1940; April 11, 1942; April 22, 1942; March 11, 1946; May 17, 1946; July 11, 1947; July 14, 1947; November 10, 1948; November 19, 1948; March 9, 1949; March 20, 1949; April 6, 1949; April 16, 1949; May 11, 1949; May 15, 1949; July 19, 1957; July 12, 1959; February 2, 1960; September 8, 1969; May 17, 1970; July 24, 1971; March 30, 1972

San Francisco Examiner: May 15, 1917; May 19, 1926; March 8, 1949; May 15, 1949; February 2, 1960; October 7, 1968; September 4, 1969; May 27, 1970; May 18, 1970; July 24, 1971; July 27, 1971; July 28, 1971; July 29, 1971; July 30, 1971; April 20, 1972; February 2, 1973;

San Francisco News (Letter and Wasp): January 1, 1939; December 15, 1939; January 26, 1940.

Scandinavian Times: November 5, 1971.

Sannes, T. B.: FRAM (Oslo, 1989)

Sea Breezes Magazine (Isle of Man, 1924-1992)

Steenstrup, C.: Firemastet Fullrigger LANCING, *Norsk Sjøfartsmuseums Skrift No. 36* (Oslo, 1942)

Steenstrup, C.: Stålbark LINGARD, *Norsk Sjøfartsmuseums Skrift No. 24* (Oslo, 1936)

Sverdrup, H. U.: *Tre Aar i Isen med Maud* (Oslo, 1926)

Sverdrup, H. U.: *Hos Tundra-Folket* (Oslo, 1938)

Sverdrup, O.: *Nyt land. Fire Aar i Arktiske Egne* (Christiania, 1903)

The Atlas, April 14 (Boston, 1853) pp. 16-17

The Illustrated London News, September (London, 1929) p. 424

The Norseman, January (Oslo, 1991)

Torr, C.: *Ancient Ships* (Chicago, 1964)

Tønnessen, J. N.: *Kristiansands Historie 1914-1945,* Vol. 3 (Kristiansand, 1974)

Train, G. F.: *My Life in Many States and Foreign Lands* (New York, 1902)

Underhill, H. A: *Sail Training and Cadet Ships* (Glasgow, 1956)

Underhill, H. A.: *Deep-Water Sail* (Glasgow, 1963)

Vikings, The North Atlantic Saga, W. W. Fitzhugh (ed.) (Smithsonian, 2000)

Villiers, A.: *By Way of Cape Horn* (London 1939)

Villiers, A.: *The Set of the Sails* (New York, 1949)

Wallace, B. L.: *Westward Vikings, The Saga of L'Anse aux Meadows,* (St. John's, 2012)

Washington-Posten: April 21, 1939; May 4, 10, 31, 1939; September 15, 1939

Weekly Commercial News: April 27, 1939; November 11, 1984

White, L. G. W.: Nourse Line Square Riggers, *Sea Breezes, Vol.16* (ns): No. 94, 1953

White Star Magazine (various editions)

SILENT MOVIE

With Maud Across the Arctic Ocean, photo: Odd Dahl, 35 mm, 76 minutes, 1926

INSTITUTIONS AND ARCHIVES

Australian National Maritime Museum, Sydney

Bartholdi Museum, Colmar

Det Norske Veritas HQ, Oslo

Fish Club, San Francisco

FRAM Museum, Oslo

Gjoa Foundation, San Francisco

Glasgow City Archives, Glasgow

Kristiansand Museum, Kristiansand

Los Angeles Maritime Museum, San Pedro

Maine Maritime Museum, Bath
Mariners' Museum, Newport News
Maritime Museum of Gothenburg, Gothenburg
Model Shipways, Bogota NJ
Museum of the City of San Francisco
National Archives of Norway, Oslo
National Maritime Museum, Greenwich
New South Wales State Library, New South Wales
Norskeklubben, San Francisco
Norwegian Maritime Museum, Oslo
Norwegian Maritime Museum Library, Oslo
Østlandets Skoleskip's Archives, Oslo
Penobscot Marine Museum Archives, Searsport, Maine
Porsgrunn Kommunes folkebibliotek, Porsgrunn
Port Elizabeth Museum Library, Port Elizabeth
Royal Norwegian Navy Museum, Horten
San Francisco Maritime National Historical Park, San Francisco
San Francisco National Maritime Historical Park Library, San Francisco
Scripps Institution of Oceanography Archives, La Jolla
South Australian Maritime Museum, Port Adelaide
South Street Seaport Museum, New York
Statue of Liberty Museum, Liberty Island, New York
Stiftelsen Christian Radich's Archives, Oslo
Sydney Maritime Museum, Rozelle, New South Wales
The Maritime Museum (Sjøhistoriska), Stockholm
U.S. National Archives, Washington DC
Åland Maritime Museum, Mariehamn

SPECIAL THANKS (PERSONAL COMMUNICATION)
Lisa Benson, Christian Blom, Ben Brynhildsen, Bob Craft Sr., Nickholas B. Dean, Kristian Djupevåg, Bård Kolltveit, Bill Kooiman, Karl Kortum, Rita Kvål, Ted Miles, Mike Porter and Else Marie Thorstvedt.

ILLUSTRATION CREDITS
·Front page: Original painting at Frank G. Dean, Maryland
·Endpapers: Painting by Reginald A. Borstel. Photo William Hester 1893-1905, San Francisco Maritime National Historical Park, P84-001.00159g (SAFR 17804)
·Dedication page: CHRISTIAN RADICH in the Pacific, San Francisco Maritime NHP, J7.6.872pl (SAFR 21347)

INTRODUCTION
p. 12: Photo Olaf T. Engvig
p. 14: Photo from painting Olaf T. Engvig
p. 15: Photo Olaf T. Engvig

CHAPTER 1
p. 16: Photographer unknown/Engvig
p. 17-18: Gjoa Foundation/Engvig
p. 19: Norskeklubben, San Francisco
p. 20-21: Gjoa Foundation/Engvig
p. 22: San Francisco Maritime NHP
p. 22-24: Gjoa Foundation/Engvig
p. 24: City Museum of San Francisco
p. 25: Drawing Olaf T. Engvig
p. 26: Mural at the former SF Stock Exchange, photo Olaf T. Engvig
p. 27: Gjoa Foundation/Engvig
p. 28: Gjoa Foundation/Engvig (three b/w photos)
p. 28: City Museum of San Francisco (colored post card)
p. 30-31: Gjoa Foundation/Engvig
p. 31: Dust jacket Olaf T. Engvig's book Shipping and Culture
p. 31: Post card Sons of Norway, Lodge 007 Henrik Ibsen, San Francisco
p. 32: City Library of San Francisco
p. 32-33: Facsimile from San Francisco Chronicle
p. 33: Photo Karl Kortum (two pictures)
p. 34: Star Shipping. Bergen (from a pamphlet)
p. 35-37: Photo Olaf T. Engvig
p. 37: Photo Mona Beichmann Engvig
p. 38: Photo Olaf T. Engvig
p. 39: Painting at Norskeklubben San Francisco, photo Olaf T. Engvig
p. 40-41: All photos Olaf T. Engvig

INDEX

251